Political Communication

Political Communication

A Critical Introduction

Heather Savigny

First published 2017 by
PALGRAVE

Palgrave in the UK is an imprint of Macmillan Publishers Limited, registered in England, company number 785998, of 4 Crinan Street, London, N1 9XW.

Palgrave is a global imprint of the above companies and is represented throughout the world.

Palgrave® and Macmillan® are registered trademarks in the United States, the United Kingdom, Europe and other countries.

ISBN 978–1–137–01138–1 hardback
ISBN 978–1–137–01137–4 paperback

This book is printed on paper suitable for recycling and made from fully managed and sustained forest sources. Logging, pulping and manufacturing processes are expected to conform to the environmental regulations of the country of origin.

A catalogue record for this book is available from the British Library.

A catalog record for this book is available from the Library of Congress.

Printed and bound by CPI Group (UK) Ltd, Croydon, CR0 4YY

To My Mum

Contents

Acknowledgements

There are many people that have influenced and shaped my thinking over the years, and I would like to thank them for that input. In particular, all of my friends and colleagues from UEA, including Henry Allen, Vanessa Buth, Tori Cann, Emma Griffin, Juliette Harkin, Sanna Inthorn, Lee Marsden, Brett Mills, David Milne, John Street, Helen Warner and Nick Wright. I'd like to thank those who have taken the time to read and offer invaluable feedback, the anonymous reviewers, to Simon Gerrard for his support, patience and critical questioning of my ideas and to Sam Sleight and Mark Smith-Thomas for their curiosity and insights. I'd like to thank Martin Williams for his friendship and help towards the end! I'm also indebted to the generosity of my friends and colleagues at Bournemouth University, for their enthusiasm and encouragement, in particular, Jenny Alexander, John Brissenden, Sue Eccles, Nathan Farrell, Anna Feigenbaum, Dan Jackson, Darren Lilleker, Marian Mayer, Tim McIntyre-Bhatty, Julia Round, Iain McRury, Barry Richards, Richard Scullion, Bronwen Thomas and all of NRG, and Candida Yates and to the Bournemouth University Fusion Fund for awarding me study leave where I was able to write a large part of this book. I'd especially like to thank Steven Kennedy for his enthusiasm, wisdom and energy and to all at Palgrave – Lloyd, Helen and Tuur in particular – for their insights, input and all of their hard work.

Introduction

Green Day's 'Holiday' and Plan B's 'Ill Manors'; the Tunisian Revolution and subsequent uprisings across North Africa; the sexualization and objectification of women in popular media content; the relative lack of public discussion about the role of the arms industry in our news media. These are all forms of political communication: the communication of differing types of politics. Yet this might not be what immediately springs to mind when we think about 'political communication'.

The basic premise of this book is that there are myriad ways to communicate politically. When elites from the worlds of showbiz, formal politics or business communicate with us, directly through news programmes or through the press, through TV quizzes or reality programming, this is political communication. When elites communicate indirectly to us, inculcating values, moral codes and social norms, this is political communication. When the public protest and tell their governments they disagree with those in power, through violent or non-violent protest, this is also political communication. When ordinary people engage in collective action such as the global Occupy movement or when people sit down in protest – as they did in the United Kingdom at Philip Green's tax avoidance in Topshop – or boycott products and companies for their use of sweatshops and child labour, these are also types of political communication. Clearly, then, we could assume that every time we act politically, we are communicating. Conversely, it could also be argued that every time we communicate, we are making political statements. Of course, this can mean that political communication is everything and it becomes impossible to pin down. In asking what we mean by political communication, it seems that we are asking questions about the analytical strategies that we are using to make sense of the world around us.

This book reflects on how the largely empirical field of political communication has developed, which is highlighted through the choice of chapters in this book. However, the central argument of this book is that we need to restore politics to our analysis. Restoring politics, in the pages that follow, means that we look beyond the surface and engage in a discussion of the wider trends and issues at stake in each area. Primarily, this means asking questions about how power is conceptualized and operationalized when we talk about, engage in and analyse

1

political communication. In this way, political communication is viewed in this book as a dialectical process which is iterative and interactive, and ultimately a site of both oppression and resistance.

Viewing political communication as fluid rather than static, and as a set of interlinked and underlying processes, we can make our own political choices about the political communication we accept, how much, in what form and how. In this sense, viewing political communication as not only enacted by elites but something that we as citizens can also engage in opens up opportunities for us, as students of politics and as citizens, to decide how we respond to the politics that is communicated to us. Rather than being passive recipients of elite-level processes, we may also choose to resist, reframe, rewrite and recommunicate politically. It is argued here that while conventional understandings of political communication tend to focus on the actions and communication processes of elite-level actors, unpacking the power relations which are embodied in these processes facilitates a more nuanced understanding of how political communication itself, as a series of practices and processes, can be intensely political (as expressions of embedded power relationships).

This book takes as its starting point the idea that if we want to make sense of how our society works, we need to think about these relations of power and how they are communicated to us, through practice, through ideas, instantiated in the language we use and discourses that circulate. Societies rest on a complex interaction of people with each other and with systems that have become embedded. Citizens and elites play a role in creating these systems, their interaction, their continuation and/or their disruption. But citizens and elites also play different roles depending upon where we, or they, are located in that system. Not only does our position as citizen or elite impact our capacity to effect change but citizens and elites are not homogenous groups. Rather, this positioning is also affected through socially constructed categories such as gender, race, class, sexuality, religion, physical ability or disability. This positioning through categorization in social structures matters because this impacts upon the possibilities and opportunities that are both available to us and denied to us.

Ultimately, to make sense of how political communication takes place, we need to understand how systems position individuals and groups, which in turn affects their capacity to effect change within existing systems and structures. And it is at these points of interaction (or the prevention of interaction) that we uncover relations of power. To get to this argument, the book takes as its starting point the more 'traditional' objects of analysis within the field of political communication and so we begin with an overview of how political communication is conventionally understood.

Political communication as a site of academic study

Say 'political communication' and some simple three-word association might conjure up: politicians, parties and spin doctors; or states, newspapers and propaganda; or elections, campaigns and advertising. Depending on how we view the world, when we think about political communication we could be referring to politicians seeking to manipulate media for nefarious ends, or media's role in speaking truth to power, holding elites to account.

As a field, political communication has been conventionally concerned with the study of the interaction between the respective goals of politicians and media. Starkly put, this can be viewed as a tension between the desire to win elections and the desire to attract an audience and/or make a profit. It is at this intersection of these desires that the field of political communication sits. The 'political' tends to refer to the agents and institutions of the state, and is narrowly defined as politicians, legislatures and elections. The 'communication' component tends to refer to media institutions and the techniques employed by those within media (i.e. journalists, editors and media owners and/or the particular media form: usually press, TV, new media). Where 'political' and 'communication' come together is in highlighting the active role that mainstream media play in interpreting the political agenda, and transmitting it to audiences/citizens. Crucially, political communication highlights how mainstream media 'mediate' political messages, and how politicians respond to this by investing enormous resources and energy in promoting a positive self-image. This is often seen to date back to the Nixon/ Kennedy debate, whereby although Nixon was assumed to have won the debate by those listening on the radio, TV viewers argued that the 'telegenic' Kennedy had won (Street, 2010).

Within the field, focus on media is often centred on technologies or the form of media: such as press, TV and new media. Or it may be on the techniques politicians use to manipulate the media: PR, marketing and spin. It may be concerned with the influence of owners (such as Rupert Murdoch) on the political agenda (be that Fox News, or the *Sun* newspaper) and subsequently the assumed (debatable) effect that has on citizens. The field is also concerned with how the news media frame debates and what this might mean for audiences: in the coverage of disasters, or war, and how changes in public opinion may impact electorally sensitive politicians (cf. Robinson, 1999). Political communication as a site of study also focuses on the production and consumption cycle of news. Throughout these analyses, there are a number of common themes: a focus on formal politics as enacted by politicians; the interaction of politicians with press, TV and more recently new media; analysis informed by liberal theories of the role and function of the media in a democracy. Mark Wheeler (1997) reminds us that in liberal theory, media are supposed to function as a fourth estate, holding elites to account. They stand separate from the 1) legislature 2) judiciary and 3) executive. In short, this approach assumes that media 'speak truth to power'. Critically, we might ask political questions about the nature of the power relationships here: is it possible for media to always speak truth to power, or are there constraints to this freedom? Restoring these kinds of political questions to the site of study is of central concern to this book.

The emergence and consolidation of political communication as a field of academic study

The field of political communication has largely emerged from and been consolidated around three main areas: political studies/science; media and mass communications; and social psychology. Underlying these diverse entry points to analysis, there are two competing narratives which make normative statements about the impact and desirability of this relationship. A negative narrative draws our attention to the deleterious effects of the media on our political life. In this view, the media are responsible for: an increased cynicism towards our politics; an increasingly apathetic public; severing the link between citizens and the political process; dumbing down our news and cultural content – style over substance; marginalizing particular viewpoints which do not fit the dominant narrative; shoring up power; reinforcing the status quo. In contrast, the positive trope or narrative suggests opportunities for: emancipation and empowerment; increasing accountability of elites and exposure of corrupt power structures. Often, positive narratives are linked to the advancement and development of new technologies, as solutions not only to the technical problems of the past but also the political ones too. (While the phrase 'new media' tends to be assumed to mean the internet, it is worth noting that historically it referred to the introduction of radio and TV. This suggests that the phrase 'new media' itself is historically and temporally bound, its meaning reliant on the historical moment it is situated in.) History has been important to the discipline; much of the way the discipline has developed is with a consciousness of that which has gone before. As Ryfe (2001) observes, however, history as methodology has been less prominent in conventional analyses. History is important for understanding and analysis, and while the brief history of the discipline below draws attention to the relationships that the field looks at, much of its contemporary focus has also served to obscure a wider set of relationships and power structures which remain undiscussed and unchallenged. That the field has focused on technological and descriptive developments, as Bennett and Iyengar note, has tended to add new data to existing categories, but can be seen as 'adrift theoretically' (2008: 713).

The field has also 'evoked criticism over the years for being too formalistic, too bound to the prevailing political/institutional arrangements, too state centered, too wedded to narrow methodologies' (Dahlgren, 2009: 5). At the same time, Couldry argues that in media literature there is a significant absence of social theory's capacity to engage with media as part of its analysis, and as such often forms a constraint rather than an asset; in this way 'there is, as yet, no comprehensive account of how media change social ontology' (Couldry, 2012: viii–ix). As such, these wider concerns form the conceptual, theoretical and methodological backdrop to this book. One aim within this book, then, is to move the debate beyond these restrictions. I seek to do this by focusing on the kind of questions a student of political communication might ask, rather than solely focusing on the object of those questions. The issue is not what the object of our analysis is but what kind of questions we should ask. In essence, the argument is that we should be asking questions about the nature of power: its distribution, negotiation, contestation and impacts on all of our daily lives.

Politics as a subject of study

Whereas once politicians were remote figures who sat in Parliament, now they appear on our TVs, computers and smartphones. We can know much more about the personal lives and thoughts of our politicians than ever before. But does this mean we know more about our politics? What we mean by politics is a wider theme that animates this book; as discussed in the following chapter, it is a definition that goes beyond the actions of politicians. However, the actions of politicians, for many, provide a starting point in political communication.

The focus on politicians, government institutions, and more specifically elections and campaigns has been central to the development of political communication as a field. For some, the development of political communication is closely linked to the actions of politicians and their harnessing and embracing of media technologies and their attempts to manage media technologies, outlets, owners and content. As Chapter 4 shows, contemporary Western election campaigns see politicians devote millions of pounds to conducting of market research, opinion polls, surveys and focus groups, to advertising on posters and billboards, as well as through broadcast media and new social media. This approach, however, begins with an observable focus on the actions of politicians, the power they are seeking to gain access to, the elections they are trying to win or the policies they are wanting to implement.

Traditional literature in political science draws our attention to the politician, or the political party, as the focus of analysis. The starting point is often on motivation, and tends to assume that politicians either are rationally driven by self-interest and the quest for power (cf. Downs, 1957) or are motivated to gain office in order to enact a set of public policies and are ideologically driven by notions of a good or just society. These motivations are attributable to the individual with an emphasis upon the individual politician. While literature explores the nature of the political party, and its linkage to the state and its relationship with members (Wolinetz, 2002; Quinn, 2004), there is also a more focused recognition of the professionalization of the politicians (Panebianco, 1988). For some analysts, power has become increasingly centralized in the office of prime minister and the use of media and marketing techniques from the United States has led some to term this presidentialization (Jamieson, 1992) or Americanization (Mancini and Swanson, 1996; Scammell, 1998). In this view, assumptions about the behaviour and motivations of politicians (whether explicit or implicit) inform much of the analysis of politicians and how they behave in mediated environments.

This focus from political science draws attention to how politicians act in their mediated environment. Depending on our perspective, this may be in the form of media management, or attempts at manipulation of the media. While politicians may engage in extensive advertising and marketing campaigns, not all communication by politicians is paid for and politicians often seek to get their message across for 'free'. This might take the form of favourable press releases (spin and its development is the focus of Chapter 4), but it might also take place beyond the news through appearances on popular culture TV shows, like *Ellen* in the United States, or *Richard and Judy* in the United Kingdom. Street's analysis of the linkage between politics and popular culture (1997) has challenged conventional understandings that politics was what only occurred within the news. Muntz (2001) suggests that more recently the field of political communication is about redefining and questioning what is meant by the political (2001). For her, this redefinition comes about as politicians engage in celebrity-like behaviour (Street, 2004), combined with the blurring of boundaries between news and entertainment (or the emergence of 'infotainment'; cf. Brants, 1998) (see Chapter 6).

Beyond the news, politicians also enact, and seek to enact, policy – domestically and internationally. How we as the public gain knowledge of this is through our media, and nowhere has our foreign policy been more overtly in the public domain than in the televising of war (which started with the launch of Operation Desert Storm against the Iraqis on 16 January 1991). The fundamental importance of the media for the success or failure of politics is emphasized in successive statements and strategies regarding the need to align the media's interests with those of political actors: in March 2011, when Hillary Clinton appeared in front of the US Foreign Policy Priorities committee, she argued that the United States is in an 'information war and we are losing that war', and later added that 'Al Jazeera is winning'. The desire of politicians to conflate the interests of state and media is often successful. For example, newspaper headlines proclaiming support for 'our boys' and reporting singular personalized stories of our 'own' war dead, while routinely downplaying or marginalizing the countless civilian deaths rebranded as 'collateral damage' align media coverage with state interests. This attempt to manage media as an adjunct of policy has witnessed, for example, the increase of government media strategists in military sources, and the embedding of journalists in war zones brings its own tensions (as discussed in Chapter 7).

Whatever the issue, elections, celebrity behaviour or war, much of the literature has emphasized the new, how the relationship between politics, media and society represents something qualitatively different from what has gone before. The larger societal transitions are embodied in the small: new campaigns, new technologies, and new messages are all thought to reflect profound social changes (for example, see Norris, Curtice, Sanders, Scammell and Semetko, 1999; Sanders, 2008). The focus is on change, and the 'new', an underlying commitment to the advancement of modernity. Yet this focus on the new, the different, on new technologies as the source of social transformation and opportunity, misses that which remains unchanged. More critical accounts draw our attention to how underlying power structures, capitalism and patriarchy remain unchallenged and unchanged: this wider concern that underpins the critique which runs throughout this book.

Media technology as a site of study

Media technologies have never been more available, more usable and more instant. We live in an increasingly networked world (cf. Castells, 1996) where, for some, our communications technologies reflect or shape profound social, economic and political change. And so an alternate route into the understanding of political communication may focus on media themselves. So rather than being about politicians communicating, we need to look to the site in which politics is communicated. From this perspective, political communication begins with media and how they discuss politics, or report politics to us, the public. Political communication, then, is often concerned with: media as a technologi-cal driver of change; the producers of media – owners, journalists and editors; media content; and processes of production and consumption.

Media studies have been incredibly influential in the development of the field, which have focused both on audiences, as well as technological developments. These developments have often been historically mapped in a linear way. Each technological invention has been heralded as 'new', offering opportunities to redefine, to enhance and improve society, or as a mechanism to understand social and economic transformation. Many of these analyses suggest a teleological linear unfolding of history, seam-lessly moving from one stage to the next; media technologies drive polit-ical processes in the onward unfolding of modernity.

Blumler and Kavanagh (1999) characterize the development of the field of political communication as comprising three chronologically linear stages. They argue the first stage was in the post-World War II era, when the media often relayed political messages faithfully to audiences. Oppo-sitional ideologies characterized the political context at the time, and this, combined with a cultural context of deference, provided the condi-tions in which journalists were conscious of their 'fourth estate' role (as independent from the state); still, the public largely received the news political elites wanted them to. A second stage is marked by the develop-ment of technology: the proliferation of TV. This technological develop-ment had social consequences; audiences had choice, and were able to be selective. For Blumler and Kavanagh, this also meant partisan ties were broken, and traditional notions of cultural deference challenged. Their technological focus on media as the driver of politics and social change leads them to identify increasing and rapid proliferation of new media technologies as constitutive of a 'third age'; at their time of writing, this was cable and satellite TV and the rise and spread of the internet.

Their key point is the interrelationship between politicians and media technologies; as technologies develop, politicians and society respond to their emergence. No doubt the new social media landscape provides the opportunities to define a 'fourth age', with dominant narratives chart-ing social media as a source of public empowerment. For example, con-sistent with the 'decline of deference' narrative, citizen journalists are now able to challenge the way we make the news (and we touch on the emergent issues in Chapter 5). Blumler and Kavanagh's evolution-ary account is presented as one of the opportunities for progress and development. Many accounts of new media present this technology as empowering, as a positive development for the masses. The North Afri-can uprisings were widely linked in mainstream media to the use of social media as a mechanism of organization. However, at the other end of the spectrum, the fragmentation of media contains seeds of social disruption. The move away from communal, shared sources of news, and its contributions to community cohesion, can also have reverse and more serious consequences. Pluralism in news, expression of opposi- tional and alternate views, is long considered to be a central component of a healthy democracy. For the positive narratives, social media, like the internet beforehand, offer the opportunity for individual empower- ment against the mighty Leviathan of media and political elites. More critical accounts, however, might draw our attention to how extremist views can flourish, unchallenged and unchecked. For example, Anders Behring Breivik's massacre in Norway was informed by his knowledge gathered through engagement with limited right-wing internet sources which reinforced his narrow views.

The emphasis on technology and its role in shaping social and political relations has led some to ask what the media are doing to our politics (Lloyd, 2004), or talk of how the media have come to colonize democ- racy (Meyer, 2002) resulting in a 'packaged politics' (Franklin, 1997) and 'public relations democracy' (Davis, 2002). In 1995, so deleterious had this relationship become that Blumler and Gurevitch (1995) argued we were witnessing a crisis in public communication. They observed that politics was no longer something which comprised a direct and straight- forward relationship between politicians and the public. And this had created a problem. For politicians' acts had become 'less savoury' and 'watchdog [...] journalism often shunted into [...] witch-huntery, soap- operatics and sundry trivialities' (Blumler and Gurevitch, 1995: 1).

This focus on technology, politics as taking place at the site of the observable, the interlinkage of the social, technology and progress, the emphasis on change, and the often implied assumption that this is a pos- itive force, misses that which remains unchanged. In detailed analyses, Herman and Chomsky (1994) offer accounts of how media function to maintain political and economic power structures. Media coverage reinforces the status quo. Elite interests coalesce and are reinforced through narratives which fail to challenge the fundamental structures of power in society (McChesney, 2008). Media systems function as forms of propaganda, as means to ensure that existing political and economic power structures remain unchallenged. Systems of production and con- sumption, premised on exploitation, are the foci of analysis, and as van Zoonen (1997) reminds us, this mechanism also serves to reinforce patriarchal relations of power.

Media or politics: Which came first?

The development of political communication as a field is one which maps the emergence of media technologies and politicians' attempts to harness them. The crucial insight and argument is that if we want to understand contemporary politics, and how politicians behave, then we necessarily need to factor in the active role of media; media themselves are not passive in this process (cf. Street, 2010). When we think about media, in order to reflect on and remind ourselves of the plurality and diversity of media outlets and content, the term 'media' is used rather than 'the media', which suggests a homogeneity. In all their forms, media have their own agendas; they may not necessarily want their news items hijacked by eager baby-kissing politicians. Those working within mainstream media would also argue they maintain a journalistic integrity, and that integrity drives their journalism, not the demands of politicians. The point to be made here is that how political communication functions and has developed is not as straightforward as a linear track of technology driving political action. Media themselves are not monolithic actors, nor are they simply passive conduits of information. They do not neutrally relay the words and images that politicians want them to, rather the media have their own agenda. Analysis of political communication thus leads us to look at relationships and interactions; we need to understand political communication as an interactive process, rather than a linear unfolding of technologically driven developments.

On the one hand, media are an instrument to be engaged, deployed and manipulated for the benefit of the politician. On the other hand, media also provide a context, an environment, a landscape or a stage on which politics is played out. But media themselves have differing motivations. They may be concerned with exposing wrongdoing, speaking truth to power. For others, the main aim of mainstream media is to attract an audience, for without an audience there can be no profit. But then this clearly raises the question: who are the audience? Are the audience the general public, the purchasers of newspapers, consumers of TV? Or are the audience advertisers? Or politicians? Or businesses? Or all of the above? This complexity of motivations provides a densely structured, nuanced and complex environment where consequences, intended and unintended, take place; this is *a* site where political communication takes place. This political communication is explicit; the tensions between those engaged in its construction yield differing outcomes. But political communication is also implicit, part of a wider social and cultural context. But it is not the only site where political communication happens and implicit political communication, the communication of wider political ideas and power structures, is of central interest within this book; by focusing on the actions of politicians and their role in the communication process, we are missing wider political messages that are being communicated.

Mass communication as a site of study

While much of the focus thus far has been on the actions of elites, be they politicians or media, the third corner of the triangle in the field is the audience. Media need an audience; politicians need to be elected. Clearly these are not the same thing. The terms 'audience' and 'public' tend to be used interchangeably, but as Higgins (2008) has so eloquently observed, 'public' exists in multiple spheres. What do we mean by the words *public* and *audience*? Are they monolithic categories, or more recently, again linked to changes in technology and societal progress, are they assumed to be fragmented? How do we know what they think and want? Or how can they be manipulated to think and want what elites want them to? These wider ideas and issues have been reflected in the field by the insights afforded in the mass communication literature, often informed by social psychology (and this is reflected on in more depth in Chapter 3).

For Bennett and Iyengar (2008), the great thinkers in political communication were concerned with understanding the 'political, social, psychological, and economic transformations in modern industrial society' (2008: 707). But to understand this, they argued, we have to focus our attention on audiences, on the effects of political communication. Who were the 'mass' in mass media, and how did they respond to media messages and media technologies?

For some, the emphasis was on the techniques of propaganda and/ or persuasion. How could the masses be 'encouraged' to want what elites were purveying? Edward Bernays' understanding of propaganda (1928) had a profound effect on political elites. While Goebbels' films may be an obvious source of reference here, Bernays' techniques of persuasion remain in place in the world of marketed politics today. Part of his success lay in his linkage of his own interests and an understanding of how the public psyche could be manipulated. For example, one of his most notable campaigns saw him succeed in linking economic imperatives with political discourses of the time; cigarette smoking was (successfully) promoted to women linked with the liberation for women discourses of the time. His techniques which promoted cigarettes as 'torches of freedom' heralded a new era in public opinion manipulation and formed the basis of modern marketing (see also Yates, 2015).

Public opinion, its identification and its opportunity for manipulation to achieve the ends of elites form a key strand of political communication analysis. The idea of the public is often invoked with respect to political communication, but who are the public? And how do we know what the public's opinion is? Walter Lippmann's

Public Opinion (1922) highlighted the key role that media played in the construction of public opinion but for him, this was not a good thing. For Lippmann, media were the source of the problem in creating ill-defined 'public opinion'. The media sought to pander to the masses; in so doing they incorporated notions of 'public opinion', but these notions were designed to appeal to the lowest common denominator, ill-thought through and uninformed. In this view, any capacity media might have to speak truth to power, or to guide or inform public debate, is limited by public opinion. Not only was public opinion problematic for informed debate, but it also had the potential to stifle alternative views. In *The Spiral of Silence* Noelle-Neumann (1977) observed how the existence of public opinion would induce those not in tune with prevailing opinion to change their views, or keep quiet.

The idea that media were able to influence how people thought was also a concern of the critical theorists in the Frankfurt School. In tune with the propagandists' approach above (although highly critical of them), these critical theorists highlighted how the media were successfully able to 'inject' messages into passive, unwitting audiences (cf. Marcuse, 1964) (in the context of sense-making action of theorists who had fled Hitler's Germany, trying to make sense of their compatriots). This focus on the effects that media have on audiences generated a wide-ranging debate. From social psychology, Lazarfeld et al. (1944/1969) argued that media simply reinforce existing viewpoints (the assumption being these viewpoints were formed elsewhere). For others, however, the argument went that media may not necessarily have told us what to think, but they certainly defined the parameters of what we think about. McCombs and Shaw (1972) argued that media 'set the agenda'; our opinions, thoughts and debates are influenced by the fact that they are discussed in media. The logical corollary being that if media don't talk about a particular issue, that issue is much less likely to form part of our daily (political) discourse. That we have little conception of alternatives to Western capitalism, for example, suggests that the way the media agendas are set discourages active discussion around this point.

The notion of agenda setting was one which had resonance and others then moved to focus specifically on how media content is 'framed' (Entman, 1993). Framing refers to the subtle privileging of some inferences and knowledge and the suppression of other perspectives. For example, Laura Mulvey's (1975) ground-breaking work on 'the male gaze' drew attention to the way women were presented on screen was directed at *male* audiences, rather than male and female audiences. What this reminds us is that while media may be sending explicit messages, there is also an implicit level of communication taking place.

Within the 'effects' debate, some have argued that there are some problematic assumptions being made about audiences. While accepting framing may take place, Capella and Jamieson (1997) argued that audiences learn and are perhaps more sceptical and cynical about the media content that they receive than might have previously been implied. This focus on how audiences receive media content has also led to the development of extensive models and concepts concerned with exploring how audiences 'decode' messages (Hall, 2010), or the interactive way messages may be communicated and received with differing effects (McQuail, 2005) (and we return to this in Chapter 3).

This discussion about media effects has also influenced research in political science and here political communication analysis has drawn attention to the potential effects of the media in voting behaviour (see for example Newton and Brynin, 2002). While direct attributable causal effects remain unresolved conclusively, in analysing the role of the media in the public's intentions or understandings of issues, the assumption made within the research is that the media have some effect. This may be direct, more likely indirect, shaping of the values and beliefs that inform our political discourses and in turn provide the context in which we as audiences perceive, interact with and form our own politics. Ultimately, I would suggest that the question then becomes not whether media have an effect per se but what kind of effect media have, and to what degree.

Much of the research located in this perspective begins from the assumption that the media direct their attention to an audience, and this audience is the public (variously defined as homogenous and/or fragmented, as voters and/or consumers). Aeron Davis (2005) challenges this notion in his analysis of media effects of financial press coverage. Here he argues the audience are not 'the public' or citizenry; his crucial insight is that the audience are other elites (and we return to the notion that media communicate beyond the citizenry in Chapter 3).

Within the field, not only are media assumed to have effects on individual audiences but they can also be responsible for wide-scale, wide-ranging social effects. Robert Putnam's *Bowling Alone* (2000) firmly situates mainstream media as central to the demise of civic relationships. In his account of post-war America, the decline in social capital he charts is directly attributed to the rise in television watching. Here, then, the effects of the media are directly observable, causally attributable to decline in social capital. The interrelationship between media (systems, processes, journalists and owners), politics (politicians, elections and presentation of public policy) and the people (audiences, citizens, publics and other elites) has conventionally been the preserve of political communication. But this interaction takes place in a wider social and cultural context, and it is to this area that we now turn.

The temporal, social and cultural as a site of study: Implicit political communication?

The arguments presented within the book also rest on the notion that history matters to the study of political communication (Ryfe, 2001). As noted in more detail in subsequent chapters, history is important in enabling us to make sense of the present (Norton, 2010). For Ryfe, this process is a result of outcomes of past actors' struggles with social structures. Just as different struggles take place in different times and in different places, historical understandings matter (Ryfe, 2001: 414–5). Yet it is not only history that matters. Our understanding of politics, of communication, is intensely interlinked with our cultural understandings and how meaning is socially constructed. Political communication is situated as both something that operates within a wider context and something which reconstitutes that wider context.

This means that political communication is socially and politically constructed, temporally and culturally bound. It also means that our understandings of political communication necessarily go beyond the narrow focus of the actions of power-seeking politicians. Feminist analyses draw attention to how politics takes place beyond the formal institutions of the state. While there is some excellent literature which reflects on the role of women in the political process (e.g. Ross, 2005; Norris, 1997; van Zoonen and Harmer, 2011), there is considerably less in the field which reflects on the wider political questions that feminist analysis raises for political communication; as such, a feminist approach is adopted here, which helps us ask some of those bigger political questions about the nature of power. Drawing on feminist literature, I use an expansive definition of politics, which enables us to think about how power is diffused, circulated, negotiated and contested. Moreover, this widening of the definition of politics enables us to think about how politics takes place in many areas of our mediated lives; politics can be intensely personal, as well as taking place in the 'public' realm of the legislature.

Widening our definition of politics, as we do in the following chapter, can also enable us to think how politics takes place outside of news, in popular culture (which we come back to in Chapter 6). As Street (2004) observes, this may be both the preserve of politicians behaving like celebrities (Clinton playing sax, Blair with his guitar), or celebrities behaving like politicians seeking to influence the policy agenda (Bono or Bob Geldof). But this is not the only way our popular culture may be intertwined with politics. Popular culture may make its overt political messages, such as that contained within Green Day's anti-war 'Holiday' or more subtle political messages in our popular culture which reinforce dominant power structures such as patriarchy and consumerism, challenged, for example, in P!nk's *Stupid Girls*. Given the significance of power for this study, we return to a discussion of the nature of power in conclusion.

The challenging of the boundaries of traditional politics is a theme that runs throughout this book, and so the idea that the nation state is no longer the key site where politics takes place is returned to in Chapter 7. The contemporary environment is characterized by interconnected economies and enormous multinational corporations, the rise and interconnectedness of new, existing and social media technologies, as well as the continued existence of war, and it is the idea that politics can be defined to the geographical boundaries of the nation state that is increasingly under pressure.

Much of the research and focus in the field of political communication rests on the notion that political communication is the preserve of elite actors – be they in mainstream media, in Parliament – creators and producers of culture or elites in the world of business, military or industry. But this focus misses the political communication of ordinary people, how citizens, the public, communicate about the political environment that they find themselves in. The argument here is also that it is not only elites who take part in politics; the public, voters, citizens and subjects are all political actors. They may not have control of the mainstream media means of production, although new technology is ushering in debates around possibilities of empowerment for electorates and audiences. The role of citizens as communicators of politics is discussed in Chapter 8.

Vision and underlying philosophy of the book

As it stands, the field of political communication is largely concerned with how politicians communicate with audiences, and the questions about how (formal or legislative) politics is publicly communicated. Within this approach, political communication tells us that media play an active role in the political process, and are not simply passive conduits of information, highlighting also how the media themselves may act politically, or attempt to influence the political agenda. The assumption is usually made that this increasingly significant subfield is concerned with a tripartite relationship between politicians, the media and voters. While there is much literature which describes this relationship as a process, or transformation, or in terms of its outcomes, there is very little which discusses the theoretical basis, and conceptual underpinnings. To date, much attention has been focused on the *what* of political communication, describing techniques, content analysis, practices and behaviour of journalists, media owners, spin doctors or politicians. Here, in the discussions that follow, the concern is also with the *why*.

In essence, the field is broadly empiricist, and crucially, while the literature describes these trends and processes, what it doesn't do is discuss the politics underlying these interactions. This book rectifies this by asking political questions about political communication. It also restores the key concerns of politics and media studies – power and ideology – to the centre of analysis. It asks the questions: what is being communicated? By whom? How? In whose interests? And with what effects and implications? The book adopts a poststructuralist approach to analyses of political communication, as these types of questions have yet to be directly tackled by the existing literature. How we know (epistemology) about political communication, I argue here, is interlinked with mechanisms of disseminating that knowledge. As such, this book also adopts feminist thinking as a mechanism of critique and analysis within the field. This challenges the notion of the masculine 'norm' which underpins much of the extant literature and enables us to ask wider questions about the nature of power, how it is manifested and may be challenged. What do we accept unquestioningly as 'normal' political communication and why? Relatedly, this book also works with an awareness of cultural difference. Western 'norms' and how political communication is conducted are not 'globalizing' norms. And while this book could have covered how authoritarian regimes, for example, engage in political communication, the starting point here is to offer an alternative way to think about how political communication is conducted and analysed in the West.

Summary

Political communication is often assumed to be something which is the preserve of governments, politicians and political parties. As a consequence of this, an academic area of study has emerged to map these changes; political communication can function as a verb – 'to communicate politically' – and as a noun, which refers to a field of study. The traditional focus on the academic literature has been around the idea of political communication as a noun, that is, as a field of description and analysis. It has asked the 'how' questions: how have politicians communicated? How have the media responded? How has this message been translated? How has it been received by the public(s)?

The emergence of the field has challenged the conventions within political science, which assumed that only political parties mattered to our understanding of how politics worked. Political communication as a site of study highlighted how media technologies and systems have a role to play in the communication of the actions of political parties and politicians. This, however, is not to suggest a monolithic media. When we talk about media, there are a range of actors and technologies that we refer to, all with different and similar, competing and coalescing, interests and these interests can all coexist in an interactive context. An awareness of this densely structured relationship is a key theme within this book; this context is both structured by politics and by media. The relationship is not unidirectional, with one causing the other, but rather it is circular, dialectical, interactive and iterative.

Politicians, media actors and political or media structures are not passive. 'Political communication' is also a verb; it is active. It is the communication of politics, which takes us beyond thinking about political communication as only the preserve of the political classes. Political communication is both descriptive and active; it contains conceptual toolkits and theoretical toolkits. These wider methodological concerns enable us to reflect on the 'why' questions: why does political communication take the form it does? The answer to that question, I argue, is an intensely political one. And so if we are to make sense of 'political communication' we need to restore 'the political' more explicitly to analysis. We do this by asking those fundamental questions which are at the core of political analysis. We need to ask political questions about the form, nature and distribution of power: who has it? Where is it located? And in whose interests? With what effects? Who wins and loses? Who writes the rules of that game and with what impacts? Asking these questions is informed by theoretical reflection; these issues are addressed in Chapters 1 and 2 and the substantive chapters are subsequently informed by the asking of 'political questions' about our political communication.

A poststructuralist approach means that this is necessarily a book about questions. While books can often be assumed to provide definitive answers to questions, the aim here is not to provide answers, but to ask questions about the nature of the world(s) around us. The purpose is to generate conversation and dialogue about the differing ways we might talk about political communication and what we might learn about how power is dispersed or concentrated. In this sense, the book is highly political. Each chapter asks a question about the nature of political communication, and each chapter is structured around the asking of these questions. Another central feature of the book is that it uses theory to guide the questions and discussion of those questions. Much of the field to date had focused on empirical data – and the argument here is that we need a rigorous theoretical basis to our work if we are to have a conversation and make sense of the complex mediated social and political world we see and experience around us.

Reflection/seminar activities

Spend 24 hours without media/communications technologies. How have you defined the media you have/have not engaged with? Keep a diary of what you notice about the world without communication/media technologies? What does this tell us about how we see the world?

What is communication?

In what ways are politics and communication connected?

Group A is in charge and wants Group B to do something they don't want to do (such as give them all their money/sweets/cake). How does Group A decide what to tell people and how to motivate them? How does Group B find out what Group A is doing?

Chapter 1

What is Political about Political Communication?

Introduction

In 2011, an image of a female protestor being beaten by military police in Egypt went viral and sent shockwaves around the world. In 2014, climate change protest marches took place in over 100 cities around the world. In June of the same year, French President François Hollande made the headlines over his extra-marital affair.

These are all forms of communication about politics, and as I began to discuss in the previous chapter, there is also a political component in their communication. On one level, we could argue that to engage in protest is a form of politics and so in that context we might consider that protestors are managing to communicate dissatisfaction to elites. However, media are not passive in this process and they 'frame' what we see in particular ways, which serve to reinforce particular world views and narratives. Media can add emphasis to a debate or issue; they can ignore it, so that it does not get discussed; or they can frame it as newsworthy but insignificant. The way that media frame what we know about the world 'out there' is densely political. It is political in the sense that it shapes what is and isn't possible for us to think about, to know, and so it ultimately frames and contextualizes for us how power is distributed in society.

This chapter picks up on the themes outlined in the introduction and explores how communication can be political. This chapter begins with a discussion of the term 'political communication'; it asks questions not only about the nature of political communication, as interlinked with this are questions about who is doing the communicating. Conventionally political communication tends to be associated with the communication of formal politics (the actions of state elites) and throughout the book, this provides us with a starting point. This seemingly obvious statement, however, has meant that the field to date has been narrowly defined. Traditionally, the notion of the 'political' is often taken to mean the actors and instruments of the state and, as is discussed below, politics is a contested term. Within the field of political communication, the politics component has often meant a focus on political actors and the way they communicate, communications media and the way they might act politically (to influence the formal policy process) and the interaction between the two.

The aim of this text is to offer a critical reflection and so through discussion the term political is broadened to include relationships of power. This enables our analysis to go beyond the state, state actors and the 'formal' arenas of politics. This provides the possibility of the asking of *political* questions and bringing the politics back into political communication. Theorists as far back as Machiavelli (1532/2003) noted that politics is about power, and so if politics is about the manipulation and wielding of power, then the political questions this leads us to ask are: whose interests are represented? In whose interests are decisions made and not made? How are some interests prevented from reaching the agenda? With what effects? Does it make a difference who is communicating? This chapter argues that it is the asking of these questions about communication processes which engenders political communication.

The meaning of 'communication' is as contested as the meaning of the word politics, and so the chapter then moves to give an overview of some of the key debates and issues; which tend to be located around form, content and effects. Again, much of the literature tends to be polarized around these three categories, ether looking at the media form (e.g. new media, press, TV, radio), media content (e.g. news, film, reality TV) or the effects on audiences (usually assumed to be the public). The discussion then highlights an interaction between these three components drawing on the work of theorists such as McLuhan (which invites us to ask how significant is the medium itself) and Habermas (who located politics very firmly in the 'public sphere', which in today's environment has been very clearly defined as a mediated public sphere).

The final section of the chapter draws together the 'political' and the 'communicative' aspects and poses the political questions which frame the substantive chapters in the book: what is being communicated? By whom? In whose interests? In essence what is 'political' about that which is being communicated?

Contemporary political communication

Conventional accounts of political communication focus upon a three-fold relationship between journalists, politics and the people (or the media, politicians and the demos or citizenry) and their interaction within the context of a democracy. For some, this means that political communication is thus defined as being linked to the state, its actors and the mechanisms through which the connect with the public as, for example, 'public discussion about the allocation of public resources (revenues), official authority (who is given power to make legal, legislative and executive decision), and official sanctions (what the state rewards or punishes)' (Denton and Woodward, 1990: 14). This suggests that mediation of politics is an open and transparent process about the relations between elite actors and citizens. Much of the literature assumes that political communication is about the actions of politicians and how they communicate with us, as electorates, and this communication takes place through the media.

For Brants and Voltmer (2011), contemporary political communication may take place in a 'postmodern' democracy, but the primary concern is still that of the relationship between democracy, news journalists, politicians and citizens. However, in a critical evaluation they do not see political communication as something particularly positive. Rather they ask 'is political communication ... produc[ing] nothing more but grey noise of meaningless and disjointed messages nobody is listening to?' (2011: 1). In this sense, they point to the way representative democratic politics has changed. And it is this change in the activity of politics that they suggest generates a negative kind of political communication, for 'what does it mean for modern democracy when those in power lose their ability to communicate with those they are supposed to represent?' (2011: 1). Declining levels of trust in politicians and political systems, and the demise of democracy itself, has been widely noted across the Western world (Nye et al., 1997; Zakaria, 2003; Hay, 2007). A variety of explanations abound for the ways publics become disconnected and disenchanted with their political systems, or their politicians; for example, if politicians are white middle-class men, how do they connect with the working classes, those of different race, ethnicity or gender? However, what has been repeatedly noted is that civic life is left impoverished as citizens 'participate less frequently, with less knowledge and enthusiasm, in fewer venues, and less equally than is healthy for a vibrant democratic polity' (Macedo et al., 2005: 1). These changing contexts, for Dalton, represent an opportunity to reinvigorate democracy, citizens can choose to engage and seek to influence in different ways and venues (Dalton, 2006: 11). However, in all this literature and in our media more widely, the assumption is still that politics is taking place at the site where politicians operate (and this will be discussed in more detail below).

The second assumption that tends to be made is that a decline in connectivity with voters and their representatives is fundamentally linked to how politics (in this sense, the actions of political representatives) is communicated. A critical reflection encourages us to think about not only the matters of the state that are being communicated but also the communication of wider political concerns about the nature of power. First, an assumption is being made that power lies with elected officials and can be directly observed as being located with these officials, evident in the decisions that they take (Dahl, 1961) or don't take (Bachrach and Baratz, 1962). This, however, precludes the notion that power is located in wider social or economic structures, such as capitalism or patriarchy (cf. Lukes, 1974; Engels, 1884/2010; Millett, 1985). This might prompt us to think, not so much how is politics communicated, but what *kind* of politics is being communicated? As such, we need to ask questions about the interests of our representatives. For example, are they more likely to represent those interests that align with their own gender, race, ethnicity or class? Might they be more likely to represent the interests of those who fund their campaigns than a diversity of citizens' views? If we answer positively to these questions, this skews the notion that politics is the equal representation of all, rather what is more subtly communicated is that politics is the preserve of the wealthy, the privileged, and the white male.

Politicians and citizens rely on an active media to disseminate messages. Communication is central to politics; essential for the functioning and health of democracy (cf. Wheeler, 1997; Street, 2010). Indeed, a number of works point us to the interrelationship between media and democracy and its changing form. This has been variously referred to as 'public relations democracy' (Davis, 2002) and 'media democracy' (Meyer, 2002) where our politics is now 'packaged' (Franklin, 1994) for mediated consumption. While democracy as a term is widely contested, the debate is located historically in the works of Aristotle and Plato. It is also seen to take different forms in different parts of the world (Held, 2006), and while it might be the 'least bad form of government', the ideal of democracy seeks to enshrine and protect basic equalities and freedoms. The idea of democracy then is about discussing those limits to freedom – should there be any? How do we determine what they are? What does equality look like? Is inequality an inevitable feature of democracy or is it possible for all to have an equal voice, and equal opportunity?

These tensions at the heart of what democracy means underpin the relationship that citizens have with their politicians. In theory, politicians are elected to discuss these complex questions and to make these decisions on behalf of the citizenry. However, in order for us as citizens to know what politicians are doing on our behalf, we rely on media to provide us with this information. In liberal theory, media have a key function in a democracy as their role is to hold elites to account. Media are assumed to sit outside of government and state structures, acting as a 'fourth estate' with the capacity to expose wrongdoing and corruption, and to give voice to the views of the citizenry (Wheeler, 1997; Curran, 2002). But this is not a one-way process, and as discussed in Chapter 4, politicians have increasingly sought, and continue to seek, to shape the media agenda. Communication can also take different forms, technologically (in terms of the many different platforms available such as TV, radio, newspapers, new social media as discussed below) as well as in terms of its content and direct and underlying messages. One crucial issue at stake, for example, is that tension between economics and democracy and this is exposed once we stop to think about the primary function of media organizations. They exist to attract an audience, but the main motivation is that of profit. Media operate as businesses. And so it is crucial to recognize that the tensions between media's desire for a profit, and the needs of an 'ideal' democracy underpin how political communication can take place.

What is political?

As noted above, conventional understandings of politics suggest that politics takes place within legislatures and parliaments, and as such, we need to focus our attention on the workings of the state (Sartori, 1973; Leftwich, 2004). For our purposes, then, this suggests that we look at the state and state actors as 'political communicators' because they communicate to us about 'politics' – the conduct of the state and the managers of the state – and this is the focus of much of the literature around political communication. As McNair has noted, '…the crucial factor that makes communication "political" is not the source of the message … but its content and purpose' (McNair, 1999: 3–4). McNair suggests that the aim and agenda of the piece of communication is what makes something 'political'. This immediately widens our definition of what we mean by political, given that the source (e.g. politicians) is not what makes a piece or process of communication political.

We start here, however, by unpacking the definition of politics. What do we actually mean? And what does this lead us to study? Asking these questions helps us to think about the differing ways in which we define politics, and leads us to different conclusions and different foci of analysis in political communication. Some political scholars and commentators argue that politics is about war. Politics takes place when governments fail: war is politics by other means (von Clausewitz, 1884). For others, politics is about the absence and prevention of war. In both cases, however, the focus is upon state personnel and institutions; power is assumed to be located at this point. Leftwich (2004) argues that there are two broad approaches when thinking about how we define 'politics'. One is an 'arena' approach which links politics to the notion of states, and takes place in a certain site, or set of institutions; it asks us to think about *what* politics is taking place. Alternatively, he suggests that politics can be viewed as procedural, concerned with the processes: *how* politics takes place. Often the assumption is made that politics takes place in public life (and this goes back to Aristotle and the Ancient Greeks).

More recently, however, feminists have challenged that notion and argue that if politics is about power, then politics is also played out in private lives, in the family (e.g. Fraser, 1992) (and indeed increasingly states and businesses play a role in regulating and monitoring our private lives). This blurring of the boundaries, of the beginnings and ends of what we mean by 'politics', enables us to operate with a broad understanding of what politics means. Lasswell's (1936) famous question perhaps encapsulates this view: who gets what, when and how? There is much debate about that which counts as political and definitions have expanded beyond the institutions of the state. For Hay, a political situation must present a choice, which is publicly debatable, and where people must have agency (2007: 65), and so it is clear perhaps that politics can then operate in the realm of popular culture (Street, 1997, 2012; Savigny and Warner, 2015). However, by emphasizing the need for public debate, this misses the role of wider structures where power is exercised and contested. Indeed this assumes that politics is evident in public action or debate. But this misses the notion that politics can take place where voices are marginalized or silenced (cf. Arendt, 1951). If, as Couldry (2010) observes, a voice is prevented from being expressed, and debate denied, we could argue that politics is still taking place: politics is about the exercise of power; rather than simply a positive publicly debated choice of individuals. This also raises the question: if an issue is not debated publicly, does this mean politics is not taking place?

Asking questions about the way resources are distributed, who wins and loses, is to also ask questions about how power is distributed and operates. Is power only located in the state? Is it located in the hands of individual politicians? Is it located in the hands of journalists who provide us with information about the actions of politicians? Is power located in the hands of media owners? Alternatively we might consider that power is located in social and economic structures, which frames the choices that are available to us, as individuals or collectively. These broader contexts take the form, for example, of capitalism, patriarchy and, in the West, neoliberalism (and we reflect on this in greater depth in the following chapter). Capitalism and patriarchy as structures are perhaps two of the most obvious examples where power may be exercised, where agency may be prevented from being exercised or may contribute to the performance and reconstruction of dominant norms and values. For example, agency may be expressed, but that could be restricted by lack of available material resources. Or it could be restricted by structures which are heteronormative, white and male. A choice could still be made, but restricted by the structures that agents find themselves located in. (This is why we sometimes refer to marginalized groups as structurally disadvantaged.) Once we start to think about how ideas become 'common sense' or hegemonic (discussed below), these ideas can influence how people have the capacity to exercise choice. But rather than power being located in the individual, we might observe that a Black, state-educated woman, is less likely to achieve 'top' positions in society. (For example in UK academia only 0.4% of the professoriate are Black women [Equality Challenge Unit, 2014].) At the more 'everyday' level, women were only granted the vote in Switzerland in 1971; in Saudi Arabia women are prohibited from driving. What is it about the Black, state-educated woman that is different from the white (middle class) male? Once we start to think about the structures that govern the way our societies operate, once we ask questions about how resources are distributed, in whose interests, then, we start to ask political questions about the way society works. And how do we find out what our society looks like? Through direct experience of it, through education systems but also through our media. And the focus of this book is about how the media play a political role: how far do they contest existing power relations? To what extent do they reproduce them? What kind of a challenge do the media pose to existing power structures?

What is communication?

Politics (whatever form we argue it takes) does not exist in a vacuum. Politics is communicated to us through a variety of means. One way politics (as power relations) is communicated to us is via the media. But what do we mean by 'the media'? In common parlance, the term 'media' is linked with others such as 'mass' media, new media and social media. It can take a variety of forms – newspapers, radio, film, TV, internet, theatre and art, to name but a few. The roots of the term media (plural of medium) are derived from the Latin; a shortening of *tunica* or membrane meaning a 'middle sheath' or 'layer'. In this sense, media provides the middle ground, linkage layers between elites and publics, audiences or citizens (such as authors communicating ideas to readers). It can also provide a layer of connection between audiences, such as conversations about a book, or viewing a film with a friend. But it reminds us that politics doesn't just happen 'out there'. The term 'media' suggests complex processes of production and consumption. Media provide a middle layer for politicians to communicate with citizens. But if we have a wider definition of politics, we see media not only provide us with daily information about the activities of political elites but with information about dominant power structures. Media are not passive conduits of information and play an active role in its dissemination (Street, 2010).

A number of theorists have explored how the media are active, and what follows is an exploration of this point through three key areas: media form, media content and reception.

Media Form. The use of the term 'media' to describe a plethora of communicative devices implies that all media can be categorized under this one broad heading. However, Marshall McLuhan (1964) argued that this was not so. For him, it was the medium itself which carried the message; the content was not what was at stake. The medium was embedded in the message, the medium determined how the message was received and influenced society. His first example was a light bulb – it carried no content, but altered the way that its environment was perceived. He extended this argument to suggest that it wasn't the content of media which mattered (irrespective, for example, of violent content), rather it was the effect of television on society more widely which should be the focus of analysis. He argued that media such as radio and film were 'hot' media – they required little active participation; audiences were passive – whereas media such as TV and print were 'cool' requiring much more active engagement on the part of the participant. Interestingly, while his key argument revolved around the impact that technology, in this instance, media, had on society, his book in its titling still assumed that society was 'man' (reflecting the wider underlying link between science, technology and patriarchy as noted by Wajcman, 1991). In later years, Putnam has picked up on the significance of the medium but rather than seeing TV as a medium that requires active engagement, for Putnam (2000) TV is the source of apathy in participation in wider political and social life.

For Debord, the reliance on media has meant that society has become nothing more than spectacle; experience is lived through imagery and representation; the spectacle is social relations mediated by images: 'The spectacle grasped in its totality is both the result and the project of the existing mode of production. It is not a supplement to the real world, an additional decoration. It is the heart of the unrealism of the real society' (Debord, 1967: ch 6). And for Baudrillard (1994), the media now serve to construct reality, but this reality is a mediated one – a simulacrum – giving us false beliefs, hopes and perceptions about what society is really like. While adopting differing perspectives, Baudrillard and Debord collectively suggest that the media *en masse* play a powerful role in shaping our perceptions of what society looks like. This capacity to create society, to shape what we perceive as reality implies an incredible amount of 'power' located in both individual platforms (such as TV or Facebook) and the media more widely. This suggests, however, that the content is almost unimportant, it is the way the technologies exist and function that shapes and controls, defines what is and isn't possible for us as individuals, and for us collectively.

Content. In contrast to an emphasis on media technologies, we see a great deal of focus on attempts to manipulate the message that is being communicated. Bob Franklin (1994) tells us of 'packaged politics', that politicians, for example, now pay a great deal of attention to the way a message is communicated. Legions of spin doctors are employed, press releases and photo opportunities ensure that politicians retain as tight a control as possible over the message they give us. This suggests a degree of control and agency that politicians have over media agendas. But politicians are not alone in seeking to manipulate or control those media agendas. Our attention is drawn to the ways financial elites use news media to speak to each other (Davis, 2005) or the success of the public relations industry in infiltrating news agendas (Nick Davies, 2008). For Lewis, media have functioned to successfully limit the bounds of our imagination (2013). For example, that we cannot conceive an alternative to capitalism suggests structural power deeply embedded in our mechanisms of communication. And the embedding of wider narratives through media content can also be thought about if we move beyond the economic messages that are disseminated and think about some of the wider social messages communicated in media content.

Natasha Walter (2010) and Kat Banyard (2010) both describe the casual way violence against women has become interlinked with the sexualization of women ... and the way this is problematic for both women and men who reject this kind of stereotyping, and the 'pornification' of culture (Gill, 2007, 2011; Levy, 2005; McNair, 1996, 2002; van Zoonen, 1994) has become a significant issue. The ways women are represented in popular culture may not be what we would automatically assume to be 'political communication'. Yet if we think about how power relations are functioning, where women are positioned according to the desires of the 'male gaze' (Mulvey, 1975) and how this can be viewed as continuing and perpetuating gendered power relations (cf. Gill, 2011) then we can see this kind of representation as intensely political.

Reception. The third aspect of the communication process is the way that communication is received. Do we uncritically receive the messages that the media 'inject' into us as the Frankfurt school suggested (see introduction)? Do we exercise our own judgment, choosing the media which reflects our own views? It has also been argued that the media don't tell us what to think per se, but they do tell us what to think about (McCombs and Shaw, 1972). Which topics are the ones we 'should' be talking about, thinking about, publicly debating, is often 'framed' for us by the media we consume (Entman, 1993). There is wide-ranging debate in which audiences are assumed to be either active or passive; however, the issue in part revolves around the location of power. To discuss media necessarily suggests an audience. But if media come prior to the audience, then power will always be located primarily with them. Ranciere encourages us to challenge this power relationship. He argues that 'what is required is an audience without spectators, where those in attendance learn from as opposed to being seduced by images; where they become active participants as opposed to passive voyeurs' (2009: 4). At present, media derive their power from the existence of the audience(s). This power is exercised though a) ignorance of the production of the media content and the reality it conceals and b) to be a 'spectator is to be separated from both the capacity to know and the capacity to act' (2009: 2). How audiences receive and interpret media thus becomes a crucial feature of the extent to which power can be reinforced or rejected and is discussed in more depth in Chapter 3.

It is argued here that form, content, and reception are not isolated features of media output and engagement. Wary of the technological determinism which suggests media form drives outcomes (such as the claim that the revolution in the Middle East was in fact the Facebook revolution), it is suggested that there are a set of interconnected and iterative relationships between media form, content and reception, and the context in which they take place. For example, while Facebook may have enabled citizens to communicate with each other and on the surface it could be seen as a contemporary incarnation of McLuhan's hot medium, there were a series of underlying structural causes which were the trigger for the Arab spring. Politics (in its widest definition) rather than technology was at the root of this revolution. Mohammed Bouazizi's self-immolation on 17 December 2010 in protest at the abject poverty and his treatment by officials was followed by bread riots, but the actions in Tunisia were not in isolation from their position in the world order. As Gray observes, 'to an extent that has not been appreciated, the Arab protest movements emerged as an unintended consequence of Western weakness. The demand for change had a specific cause: the steep rise in food prices that was produced by the liquidity released by Ben Bernanke, chairman of the US Federal Reserve, into global markets' (2011, newstatesman.com). In Egypt, high-level graduate unemployment combined with steep rises in prices of wheat (of which Egypt is one of the world's largest importers) (Gray, 2011). As such, Gray suggests that contextual international economic decisions, combined with Western historical imperialism, had laid the groundwork for internal uprisings; a technological deterministic interpretation is too simplistic.

What is the site in which politics is communicated?

The conventional literature focuses on Habermas and the public sphere: the site where political debate and dialogue take place. In more recent literature, the public sphere has become synonymous with media and media's function in democratic politics. Habermas's (1989) notion of the public sphere was used to describe/define/conceptualize the relationship between state and civil society. For him, it was the space where politics occurred; the place where rational debate (about state policy and action) was assumed to take place. He developed this based on an idealized world located around meetings in the coffee houses of 18th-century Europe where rationality was assumed to prevail. There was also an assumption of the rights to freedom of information and freedom of speech. For Habermas, the public sphere was the site where politics was subordinated to the people. Rational dialogue would take place and accordingly the best ideas for how society should be governed would emerge through this rational discussion. This was viewed as an essential component of a vibrant and healthy democracy; ideas were tested and held to account. Social and technological developments have seen the idealized coffee shops replaced with media platforms (such as newspapers and TV). Here, mainstream media are viewed as a 'necessary element for public deliberation' (Butsch, 2009: 2). Media thus are seen as providing the site where rational discussion happens, where political elites are held to account. For example, if we look at the media as fragmented rather than as monolithic, Milne (2005) argues that the press form a site where single-issue protest is mobilized. Here, then, the press are functioning as Habermas's public sphere. Milne argues the press no longer 'manufacture consent', rather they now operate in the vacuum provided by electoral party politics, and the function of the press is to manufacture *dissent*. Here, then, the press are assumed to provide a site where public opinion can be mobilized around single-issue protests and can gain a voice (2005). This implies a very liberal role for the press – that they function to keep elites accountable, that they are the 'voice of the people'.

It is fairly uncontested that on one level media more broadly now fulfil Habermas's public sphere role. The debate has subsequently tended to revolve around the type of public sphere and the role of media within it. The proliferation of media technologies and acknowledgement of differing political identities has meant some scholars talk of 'multiple public spheres' (Squires, 2002). This could suggest that power can be held to account with a range of differing voices speaking and in a number of differing venues. This focus though links the public sphere to technology primarily rather than democracy. What it does do, however, is introduce a degree of pluralism. One of the main critiques of Habermas's public sphere is that it allowed only the voice of the male educated bourgeoisie to speak, and to be heard. Nancy Fraser (1992) noted the absence of subordinate groups in this idealized public sphere: women and the lower classes were excluded from the debate. The critique argues that gender blindness does not equal gender neutrality, indeed it manifests a false gender neutrality (Couture, 1995). And this argument can be extended to race/ethnicity and class. What this critique points us towards is that in its idealized form Habermas's public sphere ultimately serves to maintain existing power relationships: rational debate and deliberation represent the individual practices and interests of bourgeois men, other classes and groups are disadvantaged in such situations. 'Rational' debate is thus narrowly defined. While Habermas was concerned with the common good; Fraser argues that in a society already defined by hierarchies, there is limited shared interest or common good. Indeed, these kinds of societies are 'zero sum'; what is good for one group is bad for the other (1992: 129–31). For Fraser, the issue at stake in the public sphere is to recognize and define competing interests and relationships; this reintroduces power relations into our analysis.

Habermas's account assumes passivity for the 'public sphere'; while the public sphere provides a forum for discussion, for him it is not assumed to be active in shaping the discussion that takes place. Herein lies a problem for political communication scholars in assuming media as a Habermasian public sphere, because as Street (2001) observes, media are not neutral actors. Rather media have their own, and indeed differing agendas to those ideals contained with the idea of democracy. For some, media form a site where consent is manufactured (Herman and Chomsky, 1988); dominant ideologies are disseminated and as such existing power structures remain uncontested. For others, the active role of media mean that our imaginations are limited (Lewis, 2013) and in this way we see media playing an active role in perpetuating and legitimating 'common sense' hegemonic ideas which benefit existing powerful interests.

The basic premise of the notion of hegemony is that we are not ruled by force alone, that ideas matter. (As Marx had observed – the ruling ideas of the age had been the ideas of the ruling class and this points us to the importance not only of the material, but the ideational – ideas matter and may have material effects – that is, in the way society works [cf. Hay, 2001].) For Gramsci (2011), the power of ideas was fundamental to preserving the 'ideological unity of the whole social bloc'. Gramsci used the term 'hegemony' to denote the predominance of one social class over others (e.g. bourgeois hegemony). This represents not only political and economic control but also the ability of the dominant class to project its own way of seeing the world so that those who are subordinated by it accept it as 'common sense' and 'natural'. More recently scholars have identified masculinity as hegemonic (Connell, 1993); that it is 'naturally' accepted that men have a dominant position in relation to women in society. However, central to what is taking place is that this is legitimated through willing and active consent. Common sense, suggests Geoffrey Nowell-Smith, is 'the way a subordinate class lives its subordination' (cited in Alvarado and Boyd-Barrett, 1992: 51). Gramsci emphasized struggle and noted that 'common sense is not something rigid and immobile, but is continually transforming itself' (Gramsci, cited in Hall, 1982: 73). As Fiske puts it, 'Consent must be constantly won and re-won, for people's material social experience constantly reminds them of the disadvantages of subordination and thus poses a threat to the dominant class ... Hegemony ... posits a constant contradiction between ideology and the social experience of the subordinate that makes this interface into an inevitable site of ideological struggle' (Fiske, 1992: 291). In this sense, we could envisage that media provide a 'battleground' for ideas, where common sense is articulated and reinforced, and indeed we might acknowledge that media are located in broader power structures which remain undiscussed and unchallenged; hegemony is (unconsciously) reinforced. Yet the emergence of new social media also reminds us that media can provide citizens a site for alternative politics to be articulated (and this is discussed in more detail in Chapter 8).

The assumption of politics being played out in the public sphere also implies that government is able to function through this forum or these media fora. However, Foucault (1991) invites us to reflect on what we actually mean by government. Government, like media, is not neutral, and as with the definitions of politics above, government not only refers to the actions of state actors but could also refer to the self, interpersonal relations and interactions with communities. In this way, government is not a material structure, rather it is a mentality, a way of thinking and crucially a way of regulating the self and others. This idea was embodied in his phrase 'governmentality': the government of one's self and others (Foucault, 1991: 2). For Foucault, this regulation was a key aspect of society which had historical roots (he locates the 'problem' of government as having 'exploded' in the 16th century [1991: 87]). We could only understand society through analysis of the 'techniques of power' or 'power/knowledge' which were designed to observe, monitor and regulate behaviour of individuals located in a variety of social and economic institutions (Foucault, 1975). For Foucault, the state itself does not contain any intrinsic or basic properties, rather it comprises the practices of (formal) government, and the changing nature of the state is a consequence of changes in government.

Towards a politics of political communication

In what is discussed above, the aim has been to draw attention to the contested and complex relations between seemingly simple constructs as the media and politics. To reflect upon what we mean by political communication, we need to unpack what we mean by politics and what we mean by communication. This unpacking draws our attention to more fundamental questions about what is taking place in society. It enables us to ask questions about how power works, and how power is dispersed. (And we return to reflect on the nature of power in the conclusion of this book.) It encourages us to reflect on the wider questions asked in politics about the limits to our freedom, to our autonomy and what rights we have. Most recently, the *Charlie Hebdo* murders set in train public (mediated) discussion about the freedom of speech in Western democracies. At this point, not only are issues of free speech under discussion but this is a set of densely political questions which (normatively) underpin the actions of elite actors – who gets to speak? Who has 'voice' (Couldry, 2010) and if voice is denied (cf. Arendt, 1951) or alternate views silenced (hooks, 1981), does that deny the rights, autonomy and freedom of individuals and communities? If our voices are not heard in media, are our political rights and freedoms compromised? Once we start to think about who speaks, and who has the right to speak in and through media, we might also want to think about who is denied the 'right to have the right' to have voice in our modern democracies.

Underlying this book is an assumption that the world does not exist 'out there' awaiting discovery. Rather the ontological assumption is made that how we experience the world is a combination of a series of economic, social and political processes, which serve to construct what we experience and how we come to make sense of the world. Ontological questions facilitate the asking of questions about the nature of 'reality'. What is reality? What does it look like? Indeed, even prior to that we might ask, is there such a thing as a single reality or a single truth about the world? In this book, I start from an anti-essentialist position which states that there are no essential features of society, rather our world is socially constructed by us, by our interaction with it. So, for example, an essentialist position might lead us to believe that we have biological or genetically predetermined characteristics as a natural consequence of our race or our biological sex. However, I (and many others) would argue that there is nothing natural about Black slavery or the appalling way that Black women have historically been treated (e.g. hooks, 1984; Walker, 1985), for example, and subordination based on biological features is not a consequence of biology but of socially constructed assumptions. If we accept that there is nothing biologically natural about our position in society, we also need to make sense of how our interaction in society is dependent upon the structural position we find ourselves in. To be born biologically Black is to be born in to a system of structural racism, whereby biological race has been taken as a category to determine the position of people in society. There is nothing inherently 'natural' about white Western dominance, rather this is a consequence of how societies have been organized by people, historically.

This book also rejects historical determinism. While history may enable us to understand our present position, it does not determine our future; rather a historical understanding may help us shape our futures differently. Of course, asking questions about what reality looks like also invites the subsequent question how can we know what that reality looks like? So in turn we need to ask epistemological questions; how we can have knowledge about the world 'out there' (for wider discussions of ontology and epistemology see Hay, 2002; Marsh and Furlong, 2002; Savigny and Marsden, 2011).

Epistemologically, in this book, the argument is that as reality is socially constructed then the way we can have knowledge of it is to explore the mechanisms in place which contribute to that structure. This is not to deny the agency of individuals in that structure; and there is a long debate almost of a chicken and egg fashion – which came first, agents or structures? (cf. Giddens, 1984; Hay, 2002; McAnulla, 2002). However, following Bhaskar, I adopt the position that individuals are situated within structures, and while they may change them, their capacity to do so relies on the position that they hold within those structures. So, in order to have knowledge of the social world, we need to explore the structures that are constituted and reconstituted in an interactive and iterative process through the actions of agents. The argument here is that these structures 'frame' the way that politics is communicated to us and we need to understand how they function. Jessop (2005) points to underlying causal mechanisms that shape social reality; although we can't see them, we can see their effects. For example, capitalism is an underlying structure; we can't see this thing called capitalism, nor can we measure, touch or taste capitalism, but we can know of its existence because of its effects – so one effect of capitalism is the reproduction of economic inequality; capitalism relies on relations of domination and subordination to function. Perhaps more locally, we might see an effect: for example, if we want to drink something we cannot do so without a commercial exchange taking place. This exchange of money, and our prominent role in the process of consumption (in purchasing said beverage), obscures from us the exploitative processes which are in place, yet, as our current economic system is organized, we could not exist without. We see the effects of capitalism – in the way as individuals we are positioned as consumers, and collectively implicated in global and national levels of economic inequality. There is a danger of structural determinism here, and I am not seeking to deny the agency of individuals or groups, such as trade unions, anti-capitalism protestors, and individuals who make ethical consumer choices. However, what is being assumed here is that these choices are made possible by a broader social context. In that social context power relations are contested and negotiated; ultimately this is a political context. To have knowledge about how power is working, to ask political questions, is to ask about the degrees of autonomy that individuals and groups have within their structural context.

Summary

This chapter has sought to explore how we can make sense of what constitutes the 'political' in political communication. It has been argued that the 'political' is much more that the infrastructure of the state, and the actions of politicians. Rather the political invites the asking of questions about the nature of power, and the degrees of influence and opportunities to effect change in existing structures of power that may be available to differing groups or individuals.

There has also been a reflection on the differing ways in which communication may be defined and conceived, be that technologically, or in terms of media content. Crucially we need to ask political questions about the nature of that communication and such dilemmas also encourage us to ask questions about who speaks, who doesn't and who decides who speaks. And it is in a discussion of these kinds of questions that we can start to unpack where power is being reinforced or contested. Political communication, I argue, is not a thing that we can identify, rather it is a series of processes, located in a set of pre-existing structures (discussed in more detail in the following chapter), within which individuals (or agents) have the capacity to act, or not, in a variety of ways. The search to understand how power works in the processes of mediated communication is a means through which we can ask political questions about the nature of political communication.

To do political analysis is not to engage in a neutral exercise; for the notion of neutrality assumes a conservatism, an adherence to the status quo and precludes the idea that change is possible or that power may be contested. In many senses, this book seeks to communicate its own normative political agenda. The aim is to facilitate the articulation of an understanding of how politics is communicated to us, which allows for us to do something different. To paraphrase Marx, the point is not simply to observe the world, but to change it.

Reflection/seminar activities

What is politics?

How do we decide how to define politics?

Draw the Habermasian public sphere. What features does it contain? What is missing? Whose interests are represented? How reflective is this of our contemporary media environment?

Bring to the seminar something that you consider to be a form of political communication. Why have you chosen this? What does it tell us about the nature of the world around us? What assumptions are being made about what the world 'looks like' in this item?

Design a piece of political communication. What is the message you want to disseminate? Who are you trying to reach? And what impact are you seeking to have? How effective do you think your political communication will be? And why?

Chapter 2

Why does Political Communication Matter?

Introduction

According to liberal theory, an informed citizenry is necessary for the healthy functioning of a democracy, so we need to be able to read the media and the politics which are being communicated in order to take part in democracy, to know what our rights are, and to be able to hold to account those who rule in society. To be able to do this, we need to be politically and media literate. Literacy is therefore central in making sense of why political communication matters. If politics is communicated to us each time we engage in media, we make choices about the degrees of engagement or passivity we display towards those mediated messages; while the extent to which we engage (or not) may be on the surface an autonomous choice, the aim of this chapter is to situate the choices that we as individuals make in a wider social and political context.

To be literate suggests a degree of knowledge, and so the chapter begins by exploring what and how it is that citizens 'know' about political processes, the formal mechanisms of the state and government. Our knowledge of the world is predicated in the language that we use, and so the way language structures our experience is discussed, and then through reflection on ideology we can start to unpack how dominant views of 'the world' are communicated to us. In becoming literate, we need to also think about the codes and messages that are communicated to us, and the chapter follows this discussion with a series of political questions that encourage us to think about how we read political messages; this also involves a reflection on the language that we use. The discussion thus moves to the wider ideological and discursive context in which much of Western political communication is situated: namely a neoliberal, capitalist and patriarchal context. Finally, the chapter argues that when we analyse political communication we also need to be sure we are as aware of what is not being communicated as what is being communicated.

Political literacy, political knowledge

Political communication relies on a degree of literacy. However, it might also be argued that actually for democracies to function effectively, not too many people need to be engaged (Almond and Verba, 1963). Indeed, following this point is a notion that it may well benefit elite interests and the building of nationhood, communities and 'stable' states, that citizens are not 'too' literate. To ask questions about the actions of state (and other) elites is to hold them to account. While it may be in the interests of elite actors for not all to be literate, not all to ask questions, it does not follow that this is in the interests of the citizenry. When we think about the politics that is communicated to us, in all its forms, we need a mechanism to make sense of what is being communicated. At its very basic level, this sense, or meaning-making process, requires literacy.

To be politically literate is to be able to read 'behind' the text that we are presented with. It is to be able to understand how interests are represented, and how moral values and codes are expressed. Once we can understand the processes at work, we are then able to choose whether to accept how our politics is framed, or we may seek to create the spaces to resist, reframe, or rewrite it. To be literate is to understand the political processes at work in our everyday experiences; and the role that media take in facilitating (or not) communication about those processes. This matters because, as Grossberg observes, society maintains its existence through reproducing its structure and its social relationships (Grossberg et al., 2006: 193). This suggests consent is constructed and accepted by citizens and audiences. As noted in the previous chapter, one way in which 'common sense' is produced is through ideology: a particular way of thinking about the social/political world. So to be literate in this context is to have the critical capacity to unpack what is taking place in how the social and political world is communicated to us.

Literature around media and politics assumes there are a set of 'ideal' functions and roles for the media to play in a democracy (e.g. Keane, 1991; Wheeler, 1997; Street, 2010; Curran, 2002). There is an assumption of communication between elites and masses. Within these ideals falls a responsibility on the part of the media, to hold elites to account, for our political representatives to represent the interests of those who they are elected to represent. To keep our representatives representative, we need information about what they do in our name. However, as is noted below, this relationship entails a set of tensions. For example, representatives are often beholden to other interests as well as those of their constituents. Party discipline and following the party line play a key role and may supersede the interests of the voters. Party funding (cf. Katz and Mair, 1995) can also play a role in shaping how parties and politicians behave. As political parties 'professionalize' (Panebianco, 1988) so they seek to manage the news agenda favourably. As noted, however, media also can be active agents (Street, 2010) subject to market pressures and increasingly reliant upon advertising revenues and public relations as sources of news (Davis, 2007). The neoliberal idea that market pressures kept the press responsive to public demand is premised on the assumption that the marketplace provides a space for citizens to choose which news to consume.

Democracy rests on the ideal assumption that 'even if some members may know more about an issue at any given moment, we are all capable of learning' (Dahl, 2000: 36). 'Political' space often tends to be linked to political parties and mapped across a left–right continuum (Fuchs and Klingeman, 1990; Halman and Heinen, 1996; Kitschelt, 1996; Knutsen, 1995). People are assumed to have a sense of their place in relation to 'policy' positions. Jenssen et al. (2012: 140) argue that there is a link between the knowledge of 'hard news' (e.g. facts about political parties) and capacity to locate oneself on a political spectrum. This they contend is more likely than for those who may be less attentive to such news and engage with soft or entertainment media. Therefore they also argue that those who are more politically interested are likely to remain so as they perceive more to be at stake. Accordingly, those with lower levels of political knowledge will find it more difficult to locate parties on the left–right spectrum. This research draws our attention to a number of features connected to the significance of the interrelationship between elites and citizens. It suggests that all are responsible for how citizens are informed and democracy functions. This in turn implies that political elites are responsible for providing information in a manner that citizens can become informed, the media have a responsibility to make that information available and citizens have a responsibility to become informed. This kind of approach again is very pluralistic and it also assumes that politics only takes place where political parties operate (which is a contested subject throughout this book).

Studies have been conducted to explore how citizens have 'knowledge' of the actions of political elites, and how their governments function. Research conducted in the United States highlighted some alarming gaps in people's political knowledge. For example, 25% of US citizens could identify five freedoms ensured by the First Amendment (freedom of speech, press, religion, assembly and petition for the redress of grievance). But more than 50% were able to name two members of *The Simpsons* (Shenkman, 2008), one-third could name all three branches of government (executive, legislature and judiciary) but two-thirds could name a TV judge on *American Idol* (Breyer, 2010). In the United Kingdom, only 27% knew that an election did not have to be held every five years; and only 49% knew that the House of Commons held more power than the Lords (Power Report, 2006). Of course a question that will be returned to later in the book is can we equate gaps in political knowledge with an apathy towards formal politics? This may represent, for example, disinterest in the present actions of political elites, but can we assume political disengagement flows from this? As is explored in

Chapter 8, citizens may be disengaged from the formal process of politics, yet still be politically participating.

The knowledge of formal politics that citizens have is often mediated via active media. So in order to make sense of this relationship, we also need to understand how media works. For Hallin and Mancini (2004) this means a focus on media systems: how media production is organized. They argue that to make sense of these systems, we also need to understand the differing cultural, social and political contexts in which these systems are located. (Although it should be noted that this implies that the systems are constructed by that context, whereas the argument here is that media are also active in reconstituting and shaping that context, rather than being passive recipients of it.) In emphasizing the role of culture, however, they remind us that often political communication research has been located in the US. This has meant it has often tended to assume a 'naïve universalism' (Blumler and Gurevitch, 1995: 75), which suggests that what is applicable in United States is applicable in any other geographic area. For Hallin and Mancini (2004), culture matters, the structure of media markets matters, and their focus in illustrating this is on the relative strength of the press. For example, they argue, that where press circulation is low, the public are more likely to rely on electronic sources, such as TV, for news. They point to geographic differentials, with Scandinavian and Northern European countries tending to have higher rates of news circulation, while Southern Europe has lower rates, and they argue rates in the North Atlantic fall between the two. This matters because newspapers allow for more news at the pace that readers wish to digest it (Iyengar, 1991), in contrast to TV news, which tends to be shorter, less informative and have generally less coverage (e.g. Neuman et al., 1992). In short, this suggests the greater the density of newspaper readership, the greater the likelihood of informed engaged citizens in the formal processes of politics.

As Niemi and Junn (1998: 9) observe, 'for democratic decision making to be meaningful and legitimate... citizens must be capable of understanding what is at stake in politics, what the alternatives are, and what their own positions are'. For our political systems and process to function legitimately, citizens need to have knowledge of not only what is happening, but how the system (or systems) works. Access to knowledge and information about our political systems is thus essential for ensuring a healthy democracy: knowledgeable citizens are able to make responsible informed choices, and they can hold elites to account. Delli-Carpini and Keeter (1996) argue that informed citizens are 'better' citizens. More able to participate in public life, more likely to have meaningful attitudes that they can link to interests, and this provides a basis from which to evaluate candidates and governments. In order to do this, however, citizens need up-to-date information about current affairs (and how political processes function). And as scholars have noted, the plethora of media outlets mean that it is increasingly difficult to avoid the news (Bennett and Iyengar, 2008; Prior, 2005). On the one hand, the increasing availability of media sources 'empowers' citizens to choose the media that they wish to consume. This is the logic of the market. However, democratically this disempowers citizens who are able to avoid knowledge about current affairs and therefore become less likely to engage with the political process. Citizens may also be disempowered through their position in the socio-economic structure, as educated and wealthier citizens tend to be more knowledgeable and likely to engage than less-educated and poorer counterparts (Perloff, 2014: 75).

So what is at stake when we reflect on how citizens are politically literate? There are questions about how citizens use media, how elites use media and how media themselves present and re-present information. This comes with a caveat though: if citizens are not sufficiently literate or able to make sense of political information when provided to them about the government of the day, what options do they have to ask the wider questions about how our societies work? If debate and discussion is narrowed to a view of politics which encompasses only political elites and governments, then what is the space where we are asking questions about equality, globally, and about the rightness or wrongness of neoliberalism as a social system, for example, or what a global social justice would look like, or how we tackle the long-term impact of climate change?

To be media literate is to be able to: identify what news is; identify who has decided what matters; monitor and analyse events; and understand the role of media in shaping global issues (Moeller, 2009: 9). And this instrumental view of literacy provides us with an important starting point in thinking about how we might make sense of the information we are provided with through a variety of media platforms. But to be media and politically literate is to be concerned with similar issues: not only questions about who structures what we know and whose interests are reflected in the information we are provided with. But we might also want to ask wider questions about how rights and freedoms are protected, who decides who gets to speak and how citizens can have their voices heard.

Language and literacy

Public debates and discussions of what takes place are also structured and framed through language. And while this may be a self-evident point, language matters as it is used to shape our environment, our discourse, our media, and defines the limits of what is and isn't possible. To speak and to demand rights and freedoms requires articulating those thoughts through language. And political elites define what is and isn't possible in the world we live in through the use of language. For example, in the United Kingdom the Ministry of War was changed to the Ministry of Defence, giving it a more peaceful-sounding name, and therefore more likely to be accepted by the public. The language of war has been used in terms of setting the parameters of debate around setting political limits to welfare budgets (think headlines that declare 'war' on benefit scroungers), rather than discussion about the reasons behind people's need for benefits – but the words and language that we use frame debates as a mechanism to shore up support for a particular perspective. So to be politically literate we need to go beyond media information about what politicians do in office. Rather we need to be able to reflect on the *how* and *why* of this communication. When we talk about systems of communication in political communication, the focus tends to be on media systems and political systems, as above. But communication is more than the dissemination of information through media systems. Successful communication is reliant on and rooted in language (Sanders, 2009: 25–6), and as Sanders notes, there are three dimensions to this:

1. Language is an articulated system of signs – syntaxis – which must be used correctly;
2. [L]anguage is a vehicle of meaning – semantics – which implies a commitment to the notion it can tell us about truth [...];
3. That language has a practical dimension – rhetoric – [...] about knowing how to communicate in such a way that we achieve the desired effect in our audience.

This tripartite relationship thus forms the basis of what it means to communicate. We use a shared system of language through which meaning to our everyday experiences is constructed (e.g. Saussure, 1966). As Harris observes, 'language is no longer regarded as peripheral to our grasp of the world we live in, but as central to it. Words are not mere vocal labels or communicational adjuncts superimposed upon an already given order of things. They are collective products of social interaction, essential instruments through which human beings constitute and articulate their world' (1988: ix). Crucially, language is not neutral. It both constructs and contains meaning; that meaning is premised on shared social norms and values. Language is not simply about a 'thing' which is happening or exists, language contains meaning that is separate from material properties. For example, the word 'school' might entail a description of a set of physical buildings; but it also might denote a set of learning activities which do not necessarily rely on the presence of a material structure. School may denote a site where free thought and autonomy are encouraged; or it may be a site where authority is enacted, obedience encouraged and future work-forces are produced. The point is that the word 'school' has no inherent priorities, rather it is a 'sign' (word) that is attached to a 'signifier' (the thing being described) (Saussure, 2006) but the sign contains values and norms which are shared among communities and understood. 'Signs' can also reflect changes in values and norms. For example, the word 'gay' had previously meant happy, then came to be viewed pejoratively as a term of abuse for homosexual (men). More recently its meaning has changed again, the negative connotations no longer so strong, but the structure of the sign, those three letters, gay, has not changed. What have changed are the norms and values attached to those letters, that word. The word is then a reflection of changing social norms and values, which also serves to embed and reinforce, as well as reconstitute those norms and values. In this sense, George Orwell's (2013) observation 'He who controls the language controls the future' is prescient. And while Orwell was using 'he' to stand in for all of humanity, actually he reinforces the notion that it is 'he' (rather than 'he or she') that controls language; what he highlights is that the capacity to determine meaning in language rests on existing and wider structures of power. And to paraphrase Alice in Wonderland, a word may well mean whatever I choose it to mean, but I can only really effect a change in the shared understanding of that word if I am in a position to impose it, or change it for others. This reminds us that language is not only relational, but situational. The capacity to determine its meaning is dependent on our position in wider social and political structures. For example, the words asylum seeker and terrorist were commonly conflated following the events of September 11. These two words have very different meanings and are not synonymous. Yet, mediated discourses reflected a political agenda which sought to 'other' those who have been left with little choice but to leave their lives, homes and families, and link them to other 'enemies' of the state.

We are reminded then that communication is contingent upon language, and as Smith and Higgins observe, 'language...can be used to persuade, argue, inform, expose: it is never neutral' (2013: 5). Language not only contains meaning but also builds and is part of wider structures of meaning. This reminds us that ultimately all communication is inherently political, as it contains the norms and values that our society rest upon; it reminds us that interests are represented (and can be challenged) and it enables us to ask questions about how power is located in the systems of language that we use.

Not only does language serve to construct our systems of communication but it functions to embed ideology. Ideology, while a highly contested concept, broadly refers to a system of shared beliefs and internally consistent ideas. Language helps us articulate this. In formal politics, in the actions of states and governments, ideology is often expressed as a vision for a 'good society'; ideology and those internally consistent beliefs form the basis for a set of principles and guidelines as to what is right and wrong. Ideology often guides governments in questions about how resources are distributed, for example. In formal politics, ideology can take the form of a coherent set of beliefs and tends to be labelled as things like conservatism, liberalism, or socialism. In some ways, ideology functions to enable us to think about what is possible, what is logically consistent with that belief system, but it also serves to exclude ideas or principles which do not fit with that internally rigorous belief system. As with many of these concepts that we are discussing, it is useful to think about ideology as interactive and iterative, rather than preceding, or a consequence of, social systems and structures. Indeed, we could argue that ideology resides within existing structures of power. As Mannheim (1936) notes, while ideologies may emerge from a social system, they are not reducible to that system. Moreover, ideologies may exist, survive and evolve independently of a social (or political) system. In its most advanced form, ideology can be conceived of as 'common sense' (cf. Gramsci, 2011), for example, the idea that liberal democracy is the 'best' ordering mechanism of government. Common sense, for Gramsci, is achieved through the negotiation of conflict and the emergence of consensus. Conflict may take place between dominant and subordinate groups, but consensus is maintained through careful negotiation of such conflict. However, this is not necessarily imposed, rather it becomes a consequence of lived social practices and individuals' perceptions of the world around them. For Althusser, 'in ideology men [sic]…express, not the relation between them and their conditions of their existence, but the way they live the relation between them and their conditions of existence' (1969: 233). Ideology can also function to position people within a particular system (Althusser, 1969). Ideology provides a coherent set of ideas which may shape social practices, be reinforced by social practices yet, at the same time, function to position people within those social (or political) practices.

Language is thus intertwined with ideology, and functions to play a significant role in shaping how the world out there exists, how we interact with that world, and how we experience it. Ideas about the world, what is 'normal' or 'right', do not pre-exist, rather they are a product of an ideological consensus that is constructed and maintained through our usage of language. The words we choose express and shape our ideological positions. To understand what is being communicated to us politically, it is useful therefore to have an understanding of how these systems and structures work and become embedded. The focus of this book is the way these function through media and political systems, processes and the actions of elites and citizens within these systems. To make sense of this is to be literate, and it is to the political nature of that literacy that we now turn.

What is the political and ideological context for our literacy?

We use language to articulate our experiences of politics, and we read media to establish the behaviour of political elites. But a cumulative effect of this is the creation and construction of normalizing discourses: world views that set the parameters of our debates, discussions and our politics. These in turn are embedded with social norms, unquestioned assumptions about how we see the world. While language and ideology are interlinked, these in turn are part of wider trends and processes which embody ideas about how society operates. This is both ontological (in that there is a description of how society works) and normative (in that ideologies describe how society should work). If we want to understand how politics is communicated, we need to understand the wider context within which our social values and norms are constructed. Reflections on what it means to be literate remind us that we need to consider these wider ideals that have become normalized; they are communicated to us (ideologically) as 'common sense'. This communication of values and norms is political in its reinforcement of power relationships; embodied in underlying ideological assumptions about the way the world should (normatively) work and be expressed through language. In the West, the democratic ideals above are situated in a context which is characterized by an underlying acceptance of neoliberalism, capitalism, heteronormative white masculinity. These assumptions often remain implicit in much media discourse, and in much academic research around political communication. However, as these normalizing ideals are not neutral and privilege particular interests over others, it is worth a brief reflection on each of these in turn, as they are returned to throughout the book.

Neoliberalism has become the dominant Western approach to politics and economics and took root in the 1970s (Harvey, 2007). Neoliberalism 'proper' is located in the work of Milton Friedman, Ludwig Von Mises and Friedrich Hayek, historically located in the work of Adam Smith. Their approach viewed the market as the solution to all economic and political problems; state intervention was unnecessary; the market would regulate. What is interesting to note about Smith was that he was a moral philosopher, concerned on the one hand with the absence of government intervention so capital could self-regulate. However, he was also cognizant that some may exploit others, and that was where he did see a need for government intervention. Notably, however, this latter aspect of his work has been lost in contemporary readings of neoliberalism.

The neoliberal 'doctrine' espoused in the 1970s and 1980s was the 'wider set of metaphors, languages, techniques and organizational principles that have served to implement neoliberalism proper' (Couldry, 2010: 5) and it is the embedding of neoliberalism, it's normalization, how it provides a culture, a way of being in everyday life, that is neoliberalism as 'meaning'. And it is this neoliberalism as a structure of meaning that is of concern here. Neoliberalism simplifies complex economic and political problems as soluble through reference to markets, or spaces where markets can emerge. So embedded has neoliberalism as meaning become that we are prevented from seeing that alternate solutions, ways of organizing society, may become visible or realistically possible. Politicians articulate solutions to 'political' problems through recourse to market mechanisms. The language of consumerism, for example, has become rife in higher education. Markets are seen as solutions to funding of UK universities, rather than this being provided by the state. We also witness this embedding as students have linguistically (and ideology) been reconstructed as consumers, which alters perceptions of relationships and expectations. In this sense, the language of markets has reshaped the educational landscape, yet the underlying assumptions and the language used to reshape our educational reality is normalized in neoliberal discourses.

Within neoliberalism, we also witness the triumph of individualism over collectivism, which rewards those who are structurally advantaged in the current structure, in the language of meritocracy. (As will be noted below, however, if a system is set up by straight white men, in the interests of straight white men, do they not begin within a structural advantage?) In practice, moreover, neoliberalism as 'meaning' has also led to widening inequalities internationally and nationally, an increasing inequality of distribution of economic growth, and all the disadvantages that flow from that unequal distribution (Wilkinson and Pickett, 2010; Dorling, 2010). This normalization of a set of ideological assumptions stems in part from changes to how political problems are articulated, linguistically and ideologically. And thus to be literate is to be aware of these underlying guiding principles and assumptions. In our contemporary Western environment, Neoliberalism interacts with and is ideologically intertwined with capitalism.

Capitalism is a mechanism for ordering economic, political and increasingly social relations. At its most fundamental, capitalism is a system where power is located economically in relations of production and consumption: in divisions of labour. For Adam Smith (1986/1776) this meant that free exchange could take place – supply and demand would be guided by the 'invisible hand' of the market. For Smith, this entailed a reasonable and fair exchange relationship, in a free market of legal equals. For Marx, however, this exchange system was exclusively concerned with monetary profit that masked an underlying reality of inequality and exploitation. As the bourgeoisie owned the means of production, there was an unequal system of exchange with those supplying their labour available to exploitation to generate monetary profit for the owners of the means of production. For Marx, the basic exchange in this market relationship – buying and selling of labour – was inherently unequal. This material exchange formed the basis of social relations and was reinforced by the creation of state regulation. Government functioned not to redistribute the wealth created in this system, rather '[t]he executive of the modern state is but a committee for managing the common affairs of the whole bourgeoisie' (1848: 3). Government was not in the interests of all legal equals, rather its function was to protect the interests of the owners of the means of production. What this meant was that social relations had a material basis, and it was through these social relations, which were reinforced through government regulation, the capitalist system was embedded as an objective or 'natural' state of affairs. But this 'natural' state of affairs was not designated to benefit all, rather those with existing wealth.

Earlier reflections on capitalism focused on domestic effects; however, increasingly we see capitalism as a means of ordering economic, political and social relations taking place on a global scale. While the idea of globalization remains contested, Robinson (2004) argues that we have witnessed a shift from a world economy to a global economy – that is an interconnection of economies, globally all interlinked through capitalism. For Robinson, this constitutes an 'an epochal shift…in the history of world capitalism' (2004: 2). The ubiquity of capitalism, like Western neoliberalism, becomes 'common sense'. For example, we might ask: can we imagine an alternative method of ordering society? The language of capitalism is so embedded that alternative sustainable articulations remain largely marginalized and absent in public debate. Thus to recognize the underlying function of capitalism enables us to unpack, first, how neoliberalism has become so intertwined, as we witness the state being reinvented and the language of markets gain primacy. Second, we are also invited to reflect politically on systems of oppression and exploitation, which become normalized in our daily discourses. The third aspect of this normalization, of the world articulated as common sense, and which a political literacy enables us to reflect on, is how gender relations affect the language and discourses within Western society.

Patriarchy. Literally the rule of the father, alongside neoliberalism and capitalism this has become a dominant social and economic political ordering mechanism. The history of feminist literature points us to how women have been politically marginalized dating back to Mary

Wollstonecraft (1792) in terms of formal political rights in the public sphere and the existence of power politics in the home, where patriarchal legislation protects male interests (Engels, 1884), and more recently how cultural norms and values are embodied in literature's (Millett, 1985) expectations about women's behaviour (Wolf, 1991) and their representation in mass media (van Zoonen, 1994; Gill, 2007) and new media (Banyard, 2010). Judith Butler (1999) points us to how our gender and sexuality are not 'naturally' determined by our biology at birth. Rather they are 'performed' in our social interactions and social settings. The way we 'perform' gender and sexuality is governed by a set of social norms and conventions. In neoliberal terms sexuality (and by extension gender) are markers of 'success' and 'failure' (Halberstam, 2011). In this way our attention is drawn to the notion that to perform gender and sexuality is to perform our identities through codes and social norms that have been defined by heterosexual males.

Feminist critiques of patriarchy have been subject to internal disputes as Black feminists noted how (second-wave) feminism had been largely concerned with issues facing white middle-class women (cf. hooks, 1981). And reflecting on whiteness as 'common sense' also helps us think about how the world is constructed ideologically around us. The term race denotes a biological grouping (such as Black) in the same way that sex does for men and women. The term race is contested and ethnicity functions to highlight the social construction of biological divisions in a similar way that gender works in respect to biological sex. What is useful about these approaches is that they help us challenge the totalizing narratives which position heterosexual (cf. Butler, 1999; Halberstam, 2005) white (Said, 1978; Young, 2004; hooks, 1983; Spivak, 1985) males at the centre of history and analysis, reminding us also of the gendered nature of democracy (Pateman, 1988; Phillips, 1991). While the starting point in this book, in part, is those contemporaries' histories, the aim here is to invite reflection on those totalizing narratives and to encourage us to think beyond the parameters that the field and our mediated discourses define for us. To be literate is to thus be cognizant of these wider narratives that shape the language we use and the ideas we hold about what is 'normal'.

Codes and messages

As discussed in the previous chapter, questions about the nature of political communication encourage us to think about what reality, or realities, look like. In order to identify 'reality', we name it and signify it through language, imbued with ideas. But this naming does not reflect an inherent realism, rather it can contribute to the construction of reality. To understand how reality is, or realities are, constructed we need to think about how they are described and defined, and the norms, values and ideologies that are contained in that defining.

To be politically literate is to be able to recognize and identify this construction. But this is not necessarily straightforward as there are a variety of ways in which we are implicated in it. Althusser (1970) introduced the term interpellation: while people believe themselves to be subjects of their own experiences of reality, these experiences have been constructed by ideological 'codes'. Political and social reality, then, is a product of ideological experiences; for Althusser, ideology is 'the systems of representation in which people live out their imaginary relationship to their real conditions of existence' (Grossberg et al., 2006: 206). Ideology (and more broadly, dominant ideas) define what you can and can't see, or know. This focus on ideology, in this context, suggests that a single 'reality' is being created by media. But this 'reality' is not static; it needs to be maintained, repeated, reinforced; because of this process, hegemony does allow for the possibility of resistance and opposition (Down, 1996: 14). This would mean that media messages are broadly consensual, that they provide a space where social norms are generated, and common sense constructed. This perspective has been criticized for implying that people are passive recipients of media messages, with little control over their own beliefs (discussed in more depth in the following chapter).

In contrast, Fiske (1987) suggests that media messages are polysemous. That is media messages are received differently by different audiences depending on their prior socialization and their relation to the text, and so the same message may be received in different ways by different audiences. The film *12 Years a Slave*, for example, was heralded by mainstream media as a breakthrough in recognition of the issues of race in Hollywood filmmaking. In contrast, Roxanne Gay (2014) viewed this film as perpetuating the subordination and abuse of Black women. For example, while coverage of Oscar winners may focus on the successful achievements of celebrities and the film industry more widely, others may view this coverage as a broader mechanism of reinforcing the dominance and how success is defined in white, male, heteronormative ways. Scholars have noted the role of the audience in constructing mediated reality with reference to the notion of 'polyvalence' (Condit, 1989). Rather than messages having a number of meanings (as in polysemy), audiences will recognize the existence of differing interpretations in a text, but disagree about the value of those interpretations, that it is the focus of the value of meanings that produces differing interpretations. Following the Oscars example, polyvalence will recognize that diversity of interpretations, but may disagree as to which reflects 'reality'. This does highlight the importance of 'context' and the possibility of oppositional readings, or resistant readings of mainstream media messages. This also suggests that media play a role in constructing multiple realities. That our different experience of media depends on our position in relation to the medium or media messages we engage with.

However, despite the differences in assumptions about how audiences are positioned, Foucault reminds us that the contestation over struggle for meaning, for 'power', takes place in and through discourse. Discourse is more than language, but is relatively bounded, it contains socially produced forms of knowledge, and crucially it sets limits on what it is possible to know. As Barad observes, 'Discourse is not what is said; it is that which constrains and enables what can be said' (2003: 821). Within discursive contexts, there are struggles over meaning. But dominant discourses become commonly accepted as truth – for example the neoliberal logic of the market as a means to tackle social and political problems is now largely and commonly accepted as truth, limiting and constraining the possibilities of conversations around redistribution of wealth as a social ordering mechanism. When we are thinking about what is being communicated politically we need to reflect on the discursive context which is setting the limits on what it is possible and not possible to know about 'reality'.

Reading mediated political discourse

To be literate is to be able to understand how mediated messages are encoded, and to think about how we read those messages. In contrast to how media messages are received, we might also think about how those messages are constructed, and how these messages contribute to and are negotiated within wider discourses. In reading mediated discourses, we also need crucially to ask, who gets to speak? And perhaps more significantly, who decides who gets to speak? These are intensely political questions, but on one level we could argue this hinges on decisions of journalists and editors, and media owners (see Chapter 5). But these questions are also intensely political as they are located in a power relationship. Couldry's work is useful here as he argues that to have 'voice' is not only to have practical resources (such as language) but also to have symbolic resources – such as the status necessary to be recognized by others as having a voice (2010: 7). Articulation of interests is thus reliant on others' acknowledgement, recognition and legitimation of those interests. We might think about this for example in relation to energy companies. They are able to have voice by discussing price increases with politicians in media such as TV, press and radio. But what happens to the voices we don't hear? In the energy example, we are much less likely to see a customer given equal footing to those with legislative or economic 'power' in this context. Voice is thus articulated and legitimated in a context of dominant interests; in this example, those of big business (cf. Allen and Savigny, 2012). So, in extending Couldry's argument, to be able to express 'voice' is intensely political. Capacity for 'voice' is not only reliant on the individual, but upon the wider ideational (social and political) context in which voice is expressed or (crucially) denied.

If there is unequal access to expression, it follows that some voices are louder, some groups and individuals are more vocal than others. And if those others do not see or hear their voices represented, how can they make their own voice heard? If their voices are denied, this represents a deep form of oppression (Couldry, 2010: 9). This oppression can be described as 'double consciousness' and 'the sense of always looking at oneself through the eyes of others' (Dubois, 1989/1903: 3). This form of oppression denies voice, and potentially alters how voices may be heard and represented. For Tuchman (1978) there were gendered consequences of the lack of capacity to express voice. This, for her, led to the 'systematic annihilation of women'. Women (of all colour) were annihilated in their media representation and the under-and misrepresentation of women in media coverage in a variety of forms has been addressed empirically by the WACC Global Media Monitoring project (and this is discussed in more detail in Chapter 5) and by scholars such as van Zoonen (1994), Ross (2007), Garcia and Wahl-Jorgensen, Savigny and Warner (2015).

So when we ask questions about what is being communicated, we are asking political questions about the location of power. Who is speaking? Whose interests are being articulated? What is the context that gives rise to these views being privileged over others? How are these interests negotiated? How does consensus emerge? What underlying power relations are shaping the discussion? When voices are heard, who is being marginalized? And what are the consequences of such marginalization? In order to think about how we might enact our literacy, we might also ask the following questions:

1. Why is this topic being written about?
2. How is the topic written about?
3. What other ways of writing about the topic are there? (Kress, 1985: p7, cited in Cranny-Francis et al., 2003: 95)

This enables the analyst to go on to consider:

1. The strategy involved in generating a particular discourse
2. The rhetoric it uses
3. The alternatives suppressed by this discourse (ibid)

What is not being communicated?

As much as political communication assumes that something political is being communicated, we are also reminded that political communication entails the act of non-communication, and this in itself is a political action, with political consequences. Couldry (2010) argues that 'voice' is an essential feature of the democratic process; indeed it is fundamental to legitimating modern democracies. But it is not sufficient to have 'voice', he argues, rather we also need the capacity to exercise that voice if democracy is to be meaningful and legitimate. For our purposes here, we are looking at how people have a 'voice' within the media. Couldry talks about voice as value as important to the way we organize socially and culturally. Voice as value, for Couldry, means valuing, and actively choosing to value the frameworks which themselves value the expression of voice. On the one hand, for example, we could say that the media is absolutely intrinsically about voice as value – in that its raison d'être is to 'value' voice. But as above, we might think about whose voice.

Couldry (2010) argues that at present we are witnessing a 'crisis of voice' where, within Western democracies, we increasingly behave as though 'voice' does not matter. To express voice is an act imbued with knowledge and assumptions about the legitimacy of that voice. But what if that voice is denied? Or suppressed? Debate, discussion and a free exchange of ideas are at the very heart of what it means to be in a liberal democracy. But what if we don't talk about, or give 'voice' to, particular issues? Or what if they are kept out of the public eye? Does this disempower groups or individuals affected by those issues? Can interests be expressed if they are not given a voice? What are the consequences for our politics and society of this kind of silencing? If voice is marginalized or silenced, rather than challenge power structures, we see media functioning to shore up and consolidate existing dominant interests rather than fundamentally challenge them. We see media coverage that focuses on the interests of business and wealthy elites, for example, in the downplaying of tax evasion as crime while simultaneously 'othering' benefit claimants. In the period 2013–14, £73.4billion was lost to tax evasion (Murphy, 2014) compared to £4.91bn in the previous year spent on job seeker's allowance (*The Guardian,* 2013). Economic logics play a role in determining who gets to speak. For example, Guy Standing (2011) has argued that we are witnessing the emergence of what he calls the Precariat – a growing number of people across the world living and working precariously, usually in a series of short-term jobs, without recourse to stable occupational identities or careers, stable social protection or protective regulations relevant to them. Standing argues that this class of people could produce new instabilities in society because as this group becomes increasingly frustrated, they become dangerous because they have no voice. In turn, he argues this means they become vulnerable to the siren calls of extreme political parties.

Hannah Arendt drew our attention to how voice, and the capacity to express ourselves, is linked to formal political conceptions of statehood. Her work was focused on how citizenship is reliant on recognition by the state. Migrants forced to flee, who are not able to claim statehood, for her, were denied not only their rights, but further, the right to have rights. She argues, 'We become aware of the existence of a right to have rights (and that means to live in a framework where one is judged by one's actions and opinions) and a right to belong to some kind of organized community, only when millions of people emerge who had lost and could not regain these rights because of the new global political situation' (Arendt, 1951: 177). In this way, Arendt reminds us that our capacity to communicate, to express our rights and interests is intimately bound up with and determined by political structures, just as the 'right to have rights' is dependent on membership of a formal political community. As rights are determined by and contingent upon a state, those who had no state affiliation were therefore not only denied rights (i.e. rights of citizenship) but they were further deprived of the 'right to have rights' in the first place. Not only were these people then denied a voice, but they were also denied the right to have a voice in the first place.

In her groundbreaking postcolonial essay, Spivak (1988) asks 'can the subaltern speak?' The subaltern, for her, are those groups who broadly stand outside of existing dominant power structures. For Spivak, the subaltern are marginalized and silenced through the prominence of Western assumptions that dominate philosophical discussions, which write subaltern identities out of dialogues, denying them the opportunity to have voice, or to speak. Squires (2002) notes how groups such as women, people of colour, religious minorities, LGBT communities find themselves marginalized in 'public spheres', where their voices are marginalized or rendered silent. Squires (2002) observes that not all in these groups have access to the same public spaces, media resources or the mechanisms to engage in political discourse. One of the consequences of this marginalization means that 'Particular groups may be targeted by government officials [for example welfare claimants] ... and have a harder time distributing their ideas' (2002: 449). Not only does this actively prevent communication, but there are also consequences in how groups may be stigmatized. The British press's demonization of British Muslims (Khiabany and Williamson, 2012) provides a problematic example here, as the repetition in the media of dominant 'prevailing social norms may instill fear into citizens of marginalized publics that their ideas would at best be met with indifference, and at worst violence' (Squires, 2002: 449). Spivak's (1988) answer to her own question was a resounding 'no'. And the marginalization and silencing of views and voices through mainstream mediated discourses, it is argued here, is in itself an act of political communication.

Summary

Political communication matters as its ubiquity means that it is a central part of our everyday lived experiences; because of this it is crucial that we are literate and able to understand what is taking place in our names. This chapter has sought to encourage a reflection on how political communication takes place; and situate this activity in its broader ideational, ideological context. Ideas about what the world should look like are often presented to us, unquestioningly, as this is the way that the world actually is. To be able to make sense of the worlds around us, this chapter has unpacked some of the wider strategies that we use as daily praxis, such as a language, and how that serves to embed and reinforce broader dominant ideological positions. These positions often remain undiscussed, taken for granted, in our mediated discourses. So our job as critical analysts is to reflect on how these discourses shape the nature of communication, and how we come to 'know' about both the formal activities of government and the more informal fluid ways in which politics is played out in mediated everyday life. Understanding the wider contexts in which our politics is communicated to us, and what is taken for granted (such as the dominance of neoliberalism as an ordering mechanism) helps us carve out a space to think about how common sense functions effectively but also helps us think more critically about what we might be missing.

Reflection/seminar activities

Choose a daily news source and keep a diary containing subjects covered for a week. What are the recurrent themes? Whose 'voices' are represented in each item that you have looked at? Who doesn't get to speak, or have their voices or interests represented? What underlying codes/ assumptions/norms are contained in those articles? How are women and people of colour and their interests represented in these items?

What might a world without capitalism; patriarchy and/or neoliberalism look like?

Why do you think media studies has a bad reputation in the media? Why don't we learn media literacy at school?

Chapter 3

Who are the Audience(s)?

Introduction

If there was no audience to read, listen, watch and consume media, then media would struggle to function or, indeed, to exist. This claim makes audiences central to the process of political communication. Not only in the communication of formal politics, the actions of political elites (as discussed in Chapter 4), but also in the sense that the existence of an audience and its relations to media implies a negotiated political relationship. Communication relies on a receiver; and so media rely on audiences. In order to make sense of the way power may be distributed and operates we need, therefore, to also understand what is meant by the term 'audience'. Indeed, this is an ontological question as we need to begin by asking, is there such a thing as 'the' audience? To suggest there is a singular audience assumes that there is an homogenous group that exists 'out there'. We might, therefore, think that there are multiple audiences with differing interpretations of the same content. Moreover, these multiple audiences may use different media platforms and bring different beliefs and behaviours to the media content that they consume. This matters because if media rely on audiences, then surely media will need to respond to audience demand. It is often assumed that audiences comprise the masses (again implying a homogeneity) but if media audiences are elites, what does this mean for the masses?

As such, the ways audiences are positioned, constructed and communicated to are of central concern in this chapter (and throughout the book). An underlying premise throughout is that each act of communication constitutes political action; power relations are reinforced, negotiated, reconstructed and sometimes challenged. This political power play also takes place through ways audiences are positioned: is the aim of communication to silence or marginalize an audience? Is the silencing or marginalization of particular audiences a function of existing dominant ideologies? When we are thinking about who gets to speak, as we are through much of this book, we also need to think about who is assumed to be listening.

What is an audience?

The Oxford English Dictionary defines an audience as 'The assembled spectators or listeners at a public event such as a play, film, concert, or meeting'. What is significant to note here is the importance of this being a public event, which implies a form of mediation. Audiences exist in a public space (as opposed to the realm of the private). This definition reinforces the idea that it is this engagement with publicly disseminated content (that comes to us via media outlets) that is central in constructing the notion of audience. In this sense, we could argue that communication via media has both political and ontological functions. To deconstruct this, we might think about what is taking place in this relationship. Audiences are assembled spectators, and in thinking through the underlying assumptions and power relations contained in the notion that audiences are spectators (or listeners), it is useful to turn to the work of Jacques Rancière. In Rancière's analysis of the relationship between art and politics, he argues that 'there is no theatre without a spectator' (2009: 2). It is the existence of the art itself, or in our case media, that creates the viewer, voyeur or audience. This attributes enormous effect to media as powerful in construction of a particular version of reality. This is an interdependent relationship, but one which creates possible problems for audiences; are they simply passive recipients of political communication, or are they active on their deconstruction and knowledge of what is presented to them?

For Rancière, the way audiences are constructed as voyeurs is enormously problematic. This is because of the passivity encouraged on the part of the spectator. He argues that 'viewing is the opposite of knowing: the spectator is held before an appearance in a state of ignorance about the process of production of this appearance and the reality it conceals' (2009: 2). As voyeurs, as viewers, we are rendered passive, uninformed, unchallenged, and required to accept rather than critique or understand. His argument suggests that a lack of deeper knowledge about the power relations that have been played out to produce the 'spectacle' on the part of the spectator means that audiences do not learn, do not gain knowledge, have no awareness of the power relationships which are obscured by media which they receive. This has consequences, and in some ways his second observation, that viewing is opposite to acting and renders audiences passive (ibid), is in line with critical theorists who assume a passivity on the part of the audience. However, while for critical theorists this passivity is a product of audiences themselves, for Rancière this is a consequence of how audiences are constructed and positioned by cultural forms with which they engage. But, as he observes, 'to be a spectator is to be separated from both the capacity to know and the capacity to act' (ibid). He argues for a different kind of theatre to be constructed; one 'where those in attendance learn from as opposed to being seduced by images; where they become active participants as opposed to passive voyeurs' (2009: 4). This suggests a change in the nature of power relations, and is almost a 'call to arms' for a more informed, engaged, resistant audience. One of the aims of this book is to encourage us to reflect on how we watch, listen to and engage with a range of media outlets, forms and contents. Rancière's work reminds us that power relations are taking place and being communicated, not only at the site of media content (as discussed in later chapters) but at the intersection where audiences are constructed by, and meet, media output.

Indeed, it is understanding and challenging these power structures that contain the roots to our emancipation; 'when we understand that the self-evident facts that structure the relations between saying, seeing and doing themselves belong to the structure of domination and subjection' (Rancière, 2009: 13). So emancipation comes from knowledge; not just knowledge of the content of the political communication that we receive through media output, but through knowledge of how audiences come into being: their ontology in relation to mediated political communication.

Why do audiences matter?

If media could not exist without audiences, this implies incredible power located within an audience. If audiences for a particular media outlet did not exist, then that media form would no longer exist. An example, perhaps, is the *Today* newspaper, which was launched in the United Kingdom in 1986. Low readership and audience engagement were among the reasons that the newspaper folded in 1995. In this way, we can see just how important an audience is for media, and this implies a considerable amount of power to be located in audiences en masse. Yet, much existing research reflects a concern with the opposite relationship. Rather than explore how audiences might affect media, attention tends to focus on how media might impact audiences.

Earlier analysis was concerned with how mass media might be able to manipulate audiences, who were seen as passive receptors of media content (Lippmann, 1922; Lasswell, 1927). A range of research from voting to violence linked audience responses to information and media depictions (Lazarsfeld et al., 1944; Bandura and Walters, 1963) and assumed that audiences could be manipulated in a manner that may not be consistent with their own interests. This was followed by work from the Frankfurt school, who, concerned with the effects of Nazi propaganda, argued that media audiences were passive recipients of media and cultural texts, empty vessels in to which messages from media and cultural texts were simply injected (cf. Adorno and Horkheimer, 1979/1947). Latterly, scholars argued that things were not quite so simple, and the masses not quite so easily duped. Rather the 'uses and gratifications' approach suggested that knowing audiences actively consumed media and cultural texts, in contrast to the passivity implied by the earlier critical accounts. Here it was argued that audiences consumed media and cultural texts for their own pleasure and reinforcement (e.g. Blumler and Katz, 1974; Morley, 1980; Ang, 1986) and that audiences consumed media 'selectively' (Klapper, 1960). In 1972, McCombs and Shaw observed that we may not be able to establish a direct causal influence in the media telling us what to think, but they argued that media are stunningly successful in telling us what to think about. The idea that media have effects has been researched in a range of areas including attempts to ascertain influence in areas such as 'moral panics' (Cohen, 2011; Critcher, 2006), media violence (Barker and Petley, 1997), voting behaviour (Curtice and Semetko, 1994; Newton and Brynin, 1997) to name but a few. Researchers have argued that it is the social context rather than a media context that creates beliefs and attitudes (Barker and Petley, 1996; Gauntlett, 1998; Norris, 1999). However, it is argued here that while analytically it may be possible to separate media and social contexts, ontologically, that is not so straightforward if we accept that media play a role in creating the social reality that we experience.

The debate about the extent to which media can influence their audience underpins much of the discussion in this book. As noted, McCombs and Shaw (1972) argued that media may not tell us what to think, but they tell us what to think about. Media frame the issues of the day, so audiences are implicitly told that these are the things we should be thinking about. For example, we may not be told what our views on the Western financial crisis, or austerity measures imposed by governments should be, but we are told that these are important issues of the day. Within this book, I extend this point to say that they also tell us *how* to think about the world. For example, in the framing of austerity and the Western financial crisis, not only is the capitalist frame reinforced, but we are encouraged to think that the world out there is dependent on this mechanism of economic exchange in order for society to function.

The general public and public opinion

Perhaps the most common assumption made about audiences is that they comprise the general public. And so we might tend to think of people reading newspapers, watching TV, blogging and reading online. News media have a remit to operate in the public interest, and this ties in with the idea that the public are audiences for news and other forms of media consumption. Elite actors often make reference to 'the public' and it is not uncommon to see 'the public' invoked as a justification for policies and action (cf. Lewis et al., 2005). In our news media, we see individuals are invoked as representative of 'the public' so politicians will increasingly use phrases such as 'I was speaking with Dave, a manual worker, who told me that...' or 'when I saw Joan, a hospital worker from Kettering...' to legitimate and justify their policy positions. So in this way the personalization of 'the public' is used as a device to connect with audiences. Public is a key term in thinking about audiences, but it is useful to reflect on who and what the public are and how the public is identified.

One way the public has been historically identified is through reference to public opinion. This has spawned an entire industry devoted to the 'measurement' of public opinion. Public opinion is often invoked by political actors in justification for their actions, but this implies a neutrality, that there is such an unbiased thing as public opinion available to be quantified and democratically legitimate. Yet public opinion is not a neutral concept, in its expression or its construction. For Walter Lippmann, an early analyst of public opinion, the expression of public opinion could be a dangerous thing. In liberal theories, the 'public' are assumed to legitimate political systems and earlier perceptions were that the opinions of the public were formed by the media of the day (Higgins, 2008: 23). Walter Lippmann's *Public Opinion* (1922), however, was critical of this idea. His hostility stemmed from the thought that individuals in mass society were not competent to think beyond their own self-interest. As he saw it, problems lay in the suggestion that media sought to pander to the masses because, in his view, public opinion was uninformed and ill considered. This meant that there was an appeal to the lowest common denominator, and in this way media's capacity to contribute to public debate, to fulfil its function in liberal theory, becomes curtailed by public opinion. So Lippmann's groundbreaking work argued that media reflect public opinion, but given the poverty of quality of public opinion, he argued this is damaging for a healthy democracy. In contrast, Bourdieu argues in favour of diversity, rather than the public as one homogenous mind (1979). The public, he suggests, is not one ill-informed mass; but the assumption and acceptance of Lippmann's stance enables elites to ignore the will of the people. As Higgins notes, 'Whereas Lippmann accuses public opinion of distracting the competent deliberation of the political elite, Bourdieu sees it as an establishment tool to dismiss the masses in an easy and sweeping definition' (Higgins, 2008: 24). On the one hand, then, public opinion is ill informed in part because of a poverty of information, a reliance on media which were not sufficient to enable citizens to be fully knowledgeable about public affairs. On the other, we see that the notion of public opinion can be a convenient political construct for elites, which enables them to ignore a diversity of citizens' views and continue to govern as they see fit, rather than represent their constituents.

Lewis et al. (2005) argue that it is media who create public opinion. This is done through a variety of methods: the use of 'vox pops' – in-the-street interviews, to authenticate, give depth and 'reality' to a TV news story. Another mechanism used to represent public opinion, to construct public opinion, is through the use of opinion polls. Widely seen as a legitimate measure of 'public opinion', polls are a common method of representing public views and we might regularly see headlines which remind us of public support about a particular issue (e.g. 'Public support for war on Saddam', 'Polls show Cameron as clear winner of leaders' debates'). Rationality is reinforced through the objective scientific measurement of this thing called 'public opinion', although as these examples also remind us, public opinion can be measured and mobilized to support a particular agenda.

While we see polls referred to in any area where public support is sought, opinion polls also feature heavily at election time. Again, adhering to the notion of objectivity in the scientific measuring of public opinion, polls are used to give insights as to who will win the election. These are widely reported on and often viewed as reliable indicators of electoral outcomes. However, in the UK 1992 election, the polls famously 'got it wrong' (Moon, 1999). Opinion polls had predicted a Labour victory, yet the electorate delivered a Tory government. After much soul searching, the pollsters argued that the exit polls had been wrong as people were embarrassed to admit to voting Conservative, so they lied to pollsters about their voting intentions and behaviour. Following this analysis, pollsters revised their methods in order to factor in that Conservatives voters may lie about their voting intentions. However, at the time of writing, in the UK 2015 election, a similar issue arose; the polls in the run up to the election predicted a hung Parliament, that there was no certain outcome and the possible need for a coalition. Exit polls confounded all, and the ultimate outcome was a very unexpected, and unpredicted, Conservative majority. At the time of writing, the 'shy Tory' thesis has again been advanced, and polling organizations and scholars are reflecting on why they 'got it wrong'. Throughout media discussion of how pollsters got it wrong, the focus has been on the methods the polling industry used. If pollsters use similar methods, then they are likely to get similar outcomes. A poll that is 'out of sync' with the rest of the polling industry may not be viewed as legitimate in media discourses, or seen as an anomaly. With reputations and businesses to protect, in whose interests would an outlier poll be? Sources close to the Labour Party, for example, have confirmed that they did have outlier polls, predicting a major defeat, but these were marginalized internally, favouring those which were not so catastrophic and, more significantly, were aligned with the dominant media poll discourses.

Noelle Neuman (1974) argued that the construction of an idea of 'public opinion' created what she called a 'spiral of silence' whereby views that weren't consistent with majority views, ways of thinking and dominant discourses would be marginalized. In short, this assumes that people are influenced by what they think other people think. So, if people think they are expressing a minority view, her theory argues, they withhold that view, based upon a fear of isolation where 'the individual is vulnerable ... social groups can punish him for failing to toe the line' (1974: 43). Indeed, it could be argued that this was why pollsters were unable to accurately predict the outcome of the 1992 UK election: people were reluctant to admit that they were voting Conservative (as above); at the time, the Conservatives were highly unpopular – to admit voting for them could have resulted in the kind of social embarrassment, isolation, that Noelle-Neuman directs us towards. However, it is not only 'unpopular' opinions, or views which might be unpalatable according to dominant social norms that may be silenced.

For Lewis, polls function to reinforce and validate dominant media frames, which may in turn influence public opinion (2001: 34); indeed, polls 'play a powerful role in legitimating and enforcing elite policy frames' (2001: 36). This suggests a complicity between media and political elites – implicitly or explicitly working together with a 'top-down' view of the public; the public are assumed to be passive recipients and media align themselves with elite agendas, framing polls as disputes between elites, rather than between elites and public opinion (Page and Shapiro, 1992; Zaller, 1992). In this way the representation of public opinion through polls is not about benefiting the public or giving expression to unheard public views, rather media frame polls to facilitate elites speaking on behalf of the public.

But what polls seem to be less successful at achieving is influence over political elites. Research has shown that political leaders routinely ignore results of polls that do not confirm their own political views or align with their own political goals (Sussman, 1988). As Helliger and Judd have observed, when public opinion does not fit elite interests, elites then 'have a significant capacity to ignore it' (1991: 248). At the time of writing, as noted above, there is media discussion as to why the polls were so wrong in respect of the 2015 UK election. Yet to date, there has been little public discussion of the extent to which political parties may have ignored polling data that was inconsistent with their electoral strategies and approach. What counts as public opinion, and how it is framed in mediated discourses, is profoundly political. Publics are constructed through media framing and yet this is not for the purposes of holding elites to account, rather it is a way for media allegiances to be expressed and elite agendas to be reinforced and advanced. In an era of new media technologies, however, there is potential for those boundaries to become blurred. For example, as Blumenthal observes (2005), in the US 2004 election campaign the internet and blogging became a source of challenging conventional polling and establishing public opinion;

public opinion becomes something that was constructed by audiences, without intervention or direction from elites and elite interests, although the extent to which these audiences are able to effect political change is, to date, debatable.

Advertisers and the construction of audiences

Audiences are not only constructed through their definition as 'public opinion'. While the primary motive of media may be to attract an audience, this is also coupled with the need for most media to create a profit. Purchasers of media content, such as newspapers or films, may be regarded as audiences, but it is not only media outlets that play a role in constructing these audiences. Those who have an input into media content, such as political and economic elites (as discussed below), are significant when we think of how audiences are constituted. The particular focus in this section is on the role of advertising. Mass audiences in themselves may not generate sufficient income for media outlets to survive, and many non-state-owned media outlets also rely heavily on advertising revenue.

The importance of advertising for media cannot be underestimated. It is an important source of revenue and, for example, in the newspaper industry with declining purchase of newspapers, the revenue gained from advertising is essential. In this way, we might think that media functions politically to deliver audiences for advertisers. This can be starkly seen by Peter Oborne's (the chief political commentator) public resignation from the *Telegraph*, on the basis that it was committing 'fraud on its readers' by refusing to publish negative stories about HSBC, for fear of losing advertising revenue (Oborne, 2015). In this way, rather than opinion polls being a mechanism to define, advertising companies spend large sums identifying target groups for their messages. And media outlets deliver an audience; but for a fee. Advertisers recognize the benefits of messages disseminated via differing media platforms to differently constructed audiences, while at the same time playing a role in constructing those audiences.

There is an interdependent relationship between advertisers and media outlets: where media outlets are economically reliant on advertising revenue, and advertisers reliant on media for the delivery of audiences. This has been the case with all non-state-funded media and most recently we can see examples in new social media. For example, most free-to-use sites are funded through the implied promise of the site owner to advertisers; that the sale of space will deliver audiences to the advertiser. It is usual to log on to any free social media site and get adverts specific to the preferences that users set, and advertisers pay for access and information so they are able to monitor 'likes' and 'click throughs' and amend their messages accordingly. In this way, advertisers are able to access information about individual users, and more broadly about differing audiences, so that they can then target messages in different ways to fit the demographic they are appealing to. However, social media do afford the opportunity for advertisers to be challenged as a mechanism to hold media outlets to account. For example, one innovative way in which media content was challenged was undertaken by Laura Bates and the *Everyday Sexism* project. She called on Facebook to monitor content in respect of the way domestic violence was being glamourized, normalized and treated as fashionable. When Facebook refused to amend its policies on the grounds of 'free speech' (for more on this issue see Chapter 5), she contacted advertisers with her protest. Advertisers agreed her point and threatened to withdraw from Facebook unless policies were put in place. In this way we can see that advertisers then become key audiences for the owners of media production. In turn, public interest becomes redefined not as 'what interests the public' (Street, 2010) and as assumed by Lippmann above. Rather public interest becomes what interests the advertisers, which reminds us just how deeply embedded economic and democratic tensions have become.

In part, advertisers are successful in a way that the PR industry has also been, in that they take into account those products they are trying to sell, but make their properties meaningful. Advertising sets up a connection between audiences and things, between types of people and products. For example, lifestyle products when advertised speak to us, create meaning for audiences of aspiration, of the possibility to change our roles, our positions in society. While Sender (1999) notes how advertising has consistently reflected dominant views of 'proper' femininity and masculinity, she also observes that prevailing representations of gender relations are also linked to heterosexual 'norms'. Williamson (1998) argues that advertising obscures the real structures of society, and Sender might argue that these are those which privilege the straight white man. Williamson suggests that economic power structures are obscured by focusing on the products rather than the people involved in the production process. In this way, she argues that false distinctions are made about what society looks like, ideas of class are replaced by an emphasis on the consumption of goods; yet class is reinforced by the aspirational products that are linked to class status (Williamson, 1998: 13). Class struggle is not to be overcome by changes to the economic structure per se, rather class is individualized and individuals are 'promised' class liberation through the consumption of particular products, rather than through knowledgeable challenge to the dominant order. In this way, advertising also positions audiences, not as knowledgeable and active citizens, rather it seeks to recreate audiences as consumers, which benefits advertisers (as they are able to profit from this material relationship) while reconstructing audiences as consumers of products. In studies of advertising trends, researchers have argued that advertisements also offer a site and system of cultural production and meaning creation to a consumer society (Leiss, Kline and Jhally, 1990). In this way, adverts also function to make us consumers, to guide us to a marketplace of products that can fulfil our desires (that have been manufactured by the advertisers). Advertising then is a means of creating audiences for media content and outlets, a site of aspiration creation for audiences, as well as a place where audiences are reconstituted as consumers.

Advertising constructing audiences as consumers?

In his teleological account, Marx argued that the product becomes a commodity – a 'mere moment of exchange' and so the value of the product, through the process of commodification, becomes its exchange value. So what can the process of commodification tell us about audiences? The terms audiences and consumers are often used interchangeably, but whereas to be an audience suggests a degree of passivity perhaps (as noted by Rancière above) to be a consumer changes the nature of the interaction between audiences and media. Audiences as consumers become more active, but not through autonomous choices made through their own volition. If audiences can be 'bought' by advertisers then through a process of exchange audiences become products, like any other material form, and become amenable to commodification. This in turn suggests that the value of the audience is to be found in the process of exchange; audiences become commodified.

For Baudrillard, to understand what is taking place in society and, by extension, politically, we need to understand the nature of consumption, and its interrelationship with production. Indeed, many have now come to talk of contemporary, postmodern, society as a consumer society (cf. Featherstone, 1991; Bauman, 1992). In this society, we are taught to consume (and indeed advertising may well play a key role in this process) but this consumption is individualized and atomized, consistent with the neoliberal project (in contrast to production, which was viewed as a more collective endeavour). Moreover, consumption takes place in what Baudrillard terms a 'growth society'. But growth is reliant on poverty where 'growth is a function of poverty; growth is needed to contain the poor and maintain the system' (Ritzer, 1988: 3). In this sense we can see how consumption contributes to growth both in the creation of wealth, and the maintenance of the status quo as the poor cannot escape the system of consumption through satisfaction and dissatisfaction; we gain temporary satisfaction through consumption, but then become dissatisfied necessitating further consumption. This dissatisfaction is brought about through our consumption of signs, which consumers need to be able to 'read' in order to make sense of the commodity they possess. Commodities are defined not by their function but their relationship to a wider system of 'signs' and so this potential for difference means that people are not able to satisfy their desire for commodities (as there are infinite difference interpretations of the commodity in its relation to the wider system). This positioning means that as consumers seek difference, so the need for commodities can never be satisfied.

Following Baudrillard, we need to understand the signs and their relationships to structures in order to understand consumption. If audiences become redefined and commodified as consumers, their meanings change in relation to each other; and the communication process and all that underpins advertising and the construction of audiences as consumers thus become intensely political. For Baudrillard, consumption is 'above all else a coded system of signs. Individuals are coerced into using that system. The use of that system via consumption is an important way in which people communicate with one another. The ideology associated with the system leads people to believe, falsely in Baudrillard's view, that they are affluent, fulfilled, happy and liberated' (Ritzer, 1988: 15). Our attention is therefore drawn to the denial of freedom in the name of consumption that is imposed upon the individual.

In this way, we can see how audiences, encouraged to become consumers, are also encouraged to think of themselves as differentiated through the products, services and media they 'consume' as a mechanism to express autonomy. However, what we witness is audiences simply being reconstituted as passive reinforcers of a structure which is reliant on unequal relations. So while we may think of audiences and the choices they make about what and how to 'consume' as liberated, Baudrillard reminds us that they are bound to wider systems of exploitation. 'The consumer experiences his (sic) distinctive behaviours as freedom, as aspiration, as choice. His experience is not one of being forced to be different, of obeying a code. To differentiate oneself is always, by the same token, to bring into play the total order of differences, which is, from the first, the product of the total society and inevitably exceeds the scope of the individual. In the very act of scoring his points in the order of differences, each individual maintains that order, and therefore condemns himself only ever to occupy a relative position within it' (Baudrillard, 1988: 61). Our attention is thus drawn to the wider processes which inform how audiences are constructed and positioned. Audiences are positioned within existing structures; these are structures which necessitate consumption. We also see here tensions between capitalism and democracy. While democracy requires citizens to be informed, current socio-economic structures require audiences to consume. We could argue that this is not an either/or position. Rather what this enables us to reflect on is how the tensions between the requirements of democracy and capitalism are interrelated and interactive. Audiences are not static in this relationship, and may hold multiple identities at this point of interaction. However, it is at this site of interaction and positioning of audiences that we may reflect on the politics that are being communicated.

Elites as audiences

Aeron Davis (2007) offers a different perspective on the idea of audience. He argues that audiences, for media, are not comprised of a general public, rather financial elites use the business pages to talk to each other. In his empirical study of fund managers and those working in the finance sector, Davis highlighted the significance of newspapers as a mechanism through which financial elites speak to each other. Through these pages, they gain information about consensus beliefs, about how the market is likely to react to investment decisions. As he notes, the press play a central role in this as '[m]any stories in the financial media are built around the representation of what the general feeling is of a company or trend according to what "analysts", "the City", "the market" or "major shareholders" think as a group' (Davis, 2007: 162). His interview data show that fund managers do not want to appear overly influenced by the media, but nonetheless they do use media coverage as a way to interpret wider consensus as to how the market is working, how it may react. In turn he shows how media's implication in financial elites behaving rationally in the short term has led to longer-term 'irrationally' (according to economic logic) resulting in losses on a mass scale (Davis, 2007: 168), leading to crashes. Indeed, media coverage has been argued to have played a significant role in previous financial crashes where media outlets provided a speculative forum for discussions of rising processes and trends, helping to hype new stocks and investment opportunities (e.g. Cassidy, 2002; Shiller, 2000). In this way, economic interests are provided with a platform where other economic elites are conceived of as audiences. Rather than the 'masses' or the general public, it is the interests of finance and capital which comprise the audience.

For Monbiot, the very nature of the corporate press suggests there is a degree of inevitability about the protection of economic interests. He argues that 'The men [sic] who own the corporate press are fighting a class war, seeking, even now to defend the 1% to which they belong against its challengers. But because they control much of the conversation, we seldom see it in these terms. Our press re-frames major issues so effectively, it often recruits its readers to mobilize against their own interests' (Monbiot, 2011: 29). His prescient critique of capitalism also, of course, reminds us that press ownership is gendered, which in turn has consequences for outputs. And more broadly, we are encouraged to see the world through a gendered lens: the public space is foregrounded, we are discouraged from thinking about the effects of austerity and financial mismanagement in the private sphere. Cynthia Enloe (2013) points to how masculine cultures could be seen as responsible for the financial crisis and this remains unexplored in mainstream media analyses; in *Who Cooked Adam Smith's Dinner* Marçal (2015) shows that how our economic system functions is reliant on unpaid labour often carried out by women to support the paid labour carried out by men in the public sphere. In failing to explore the gendered nature of how our economies function, media encourage us to think about the important issues of the day in a way which reinforces existing gendered power relations.

The interests of elites (in all their forms) and their construction as audiences are also evident in the work of Justin Lewis (2001). He points us to how dominant elite interests are represented, not only in how public opinion is 'framed' by media outlets (as discussed above) but he directs our attention to how opinion discourse is mobilized to 'reinforce a political economy that favours the powerful and excludes popular opinion when it contradicts those powerful interests' (2001: 45) (also seen in the work, for example, of Gitlin, 1980; Glasgow Media Group, 1980; Herman and Chomsky, 1988; McChesney, 1997; to name but a few). Lewis' work, based on an analysis of US media, showed that there was a significant bias towards the articulation of public opinion as 'moderate' or 'conservative', whereas his findings showed liberal or progressive aspects of public opinion received comparatively little coverage (2001: 45–6). And while media framing and media outlets may not directly affect the construction of public opinion, they do affect the representation of public opinion (Lewis, 2001: 70). Lewis also found that US public opinion polling showed a primary concern with welfare spending, in areas such as healthcare and education, military spending received minority support. However, he noted that there was elite consensus for maintaining vast military spending which 'operates *autonomously from public deliberation or sentiment*' (Lewis, 2001: 141, original italics). So despite not being a publicly popular priority, military budgetary spending predominates and exceeds other forms of public good spending. These high levels of spending are justified through a discourse which supports the existence of a global threat, and so the need for weapons. In the Cold War era anti-communism was the creed which was used as a justification and this was repeated through media and political expression (see for example Herman and Chomsky, 1988). In the post-Cold War era, 9/11 provided a new political identification of threat, and as anti-Islam sentiment characterized political leaders' speeches (culminating in the invasion of Iraq), so support for this was shored up through media outlets (see also Gershkoff and Kushner, 2003). Scholars have argued that media take their cues from political elites rather than the masses in deciding what stories to cover (Herman and Chomsky, 1988; Kellner, 1990; Page and Shapiro, 1992; Zaller, 1992). Political elites are discussing the 'threat of Islam', and what we see are media providing a platform for political elites to talk to each other, which is contrary to liberal views of the media which emphasize the masses as the audience.

Drawing on the work of Davis (2007) and Lewis (2001), then, we see a consistency in the processes which govern framing of opinion in the media. Reinforcing neoliberal ideology, we see a privileging of market discourses which legitimates and validates a wider ideological split between left and right which serves to privilege the values of the right. Ultimately as Lewis notes 'polls can...be seen as a vindication of dominant discoursesè...' (2001: 61). For example, following the Western financial crisis, while some media reporting has sought to vilify bankers, little questioning has taken place of the systems and cultures (cf. Enloe, 2013) that we have in place which enabled this kind of event to happen. Growing public mistrust has yet to be fully articulated in a left-wing discourse, for example one which discusses the regulation of corporations and corporate responsibility and the restrictions to corporate power. Moreover, as we see ever-widening gaps between the wealthiest and poorest within and between states (Wilkinson and Pickett, 2010), we see little in the way of public discussion about the need to redress some of these gross imbalances, to redistribute some of this wealth via a fairer tax system. These discourses of the left remain largely invisible in mainstream discourses. And whether or not you agree with these broader leftist ideals, the issue is not the ideals themselves, but the need for them to be part of a balanced debate about what our society looks like. Hegemonic discourses of what the public believe, Lewis argues, are built around a 'selective' reading of public opinion, generating the appearance of a consensus around free market ideologies (2001: 71). In this sense, the communication of opinion and construction of audiences for media outlets is highly political where we see power contested, negotiated, challenged and re-established. Hence the way opinions are created and articulated in mediated discourses is as significant, if not more so, than the data that is gathered in the first place. For it is at the site of the representation of audience beliefs and views that power is contested.

Who is not an audience?

Throughout this discussion of audiences, there is an implied assumption that the intention is always to communicate, and there is also an assumption of inclusion. But one way in which we see power operating and politics taking place may well be in the intention *not* to communicate. As we have witnessed, a plethora of spin doctors, media managers in all walks of life, from Parliament, to the military, to business, seek to manipulate what is and is not communicated to wider audiences. To not communicate around an issue is to assume no audience exists for this issue, or to not construct an audience for a particular issue. For example, audiences may be constructed around issues about the economy, or spending needs of nations, or the actions of political elites. Audiences are much less likely to be constructed around issues of benefits, welfare experiences or asylum seekers. Rather audiences for these kinds of issues tend to be constructed to reflect elite interests and elite thinking, rather than lived experiences of those in these dire situations. In this sense, audiences who have interests which do not align with elite views of the day find themselves in another arena where their voice may be marginalized and their interests unexpressed. In this way, when we think about audiences (the raison d'être of political communication), we need to also think about whose views get to dominate and who is defined as representative of the 'audience'.

As Higgins notes, historically the assumption about public opinion at the turn of the 20th century was that 'the member of the public is male and holds a senior position in business' (Higgins, 2008: 22). In this way gender, race and class relations were reinforced through the construction of public opinion. Voices of the lower classes, of ethnic minorities and women were marginalized in what was deemed salient as a marker of public opinion and so audiences did not comprise every citizen in the population, rather audiences were assumed to reflect the images of elite interests. This assumption was also maintained by later theorists; for Habermas, interactions in the public sphere were assumed to take place by a homogenous community: European, male, middle-class citizens. This also assumes that audiences and public opinion only exist in a public space, rather than in a private sphere (Sanders, 2009: 146). To assume a white middle-class male audience therefore marginalizes and silences those not in those categories yet who also constitute an audience. There is less opportunity for a diversity of audience views to be reflected, and/or this diversity is lost when audiences are constructed. This construction, in itself a political act, whether intentional or unconscious, reinforces existing power structures rather than challenges them.

We might argue that the marginalization of these particular audiences may also contribute to wider passivity in engagement with political discourses. The extent to which audiences are active in their consumption of media content has been of crucial concern (as discussed above); knowledgeable informed citizens are those who are able to participate actively and politically as audiences or citizens. Yet as Baudrillard notes, the passivity of the audience is not necessarily evidence of alienation, but is a response and a challenge to the manipulation of demand. The masses are silent, but this inertia is powerful, individuals are arguing, engaging and resisting. And in this sense, that previous audiences of mainstream media content are now choosing to engage in media that reflects their marginally constructed interests (for example the rise of LGBQT magazines and online fora) suggests that audience passivity in the face of their non-recognition by mainstream media may in turn be viewed as a mechanism of political engagement and communication.

Summary

The purpose of communication is that it is received, which in turn constructs an audience. While the content of communication may exist without receipt, it is only in its receiving that it becomes communication. But the way reception takes place is a consequence of how an audience is positioned. In this way, it is possible to reflect on an audience, not as a homogenous mass but rather as something that is constructed and positioned. The degrees to which audiences are active or passive recipients of this process relies in part on citizens' own capacity to reflect on their positioning in this way.

Throughout this chapter there has been an attempt to reflect on what is meant by audience. Who is or are the audience or audiences for political communication? And what role does the communication of politics play in constructing the audiences it needs in order to achieve its ends? Public opinion can be considered significant to: politicians (in shaping their political strategies such as the desire to gain office); the media (in responding to and seeking to manipulate public opinion in their own interests); to the public (in shaping their own opinions, agenda setting, and in silencing minority views engendering a spiral of silence). In order to understand how audiences are constituted and why they matter, this chapter has explored some of the processes behind the construction of audiences. It has viewed this construction as densely political, for here in the process of creating an audience is where politics is taking place and being communicated. Audiences are essential for communication processes, but audiences are not neutral entities and this chapter has explored just some of the ways audiences are constructed, through public opinion, through advertising, where audiences may reflect elite interests with little or no reference to the citizenry at large and where audiences may be reconstructed as consumers to further the embedding of our contemporary social economic and political systems. These debates are essential for understanding the communication processes that are discussed in the chapters that follow. Understanding the power structures behind how we are implicated in the communication of politics is central to understanding how power is operating in our contemporary environment.

Reflection/seminar activities

Choose a media item and then draw the audience for that piece. What do they look like? What is assumed in the media item about the audience? Who is featured and who is missing in your audience?

Find media coverage of a recent opinion poll: what is the message that is being conveyed in the coverage of the poll data? Whose interests are represented? Whose are marginalized?

Design an opinion poll on a topic of your choosing. How do you ensure you are not generating the answers you want to see? How can you get people to take part? How do you know they have the information that they need to answer the questions you set? Does it matter if some people don't have that information?

Who decides what an audience looks like? Why does this matter?

Chapter 4

How do Governments and Politicians Communicate?

Introduction

> INT: Tell us something or [sic] how you view the election prospects.
>
> ATTLEE: Oh we shall go in with a good fight. Very good. Very good chance of winning if we go in competently. We always do.
>
> INT: On what will Labour take its stand?
>
> ATTLEE: Well, that's what we shall be announcing shortly.
>
> INT: What are your immediate plans Mr Attlee?
>
> ATTLEE: My immediate plans are to go down to a committee to decide on just that thing as soon as I can get away from here.
>
> INT: Is there anything else you'd like to say about the coming election?
>
> ATTLEE: No.
>
> (cited in Hennessey, 2001: 170)

It's hard to imagine a contemporary politician giving the same kind of response to a TV interviewer as Prime Minister Clement Attlee did, just after the start of the UK general election campaign in 1951. Today's politicians have a whole host of speechwriters, consultants and advisers, who would provide an 'instant' reply, which would spell out a commitment to fairness, demonstrating economic competence, while at the same time pointing out than the other party, or candidate, was simply not up to the job. Much has changed...

The prominence and importance attached to election campaigns are not only UK phenomena. This chapter begins with an historical overview of attempts of governments and rulers to manipulate masses in order to achieve their aims (e.g. from Machiavelli). It traces techniques of propaganda and looks at how governments have engaged in forms of manipulation of audiences and citizens; and attempts by elites to manipulate media. It charts the rise of PR and advertising in the formal arena of politics: as an idea and as a set of techniques and media responses to it in election campaigning and beyond. But in asking political questions

71

about this form of communication, we need to reflect on what is being communicated by politicians. In reflecting on the wider values that are communicated, this enables us to rethink what is meant by electoral and governmental communication, and what collective values are communicated. How does this happen?

A brief history of 'spin'

The word spin has become shorthand for the communications activities of contemporary governments and politicians. An abbreviation of the term 'spin doctor', it has been adopted as a verb to describe methods of manipulation in attempting to communicate a message. The term was first used in 1978 by the *Guardian Weekly* (Sanders, 2009: 29) and by the 1990s had become synonymous with governments' media management. For some, this process 'emptied out' the content of politics (Savigny, 2005) leaving nothing more than 'packaging' as a replacement for policy substance (Franklin, 2004). Technology, for some, is at the root of the phenomenon of 'spin'. Seen as a logical development and response to changes in media capabilities, spin has also been characterized as a positive phenomenon, one that facilitates democratization (McNair, 2000: 138).

But to attribute spin to changes in media technology is to belie a history of attempts to manage messages and create a favourable impression in the eyes of the public (the essence of spin). In this sense, manipulation is not a new phenomenon for governmental politics. Nor is it simply a phenomenon triggered by increasing capacity to manage new media forms. While technology may advance, underlying these changes is a set of ideals and processes which influences how such technologies are put to use. The Ancient Greeks recognized the importance of persuasion in politics and the power of rhetoric. But it was Machiavelli who linked the art of persuasion and the nature of political leadership with the recognition that this necessarily involved manipulation.

Writing in the 16th century, Machiavelli was the first philosopher to separate religion and politics. (Prior to this the assumption had been that politics served the highest aims, but these aims were religious.) Machiavelli (1532/2003) was one of the first to treat politics and ethics as discrete entities. In his treatise he unmasked how rulers sought to manipulate others to gain political power; this was seen to be the aim of politics. His work has been hotly debated. Initially, *The Prince* was interpreted as a 'do it yourself' guide for rulers, which set out how you can manipulate people to advance your own interest. In his work, the separation of morals from politics meant that ethical matters, such as justice, equality and freedom, were regarded as irrelevant. Rather, all that mattered was the pursuit of power. In this sense manipulation of messages, and information, was crucial in order to gain support. Latterly, his work came to be interpreted as a treatise which exposed the 'duplicity of tyrants', and highlighted how debauchery proliferated and rulers overstepped the bounds of religious morality, in the pursuit of power. Machiavelli's work in this view was seen as a warning to the people of the dangers of despotism. More recently, Machiavelli has been characterized as a dispassionate observer of 'reality' (Boucher and Kelly, 2009). Whichever interpretation of his work we accept, what does stand out is how manipulation takes place in the pursuit of power. Some scholars have noted the Machiavellian roots in contemporary electioneering practice (O'Shaughnessy, 1990; Lock and Harris, 1996).

Foucault reminds us governments and politicians are not completely autonomous. Alongside their own interests they are bound by 'the state'; the state comprises an amalgam of interests. But Foucault points us to the elite nature of those interests... 'To know how to govern, one must know the state and the secret springs of its interests, a knowledge which in part may not and cannot be accessible to the ruled, and is liable to dictate governmental acts of a singular, unforeseeable and drastic character' (Burchell et al., 1991: 9). In this way, if we are to understand how governments and politicians work, how they communicate politically to us, we need to look beyond the spin, and explore the interlinked interests that comprise a functioning state. In this context, these interests are perhaps most easily recognizable as narratives of neoliberalism and patriarchy, and their manifestations are explored below through reference to how politicians and governments communicate to us as electorates.

As electorates, we have a responsibility to identify these interests and hold political leaders to account. For Emma Goldman, interests were endorsed and the ruthless pursuit of power reinforced through the failure of collective public opinion. She argues: 'Today, as then, public opinion is the omnipresent tyrant: today, as then, the majority represents a mass of cowards, willing to accept him who mirrors its own soul and mind poverty... A politician, he (sic) knows the majority cares little for ideals or integrity. What it craves is display' (Goldman, 1910/2013: 33). Emma Goldman suggests that actually the reason we get spin and spectacle is because that is what we the public want (raising the question, do we get the government we deserve?). Indeed, the notion that it is public opinion that determines the kind of government we get (in contrast to the features of self-interested individuals) is one that has a lineage. Gustave Le Bon (1896) warned of the power of the crowd where opinion and emotion overtook reason. But the German sociologist identified that media played a role in manipulating and shaping such opinion. He warned that because newspapers packaged information like 'grocer's goods' they were able to manufacture public sentiment in powerful ways. The importance of managing public opinion through the management of a media agenda was also reinforced by Walter Lippmann. He pointed to the capacity of US government to spin and control information during the First World War. He argued that people lived in a world that was 'out of reach, out of sight and out of mind' and so they had to rely on governments and press for accurate information (1922: 18). Crucially, Lippmann argued, however, the press did not convey deeper truths, rather it transmitted symbols, and government could manipulate these symbols to manufacture consent (Lippmann, 1922; see also Herman and Chomsky, 1988). What this points towards is a set of complex interactive processes. In a which-came-first scenario, do we think about politicians in their selfish pursuit of power, or the state engaged in protecting a particular set of interests, or how public opinion might be responsible for the state of our formal politics? What these debates point us towards is that this is not a 'level playing field'. To understand the accuracy of the information we receive, we need an understanding of how the information agenda is manipulated. Lasswell (1927) used the term 'propaganda' to denote how governments were increasingly seeking to manage information that citizens received. While contemporary incarnations of message presentation by political elites are referred to as spin, in other contexts, and as Lasswell suggests, message dissemination to the masses has also been termed propaganda. In contemporary usage the term propaganda has tended to be associated negatively with the 'darker' arts of politics, so how do we distinguish propaganda from spin? Or indeed, we might ask, is it possible to separate spin from propaganda?

Propaganda

The term propaganda is derived from the Latin 'propagandas' and had a relatively neutral meaning 'what should be propagated'. It was first used in this way to describe the process of spreading information and ideas by the Catholic Church in the 17th century. In the early 20th century, Edward Bernays argued that 'the only difference between "propaganda" and "education"... is the point of view. The advocacy of what we believe in is education. The advocacy of what we don't believe is propaganda' (1923: 212). In this sense, propaganda is a process, but it also suggests that the more informed we are the more we are able to detect what underlies the message that is being propagated. More recently it has become synonymous with lies, distortion and many other contemporary pejorative terms. During the First World War, false atrocity stories were disseminated using 'black' propaganda techniques (Sanders, 2009: 28). Of course, the term is also intimately linked with the work of Goebbels during the Second World War. Goebbels realized that the most effective form of propaganda was that which people were unaware of receiving. What the term and its nuanced usage reminds us, though, is that dominant interests, be they religious, commercial or based in political ideology, all seek to shore up public support through the spread of information and ideas. The function of propaganda is to create a set of beliefs rather than provide information about an objective truth. In this way, 'Propaganda in the broadest sense is the technique of influencing human action by the manipulation of representations' (Lasswell, 1995: 13). Propaganda in more recent usage tends to be linked, historically, to war efforts. Indeed, the state has used propaganda to marshal good will and support in wartime. However, it is perhaps useful to reflect on the above definitions. For if propaganda '... is the deliberate, systematic attempt to shape perceptions, manipulate cognitions, and direct behaviour to achieve a response that furthers the desired intent of the propagandist' (Jowett and O'Donnell, 2006: 7), then we might ask: is propaganda possible in peacetime? Indeed, it could be argued that contemporary propaganda functions to maintain Western stability and the absence of war between liberal democracies. If propaganda is about attempts to shape beliefs, feelings and emotions favourably in the interests of another, then if we are influenced to buy a product through advertising, is that a form of propaganda?

Moreover, as media play a role in disseminating ideas and messages, it is useful to reflect on the relationship between media and propaganda. Herman and Chomsky's (1985) propaganda model explicitly links media and capitalism to propaganda. They argued that news (information) is 'filtered' in order to marginalize dissent and enable dominant interests (i.e. the government and business) to promote their message. They identified five filters which skew news coverage in these interests: 1) corporate ownership (and as we identified in Chapter 2, very few companies own and control a large share of media content); 2) The importance of advertising revenue (for example, as newspapers decline in readership increasingly revenue is drawn from advertising; many internet sites also rely on advertising revenue); 3) Reliance on official sources. This is not only reliance on press releases in military circumstances, but more widely in the coverage of government and politics, and increasingly in the case of businesses (cf. Davies, 2008); 4) That media fear 'flak' – that is, withdrawal of support and criticism from established news/political sources who do not comply with established view; 5) That media share the same broad ideological outlook as their government, for example general acceptance of capitalism and neoliberalism. This interrelationship was a mechanism by which the media were disciplined to promote a particular ideological outlook. At their time of writing, this was anticommunist capitalism. Today we might argue that this takes the form of anti-Islam neoliberal patriarchal white capitalism.

However, to suggest that the media function to disseminate propaganda does imply that audiences and citizens have very little critical capacity to understand and deconstruct these 'codes'. And as Kallis, (2005: 3) argues 'the suggestion that any form of effective propaganda results in "brain washing" fails to take account the recipients' ability to resist a particular message, however successfully this may be presented to them'. The extent to which propaganda, or idea and belief dissemination is successful or not, is clearly dependent on a series of interlinked and interrelated conditions and predispositions of groups and individual recipients. However, it almost doesn't matter whether we have factual knowledge about the efficacy of these kinds of reflections as increasingly we see politicians behave as though this is possible. The management of information flows, what to disseminate and what not to, is a central consideration. Whereas media communications strategies had been an afterthought (as suggested by the Attlee excerpt at the start of this chapter) in contemporary Western politics, media management of communications of ideas and attempts to construct perceptions have taken centre stage. Media management is now a, if not the, key preoccupation of modern politicians and governments. And it is to those attempts to manage the control of information, during elections and in office, that we now turn.

Contemporary marketing and advertising by politicians

This chapter is concerned with exploring how politicians seek to communicate their messages. In attempts to manage media and message dissemination, to spin, to propagate viewpoints, more recently, marketing methods and techniques have become prevalent in the behaviours of contemporary governments and politicians, and political elites, particularly in the United States and United Kingdom, have engaged in what has become termed 'political marketing'. Political marketing has been used as a 'catch-all' term to describe the increasing professionalization of political parties (cf. Panebianco, 1988) and increased preoccupation with formal political communications. These have included (but are not restricted to) the increased use of political consultants, negative campaigning, advertising (in both paid and free media) and public relations techniques and marketing methods.

There is debate as to where the origin of this contemporary approach lies. In the United Kingdom, Scammell (1995) connects the use of marketing in formal politics to the hire of professional pollsters and publicists, which, she states, first occurred in 1964; Wring (2005) suggests that the origins are not so recent, and he traces the use of marketing strategies within the British Labour Party back to the early 20th century.

(Although he notes that it was only during the leaderships of Thatcher and Kinnock that the term marketing explicitly became part of organizational thinking [1996: 102].) In America, Maarek (1995) and Beresford (1998) suggest marketing originated in the 1950s/1960s while O'Shaughnessy (1990) charts its usage back to Ancient Greece. However, what is clear is that marketing in contemporary formal politics has become pervasive and a mechanism by which political elites seek to manage messages and communication strategies in order to realize their goals. In 1969 Kotler and Levy argued that 'Political contests remind us that candidates are marketed as well as soap' (p10). The notion that political parties and politicians are as amenable as other products in the marketplace to a marketing campaign has become a central, if not defining, feature of contemporary US and UK government and politics. Here, then, we witness a subtle shift in how communication between and from elites is enacted. It is not only political ideas which drive the messages that politicians seek to communicate, rather ideas about how messages can be marketed also play into the politics which our elites enact.

This is not to suggest total autonomy to politicians engaging in communication strategies and process. Rather this adoption of marketing in governmental politics is situated in a context of wider societal flux. It has been argued that we have moved from producer to the consumer as a driving feature of society (cf. Bauman, 2007; Baudrillard, 1988) where individual (rather than group) identities are expressed through acts of consumption. Arguably this shift has been rooted in the works of Edward Bernays, a US pioneer of public relations. His insights and experience in creating female smokers for the tobacco industry highlight for us that the mobilization and, crucially, the creation, of individual desires, which focus on the self as a site of consumption, are acts of identity construction for the purpose of manipulation. This focus on the individual as consumer also fits neatly with the neoliberal emphasis on the self, rather than group identities (and of course the destruction of group identities means that it becomes very difficult to mobilize group challenges to dominant norms if no collective identities exist). The link between mobilization of unconscious (and conscious) desires and expression through consumption forms the basis of contemporary marketing in politics.

While the development of marketing in politics may or may not be a new phenomenon (as above) what is significant is its consolidation since the neoliberal 'consensus' of the late 1970s. Marketing in politics assumes that parties behave as businesses, voters as consumers (Lees-Marshment, 2001). This is a significant ontological and normative shift. Rather than assuming parties and politics behave as *if* they were businesses, voters as *if* they were consumers, the adoption of marketing as a mentality (as advocated by Kotler and Andreasen, 1996: 37) generates a perception that there is little difference between political parties, politicians and businesses. Once this assumption is accepted and parties/politicians behave in this way, with voters encouraged to behave as they would in a supermarket, we see the 'emptying out' of formal politics. A 'politics' concerned with equality, justice and freedom is replaced with a politics of the marketplace (Savigny, 2008). Moreover, as Scammell argues, this means that political communication (in its conventional definition) becomes merely a 'subset' of marketing (1999: 723) and that campaign strategy is now driven by an understanding of, and an assumption of the existence of, a political 'marketplace' (cf. Harrop, 1990). The notion of a 'marketplace' as the arena where electoral competition takes place again is not a new phenomenon, and Downs (1957) articulated this notion, clearly located in economic theory. That economic assumptions underpin contemporary formal political strategy again (Savigny, 2004), reminds us of the consolidation of neoliberalism not only as policy ideology but its embedding in all activities of politicians' and governments' behaviour.

As such, marketing is not only confined to election campaigns. Indeed, some have argued that we now live in an era of 'permanent campaign' (the term was initially used by Blumenthal, 1980, but is now widely accepted and used within the political marketing literature; see for example: Butler and Collins, 1994, 2001; Sparrow and Turner, 2001; Wring, 2001: 914). For example, in the US, Reagan, Clinton and Bush all extensively engaged in marketing throughout their administrations (O'Shaughnessy, 1990: 193; Morris, 1999; Newman, 2001; O'Shaughnessy and Henneberg, 2007). In the United Kingdom, the Labour Party has accepted marketing as an approach to government (Gould, 1998). In essence, the adoption of marketing as an approach is not simply about the use of techniques and strategies adapted from the business arena. Rather it is a wholesale shift in the nature of formal politics. A governmentality that is grounded in consumption and the logic of the market. This governmentality is promulgated via media and we now turn to look at how this logic informs campaigns and the process of government.

Communicating election campaigns

Election campaigns essentially comprise the application of strategies and techniques to communicate and mobilize support for policy positions in order that candidates and parties may gain office. Media are central in the process of relaying messages to citizens. Democracy requires citizen engagement for elections to be legitimate. And in order to engage, citizens need information and knowledge about politicians, political parties, and also political processes (as noted in Chapter 2).

As Kavanagh notes, for most people the election campaign is what is covered in the media (1995: 177, 197). With the proliferation of powerful and privately owned media with commercial interests, politicians have to respond and adapt to this environment. Elections have become regarded as increasingly stage-managed for media (Kavanagh, 1992; 84). The growth and expansion of access to television has led some commentators to argue there has been an Americanization of politics (Mancini and Swanson, 1996; Negrine and Stanyer 1996). In this sense 'image is everything' (Iyenagr, 2005: 1). For some, this has meant the identification of a 'celebrity politician' keen to engage in entertainment media (Street, 2004; Baum, 2005); imagery thus becomes crucial. While there is much debate about whether it is media who drive the politicians' agenda, or the politicians who drive media agenda, it is important to recognize the dialectical nature of this relationship.

While there is also debate as to the effectiveness of media coverage on election outcomes (e.g. Newton and Brynin, 2001), it has been argued that there are long-term effects of news consumption and levels of knowledge and participation in the political process (Norris et al., 1999). Parties and politicians clearly assume a link as they now extensively engage in slogans designed to capture the public imagination. Labour's 'education, education, education' and Obama's 'change' campaign typify how snappy 'soundbites' are sought to mobilize public attention and conform to a changing news agenda (see Chapter 5). The roots of this 'normalization' of a focus on imagery in the United States are closely observed by McGinnis (1969) in his account of the transformation of Nixon; in the United Kingdom, we can see this most clearly if we look back to the 'transformation' of the Labour Party. A spin doctor for Labour was quoted after the 1997 election as saying: 'communications is not an afterthought to our policy. It's central to the whole mission of New Labour' (cited in Gaber, 1998: 13). More widely though we can see the shifts in how politicians themselves perceive the activities of formal politics. New Labour 'spin doctor' Peter Mandelson stated: 'If a government policy cannot be presented in a simple and attractive way, it is more likely than not to contain fundamental flaws and prove to be the wrong policy' (1997, cited in Franklin, 2001: 131). Thus we see communication and perceptions being what matters in policy making; a reversal of the notion that the 'right' policy would speak for itself.

The way that politicians and governments use election campaigns to connect with the public tends to fall into three broad areas linked to technology and marketing strategies: the use of advertising; negative campaigning; and new social media. Advertising, whether paid for or free, often comprises a significant component of campaign budgets (Sanders, 2009: 177). In the US, research has shown that voters learn more from TV adverts than from news or televised debates (Kaid, 2004).

Advertising can be useful in the provision of information for electorates. However, unlike other forms of commercial advertising, political advertising is the only time we see advertising that 'goes negative', that is, the use of strategies which are overtly aimed at undermining the opposition rather than promoting a positive message of the party or candidate. (In commercial advertising the negative smearing of an opposition product is prohibited). Highlighting weaknesses in the opposition, in terms of either character or policies, is reasonably standard practice. Despite research suggesting that this kind of negative advertising can demobilize voters (Ansolabehere and Iyengar, 1995) with high levels of negativity suppressing turnout, Lau and Pomper (2001) suggest that partisans are likely to be stimulated by negative campaigning, while independents/undecideds are more likely to be discouraged. More recently the notion that negative campaigning suppresses voter turnout has been challenged by Brooks (2006) and indeed, this literature not only relies on an assumption that direct causal effects can be established between campaign agendas and propensity to vote but also implies a kind of hypodermic effect (cf. Adorno and Horkheimer, 1944) where media messages are passively received and digested by audiences. While it may be difficult to establish direct causal effects of single adverts or their exposure over a prolonged period, and one negative advert alone may be inconsequential, there is the propensity for a cumulative build-up of negativity around the activities of politicians more broadly. If discursive interactions invite us to view political actors purely in negative terms, whether this directly affects turnout or not, this negativity plays a role in constructing the discursive environment in which formal politics takes place. A discursively constructed context in which the actions of politicians is discussed in a negative light is unlikely to be conducive to encouraging citizens to engage with political actors.

Each technological development is often heralded as providing a 'new' way of engaging the electorate. And the rise of social media has been no exception. Obama's campaign using mobile phones was seen as a mechanism to engage voters who had previously been disenfranchised (Bimber, 2014). Technology has also been developed to measure real-time efficacy of campaigns (Bode and Epstein, 2015) enabling campaign communicators to adjust their campaign in response to consumer preferences. New social media have also been viewed as a mechanism of mobilizing previously disinterested voters (Koc-Michalska et al., 2014). For Bode and Dalrymple (2014), Twitter provides a mechanism by which political engagement is enhanced, viewed as a more reliable source of information than political information that is 'filtered' by mainstream media. Mainstream news is becoming condensed to 'soundbites'. Twitter perhaps represents this ultimate reduction in 140 characters. Despite this change in technology, once we start to delve deeper, some things remain unchanged. For example, Gerodomis and Justinussen (2014) argue that although Obama extensively used social media during campaigning, the Facebook campaign was still used as top-down communication, rather than an opportunity for citizens to engage on their own terms.

So what much of the literature on campaigning draws our attention to is the role of technology in the campaign process. The tendency is to focus on how technology facilitates or inhibits campaigning and the impact that this has on the voters and how they engage. But these new media technologies do not necessarily translate into changing or challenging existing social and political relations. For example, what is less often considered in this context is the history of gender and market relations which underpins how technology is employed.

The application of marketing beyond the United Kingdom and United States in formal politics has been argued to be limited (Ormrod, 2006; Lilleker and Lees-Marshment, 2005), hence the focus on the United States and United Kingdom in this chapter. While the focus of these authors is on the institutional nature of party politics (i.e. this relies on the existence of a zero-sum game in a two-party competitive system), the wider observation is that marketing has become embedded in the two countries (United States and United Kingdom) that were at the heart of the neoliberal consensus. As Harris and Wring observe, there is now a perception that: 'managerialism has to some extent replaced traditional forms of ideology as the driving force within modern politics' (2001: 909) and this is consistent with Kotler and Andreasen's (1996: 37) prescriptive claim that, to be effective, marketing must be internalized and adopted as a guiding philosophy. And this managerialism is located in a context of economic individualism (neoliberal, capitalist relations of production and consumption). In this sense, marketing methods as used by elite political actors become not only about the employment of a set of tools and techniques. Rather they become a mechanism by which marketing is embedded as ideology, as a belief system. This is perhaps a fairly logical extension of the neoliberal marketization agenda that informs the practice of many Western governments. Yet at the same time, that implies a path dependency; the idea that politics can only be about marketing is highly questionable. This may encourage us to reflect on the degree to which formal politics should be concerned to ask what a good, or a just society looks like, rather than how market principles and practice can inform our modus operandi. When we ask questions about how political elites are communicating, we need to ask questions about the methods and techniques that inform this practice; for this can provide us with insights into the nature of the message, how it came to being, what interests may be represented, and the consequences of this for the nature of our politics. When we consider the nature of our politics, we not only consider the methods and processes (such as spin, propaganda and marketing) but in so doing, we are invited to reflect upon the 'essence' of formal politics. How is this constructed? And what are the consequences of how this kind of political communication takes place?

What is and is not being communicated?

In reflecting on the role of propaganda, spin and marketing in shaping public perceptions of formal politics, we are also reminded that scholars have long noted the role of symbols, rituals, myths and metaphors in constructing public life (e.g. Barthes, 1972; Edelman, 1988; Kertzer, 1988; Lakoff, 1996). Indeed, if as is being argued throughout, we want to make sense of the political nature of political communication, we need to reflect on how 'politics may shuffle money, votes, territory, and other material entities, where politics *itself* is a symbolic process wherein cultural identities – myths, ideologies, values, attitudes, beliefs – are evoked, arranged, and ordered in ways that produce political decisions. Politics thus is not *about* symbolic matters but is in essence symbolic' (Gronbeck, 1990: 212, original emphasis). In this sense, the interaction of politicians with media in election campaigns is symbolic, creating collective identities, shared social myths and ideologies. As noted in Chapter 2, these shared mythologies and ideologies are located in a wider discursive context, which is characterized by neoliberal beliefs about the dominance of markets and a similarly uncritical acceptance of the privileging of white masculine interests (discussed further below). But we might also want to think about the efficacy of these mythologies and collective identities.

There is a literature which highlights disengagement of publics from formal processes of politics. Hay (2007) asks *why we hate politics* but the legitimacy of governments to run countries on low levels of popular engagement remains largely unquestioned beyond the academy. If, as Dalton observes, citizens have become 'distrustful of politicians, sceptical about democratic institutions, and disillusioned about how the democratic process functions' (2004: 1), then why are media and political actors not engaging in these conversations and dialogues? As Simons notes 'mass media generate a pseudo-public sphere in which cultural consumption entails no discussion of what is consumed. When debate is presented through the media, the conversation itself is administered and treated as a consumer item...' (2000: 84). To present politics as an act of consumption is not only about the changing methods that politicians adopt as they respond to changes in technology. Rather our attention is drawn to a wider set of discursive logics and processes. The use of marketing methods and techniques by politicians, for example, serves to embed the notion that (neoliberal) market solutions are the 'correct' response to political problems (in this case getting elected). The unpacking of the techniques and thinking that inform communications strategies of political elites reminds us how embedded the notion of markets, and associated methods, are the 'go to' responses of political actors. This also serves to reinforce, and uncritically accept, a discursive neoliberal context.

Not only do we witness an acceptance of neoliberalism as characterizing contemporary politics but we might argue this also reinforces existing gendered power relationships. The accounts of the changing nature of campaigning, the focus on technology and negativity in the conduct of campaigns, all tend to treat the actions of campaigners and media as though they are gender blind. But as Fraser (1985) observes, gender blindness is not the same as gender neutrality. Research has shown that women are more likely to engage in electoral politics if they see women representatives (Karp and Banducci, 2008). Successive analyses of the representation of women in electoral politics highlight not only their descriptive underrepresentation in the legislative chambers (see for example Childs and Krook, 2006) but the women are substantively represented differently through media. For example, in the UK 2010 election, women politicians were largely absent from the campaign (Ross et al., 2013). The main focus was on leaders' wives (Higgins and Smith, 2013) rather than female politicians themselves. Female politicians are often constructed as 'other' that is deviant from the 'norm' of a politician that is assumed to be male (van Zoonen, 2006; O'Neill and Savigny, 2014) and 'men [are] taken to stand for the whole human population' (Gill, 2007: 9).

In the US, while Hillary Clinton and Sarah Palin were unavoidable candidates for media coverage, they were more likely to be framed as unsuitable candidates for office because of their gender (Carlin and Winfrey, 2009). Female politicians across Europe also tend to be predominantly represented in sexist stereotypes such as wife, mother, or in terms of their appearance (Garcia-Blanco and Wahl-Jorgensen, 2011) or with a focus on their femininity (Harmer and Wring, 2013) rather than as pronouncers of policy.

So we can see that politicians may be seeking to manipulate beliefs and emotional identities; the emphasis on perception of image has become crucial. But media play a role in this, in the way that they choose to frame campaigns and issues (what don't they talk about?); as Weaver observes, 'by making more salient certain issues, candidates and characteristics of candidates, [the] media contribute significantly to the construction of a perceived reality' (1996: 216). Could this construction of perception be linked to a declining trust that publics have in their political leaders? Norris (1999) notes that Western democracies have evidenced a decline in trust in political leaders, institutions and political systems. Newton (2006) argues that the public 'place less trust in their politicians; have less confidence in the main institutions of government; or more likely to believe that government is run for the benefit of the few big interests; and are more dissatisfied with the way democracy works in the country' (see also Dalton, 2004). The reasons for dissatisfaction are varied (Hay, 2007), although in the United Kingdom dissatisfaction also stems from the perception that 'our politicians are not like us' (Mortimer and Terry, 2015). What is interesting is the failure by politicians to address this issue. Rather it seems campaigns start from a disconnected place. What the above research also points us towards is the reinforcement of a set of 'male norms' that characterize contemporary electioneering methods and media representations, yet these remain largely unchallenged. Patricia Sexton observes that 'male norms stress values such as courage, inner direction, certain forms of aggression, autonomy, mastery, technological skill ...' (cited in Donaldson, 1993) and that these characteristics become normalized through the ways our contemporary elections are conducted.

In rethinking how campaigns are conducted, it may be worth reflecting on the notion that lack of mobilization and engagement comes not from the different technological platforms adopted but a more fundamental feature of how campaigns are conducted. We have seen elaboration on the marketized neoliberal workings of contemporary political campaigns (Crouch, 2002; Savigny, 2008), where the competitiveness and aggression of negative campaigning serve to reinforce notions of hegemonic masculinity (Connell, 1993) rather than challenge them. A different kind of campaign and electoral politics requires, it is contended, not new media technologies but a wider understanding of the politics that are being communicated. At present these politics are exclusive to many.

Moreover, that politicians are seen to be unrepresentative (i.e. not like us) in that, for example, in the United Kingdom, they are predominantly white, male, and from middle class backgrounds, which means that if we accept the premise that descriptive representation can lead to substantive representation (cf. Childs and Krook, 2006) – that the numbers of people reflecting a particular set of interests can mean that policy is developed to reflect those interests, rather than the interests of all in society – then the starting point of seeking to communicate about formal politics, is flawed due to the over representation of white, middle-class, masculine interests.

Summary

The history of 'spin' and propaganda reminds us that politicians have always sought to manipulate information provided to citizens in a bid to secure electoral victory, and in some ways this is the conventional understanding of what is meant by 'political communication'. More recently, we have seen a rise in the marketing of political elites, as both a response to changes in technologies and wider discursive political contexts, as well as having the capacity to shape those discourses.

Contemporary elite political practice requires a reliance on media to disseminate messages, myths and values. Yet the underlying premises of the messages remain often unchallenged, unquestioned in public discussion. The failure to do this means that underlying power structures remain, and continue to be renegotiated, reconstituted and restructured. To be literate and have political efficacy, we need to understand the processes by which we are communicated to, and this chapter has drawn out the historical location of contemporary electioneering practices in the United Kingdom and United States, through reference to ideas of spin and propaganda, to contemporary marketing, and situated those in their wider ideological context. The politics of contemporary electoral communication leads us currently to ask, what processes are politicians using to manage media? How do they do this? How can campaigns become more effective and connect with the voters? There is a larger set of questions, more politically useful, that might ask – what does social justice look like? How can we create a meaningful system of government? How can voices of all sections of society be expressed and represented? What role do we as citizens play in critically engaging with the information we are presented with? What do we want our future generations to inherit? In asking these kinds of questions, we are encouraged to reflect on what we understand our politicians are communicating with us.

Reflection/seminar activities

Is spin a necessary feature of election campaigning? (What would a campaign without spin look like?)

Are elections only what we see in and through media? What does this tell us about the nature of democracy?

Is politics as amenable to marketing as Coca-Cola? Does this change the nature of political activity?

Design your own election campaign. What features do you need to take into account? How do you decide how to present your message? What do you include and exclude? How will you disseminate your message? Who is your message aimed at? Is it necessary to marginalize particular groups or interests?

Choose some examples of male and female politicians engaged in election campaigning. How are they described the same and differently in your media sources? What assumptions underpin how these candidates are referred to?

Chapter 5

How is News Communicated Politically?

Introduction

News, like media, is ubiquitous, and can be accessed through a variety of differing channels from apps on our phones to TV channels, to local and national newspapers. We have myriad means to find out what our political (and other) elites are doing on our behalf in public life. News also defines for us what is taking place in society around us. News is *a* (although as this book seeks to make clear, not *the* only) crucial way in which we find out about politics: both in the formal sense of the behaviour of elite political actors and the institutions of the state and culturally through the dissemination and circulation of norms and values. News implies, however, a formality: an accurate, objective record of events, that are deemed important. To ask political questions about news is to ask how it comes into existence: from the billions of events and occurrences that happen each day, why do we know about some and not others? Why does some news make the agenda and other events not be considered newsworthy? Who decides what counts as news? In asking these questions we are also reminded that news is communicated to us, via a plethora of media platforms, and constructs for us a version of reality, rather than being the measurement and objective presentation of one 'reality' out there. This chapter focuses particularly on the way news constructs for us a sense of the 'public' – not as an audience, but as a space, a site where social and political relations are constructed, negotiated and contested. So when we start to ask political questions about the nature of news, and what is being politically communicated, we need to ask a series of prior questions.

Simply put, we need to begin by thinking what 'news' actually is. When we think about what news is, we might also think about how news is defined and what counts as news. The choices that are made in what constructs a news agenda almost inevitably expresses the interests and biases of those involved in the production of news, we could argue. We might want to reflect on the agency of those involved in constructing news and the extent to which they are bound by structural, cultural and ideological constraints. A question that regularly features in the analysis of journalism is, whose interests are being represented? For liberal theorists, news is a mechanism whereby elites are held account-able. However, the way news becomes news is not simply the collection of facts that are 'out there', rather it is the product of an interaction between journalists, news organizations, wider ideological and political interactive contexts. We also need to think about the language we use when we construct news. Journalism is often discussed as underpinned by news values. Journalism and the production, construction and con-sumption of news are situated in, and contribute to, a wider set of social and cultural discourses. These issues underpin what follows, and the chapter starts by discussing what is meant by the term news and how decisions are made as to what counts as 'newsworthy'. We then move to consider the wider context in which news is produced and constructed and focus on four key areas: the wider political context; the techno-logical environment; and how news features in gendered relationships of power; and the broader discursive social context of news.

What is news?

So how do we know what news actually is? News is the plural of new, and suggests that something novel is happening. But news is a frame, a way that we find out about the world. It is not everything that is hap-pening 'out there', rather it is a selection of things that are 'new' that journalists decide are important enough for us to know about. What is deemed important in the world 'out there' is often determined by what media choose to show us. In this way, news is a social and political institution; power relations are embedded as interests are reflected and rejected. News also reflects political and cultural values; it is constructed by professionals in an organizational context, reflecting wider societal norms. We rely on professionals, who, like us, are structurally and cul-turally situated, to inform us of what are deemed to be the pressing issues of the day. When we think about what news is, we also need to reflect on the values informing it, and how it is constructed. To make sense of this, we need to look at a number of interrelated features: the way we talk about news and world and local events, the way that pro-fessionals decide what does and doesn't count as 'news'; more widely, it is useful to explore the technological and social context in which that news is constructed.

News industries themselves acknowledge their significance in setting the public agenda, and they have also attributed themselves power in determining how people think. For example, in the (in)famous *Sun* headline following the 1992 Conservative victory, it was claimed as a success by *the Sun* who the following morning led with the front page 'It was the Sun wot [sic] won it'. Whether the press have this level of influence on voting behaviour has been widely debated (for a nuanced account see Newton and Brynin, 2001). Irrespective of the possibility of establishing causal effects of the capacity of news media to shape outcomes, we are reminded nonetheless that news media do play a role in what we do and don't know about the world out there. In this way, the 'important' issues of the day are defined for us as audiences.

The way our news is structured is an outcome of choices made by journalists (in a wider social, cultural and institutional context). Indeed, to suggest that journalists have complete agency over what they report would be disingenuous. Rather, as Shoemaker and Reese (1996) observe, there are five levels which influence what it is a journalist can report: 1) the individual level (the journalist themselves and their own characteristics such as political agenda, gender, education, ethnicity); 2) media routines level (the 'news values' that underpin the construction of news – discussed below); 3) the material media organizational structure (be that state or commercial enterprise); 4) the 'extra-media level', which describes the regulatory context in which news is produced; and finally 5) the ideological level – which refers to the implied assumptions which inform coverage.

So when we are thinking about why some items are deemed 'newsworthy' and others aren't, we need to understand the motivations that influence the news agenda; it is argued that these five levels can inform how we start to make sense of how news becomes news. How does one item get selected over another? To answer this question, in their widely cited work, Galtung and Ruge (1965, as cited in Smith and Higgins, 2013) argued that there were 12 'values' which informed how news was selected and was subsequently constructed:

1. Frequency – that an event should unfold at a rate appropriate to the medium through which it is disseminated (be that weekly in a magazine, or 'live' on rolling news).
2. There is a 'threshold of magnitude'; the bigger, or more violent, the event (for example, a school shooting; a tsunami).
3. News should be unambiguous, and simple (which means that complex political backgrounds to stories tend to be ignored).
4. News is 'culturally meaningful' in that it resonates with the audiences who will consume it.
5. News should be 'consonant' with the existing agenda of the news organization that produces it.
6. There should be an 'unexpected' element (how many headlines include the word 'shock' for example?).
7. News can be a 'continuation' of an ongoing story (such as a missing person, or a wide-scale human tragedy such as an earthquake).

8. News needs to fit the 'compositional requirements' of the news outlet, where particular kinds of story are expected – such as economic news.
9. Reference to 'elite nations' (for example like the US) takes on greater significance than those countries that are economically and culturally removed (such as many countries in the Global South).
10. News about people tends to focus on 'elite people' (such as politicians) rather than ordinary individuals.
11. There is a need for 'human interest' and empathy is encouraged with the subject(s) of the story.
12. A focus on 'negativity' means that journalists are more likely to look, for example, to disasters or corruption, to 'bad' news, and this will also feature above so called 'positive' news stories (such as celebrations, royal weddings ...).

Harcup and O'Neill (2001) argued that there were three features that were absent from this list:

i)   'Celebrity', and this is returned to in more detail in the following chapter.
ii) 'Entertainment', closely aligned to celebrity and again, something which has been argued increasingly dominates the news agenda (Turner, 2010; van Zoonen, 2005).
iii) 'The political agenda of the news organization itself'; for example, as newspapers function as businesses in a marketplace, it is unlikely they will do anything to critique more widely this system in which they currently benefit.

These news values matter as it helps us make sense of why some items make the 'news' and some don't. Recognizing these news values helps us start to unpack why some stories are chosen over others; why it is more likely, for example, that we would see reports of celebrities falling out of cars (which contains an unexpected element, an elite recognizable individual) than the plight of homeless people on our streets (a perennial politically based problem, with no eye-catching immediate features or ongoing developments to the storyline).

These news values underpin what counts as news, but the way that news is described is also of considerable significance. As Smith and Higgins argue, just like the way we talk about formal politics, the language that is used to describe 'newsworthy' events is incredibly important (2013: 5). The way, for example, news media choose to use words such as 'benefit scroungers' to reflect the lower end of the socio-economic spectrum, yet those who engage in tax avoidance, and business

illegalities are rarely subject to the same levels of demonization and vilification in the British press (Allen and Savigny, 2012). The conflation
of benefit and scrounger is used to symbolize (a Victorian ideal of) an
'undeserving poor'. This conveniently sidesteps material changes in the
workforce brought about by increasing numbers of workers on zero-
hours contracts, reliant on state support, as the state has precipitated
the structural conditions which have led to precarious working conditions for many. And so the way we talk about the world, the language
we use, serves to construct our ideals of what the world looks like, and
normatively, what it should look like.

The demands for 'objectivity' in journalism mean that as audiences we
are implicitly reassured, in our broadcast media, that the content is free
from bias. (Although this is different from UK newspapers, which have
an explicit ideological bias, the majority of which are right, or centre
right, with two left-wing exceptions [not including the low circulation
Morning Star]). However, the notion of lack of bias was challenged,
and continues to be monitored and challenged by the Glasgow University Media Group (1980). Their work drew attention to how broadcast
journalism was 'framing' union actions surrounding the miners' strike.
They observed how news coverage focused on images of violent pick-
eters, contrasted with smart, well-groomed managers presenting from
behind desks. In this way, the media 'frame' a story and 'prime' us to
receive it in a particular way (cf. Gitlin, 1980). Herman and Chomsky
described this process as the 'manufacture of consent'. Rather than news
coverage being objective or unbiased, these scholars would suggest that
media coverage is presented to encourage our reading of events in a
particular way, which suits existing interests. Robinson argues there are
two ways in which this can be identified. First, the 'executive' model
whereby news adheres to official versions of events (Herman and Chomsky, 1999: 303). The second 'elite' version suggests that news conforms
to the interests of those with political power. Even when journalists are
seemingly critical, this is only because there may be a reflection of policy
conflict between political elites (ibid, 304). So when we start to think
about the political nature of the communication of news, we need to
begin by unpacking underlying assumptions that are made as to what
actually counts as news. We then need to reflect on the way news is
described to us. As noted above, the language that is chosen plays a
considerable role in conveying intended meaning and in positioning our
responses. For example, the 2015 *Daily Mail* front page headline which
read 'Is this the most dangerous woman in Britain?' in reference to
Nicola Sturgeon, SNP leader, invites hostility towards Sturgeon, rather
than support or reflection on her views. We as audiences are also being
positioned to respond to her as a woman primarily, rather than as a
politician with policies. The language that is used to construct news

and the values that inform this do not exist in a vacuum. They are both derived from and constitutive of wider social and political contexts, and it is to those that we now turn.

Relations between news organizations and the state

In a book primarily concerned with the nature of politics, perhaps the most logical place to start when thinking about the construction of the news agenda is in reflecting on the role of the state, in this case as played out through government regulation and the tensions that emerge in this regulatory context between control and market demands. When we talk about the relationship between the media and state, one way to do this is to think about who owns the media and what regulation facilitates this. As Devereux notes, 'media ownership is increasingly characterized by both concentration and conglomeration' (2003: 92). What this means for us as audiences and citizens is that we have a narrowing of the news agenda. While liberal theories of the media assume a plurality of outlets, what does this say for the democratic function of news if there are fewer and fewer outlets? This kind of narrowing of ownership can work to a politician's advantage. For example, Tony Blair travelled to meet with News Corp executives around this issue during the 1997 election campaign resulting in a front page headline which declared 'The Sun Backs Blair'. The hostility that had been previously displayed to the Labour Party in this newspaper (with one of the highest circulations in the United Kingdom) was tamed. Of course, this would not matter if the media did not have an effect but, as has been noted throughout, an assumption of this book is that media do shape the agenda and the parameters of what we think and talk about. And so, the relationship between media owners and politicians (representatives of the state, with the capacity to determine or restrict media practices) becomes significant.

More recently, the issue of media regulation came to light in the United Kingdom during the Leveson inquiry in to the limitations on press freedom. This was a response to calls for greater media regulation following allegations that journalists had tapped the phones of a range of people, from celebrities to 'ordinary' people. One of the ways the public debate was framed around this event was in terms of free speech. The press claimed (and this is consistent with liberal theory) that free speech should be the ultimate principle guiding what media organizations can report as 'news'. When we talk about free speech, we often assume that free speech is the capacity to say anything, and to have the 'right' to do so. But not so, argues Fish, when he says 'free speech ... is not an independent value but a political prize' (1994: 102), and indeed as Howarth (1998) observes, that right to freedom of speech is something we have, rather than something that we 'own'. Free speech is, however, seen as a necessary condition of democracy, one that facilitates rather than restricts dialogue and is essential for a diversity of opinions to emerge, as well as being important for individual autonomy (Tseis, 2009).

In this sense, the issue is, then, about how we as a society, and our states and governments, in our names, define the limits of free speech and how our media adhere to these understandings of those limits. John Stuart Mill, a liberal philosopher and defender of free speech, recognized, however, the existence of tensions with other values (such as security, authority, democracy) connected with what a 'good society' should look like: 'Some rules of conduct, therefore, must be imposed – by law in the first place, and by opinion on many things which are not fit subjects for the operation of law' (1978: 5). So then how do we decide which opinions are 'off limits' and what good 'free speech' looks like? Mill argued that we know this through reference to the 'harm principle', that if the speech causes harm to another then it would not be appropriate free speech. There has been widespread debate as to what Mill actually meant by harm, but not withstanding this challenge, we can see examples of ways in which limits to free speech are defined. For example, in the United Kingdom (with reference to 'hate speech'), the Public Order Act 1986 states that 'A person is guilty of an offence if he (sic) ... displays any writing, sign or other visible representation which is threatening, abusive or insulting, within the hearing or sight of a person likely to be caused harassment, alarm or distress'. These sentiments have become enshrined in legislation such as that around 'hate speech'. In the United Kingdom, hate speech is not specifically legislated against, but is covered under statues such as that Public Order Act 1986, which forbids racial hatred against individuals or groups including colour, race, ethnic origin and nationality and was amended in 2006 to include religious hatred and in 2008 to include the incitement of hatred on the grounds of sexual orientation (civil rights movement, 2015). The incitement of hatred on the grounds of gender has yet to be enshrined in this legislation; hatred against women has been a theme on new social media and campaigners (such as Laura Bates' Everyday Sexism project and Women, Action and Media) have fought to get companies such as Facebook to self-regulate to not promote hatred against women, but this remains an issue outside of state regulation. As such, when we think about the political context in which news is produced, we need to consider how states and governments provide a broader framework, and the set of democratic principles through which news is constructed. To ask questions about the political nature of news involves asking questions about the formal political context in which news production is situated and the extent to which notions of 'free speech' are defined by both state and media and encapsulated in what we consider to be news.

The changing nature of news and journalism: The technological context

News, as we know, by its very nature, is not static. Not only in terms of events and what is and isn't possible to print and discuss publicly but also in terms of the technologies involved in its production. So far, this chapter has followed Schudson's (2011) approach, which allows for 'news' to be discussed broadly irrespective of its technological basis. Some of the literature differentiates between print journalism (which tends to include openly partisan ideological bias), TV journalism (which is assumed to be impartial in the sense of formal partisan attachment) and the kind of news which is generated via new social media. Throughout discussions of the constitution of news, we also see the way that technology has been attributed a key role in changing the way that news is collected and covered. On the one hand, we could suggest that there is nothing 'new' about new media technologies. Each technological development has often been hailed as revolutionary, from the printing press to new social media. For Castells (1996), we are now in an information age, facilitated by changes in communications media that enable us to cross temporal and spatial boundaries in an unprecedented way; this signifies a whole new type of experience. For Castells, this is illustrative of a shift from an industrial to a post-industrial age. In this arena, *information* is the key to social organization; time and space have been compressed. There is instant virtual linkage; we can know instantly what is happening elsewhere in the world. Geography no longer restricts what information it is possible to have access to (although it is worth reminding ourselves that technology alone cannot cause change, rather it is the way individuals, groups and communities use these technologies in a cultural context that means they are able to effect change, or not).

For some, therefore, technology has been deemed to play a key role in shaping the society that we live in, but in shaping what we can know about that society, scholars have argued that technology has been highly significant in altering the nature of the news that we receive. The development of the printing press was crucial in challenging the orthodoxy of the time, and led to opportunities for the 'masses' to have access to information in an unprecedented manner. Livingstone and Belle (2005) see technological developments as largely positive in altering the nature of news. News can be reported from locations previously too remote to access. The opportunity to present 'breaking news' means that journalists are 'empowered'. They do not have to rely on official sources but can convey their own observations and analysis. This suggests that technology facilitates the capacity for media to carry out their 'fourth estate' function, freeing them from formal political control. Changes in broadcast media production, for example, have meant that with the proliferation of news channels and sources, broadcast news organizations have engaged in the production of rolling news; and as Cushion and Lewis (2010) note, time has become increasingly significant in the rush for broadcasters to be 'first' with 'breaking' news – timeliness is emphasized by the immediacy of the medium. This has been viewed as a largely positive democratic development, as Lewis et al. (2005) suggest; 24-hour news can fulfil three main functions: enabling the viewer to engage whenever they wish; to show major news events as they happen; and to provide more in-depth information/background/context and analysis. These technological developments can be seen to provide increasing opportunities for engagement and interactivity among audiences (although, despite these technological advancements, the process of communication is still top down, in that elites have a monopoly on information, on what does and does not count as news). And in what follows we see that technological changes have been attributed such impact that the medium itself has been used as shorthand to define these changes.

CNN effect and Al Jazeera effect

The term 'CNN effect' came into frequent usage, as illustrative of the incredible capacity of media technologies to shape the political agenda. As Robinson observes, the term 'CNN effect' has been used to denote the way 'real time communications technology could provoke major responses from domestic audiences and political elites to global events' (Robinson, 1999: 301). This assumed impact originally came to light when scholars looked at media coverage of intervention on military and humanitarian grounds in terms of military and humanitarian intervention (for example Bosnia, 1994 and 1995; Iraq, 1991; Somalia, 1992) and non-intervention (e.g. Serbia, 1999; Rwanda, 1994): that CNN chose to focus coverage on the need for humanitarian intervention in Somalia and Bosnia, for example, was attributed as a reason why US foreign policy changed. Politicians, fearful of a mobilized electorate who reacted strongly to images of human suffering presented to them on screen, would amend policy, or engage in political action, accordingly. However, as Hawkins also notes (2002), this focus upon the direct effect of media coverage draws attention away from the lack of coverage of conflict elsewhere in the world, and the consequential lack of policy. This suggests an incredibly powerful role for the news agenda: where public policy is formulated in response to a news agenda, if an item is covered then there is a public policy response, no coverage equals no public policy. Although this somewhat skews the notion of formal political actors making policy decisions in a context of a set of political beliefs or adhering to procedures of democracy; rather it is suggested that we see media playing an overt political role in defining policy agendas.

While the CNN effect refers to how technology facilitates action by political elites, the subsequent Al Jazeera effect (Seib, 2008) has referred to how technology has enabled previously unheard voices to make their views known and presence felt (in Seib's 2008 work, this was the Kurds). So in contrast to the elite dominance assumed and reinforced in the 'CNN effect', in the 'Al Jazeera effect' elites were seen to lose their 'monopoly' on information. While the CNN effect referred to how mainstream media was dominated by elite agendas, the Al Jazeera effect refers not only to the growth and popularity of alternative sources of information, but the ease with which citizens have access to the Al Jazeera satellite network. This notion of ease of access and popularity has also been extended to other forms of 'new' media such as citizen journalism.

New social media/different kinds of journalism; citizen journalism and trolling

Much like the Al Jazeera effect, new social media may also afford opportunities for voices to be heard that have previously been marginalized. For some, the emergence of new social media and the opportunities provided via the internet have meant such a considerable difference to how news is collected and produced that as Deuze has argued 'journalism as it is, is coming to an end. The boundaries between journalism and other forms of public communication... are vanishing, the internet makes all other types of news media obsolete' (2007: 40). This attributes enormous political influence to media technologies in the hands of citizens. The term citizen journalism' has been used to denote how citizens themselves are producing media content and challenging traditional forms of distribution by using new social media sources. For Atton (2003), this technology presents a radical challenge to how professional journalism has been institutionalized in mainstream media; traditional elites no longer have a monopoly over what counts as news. Indeed, as Forde notes, 'the advent of the internet with all its empowering, democratic potential is a significant moment in the development of alternative journalism... it is another way for alternative journalists to organize and to impart their message' (2011: 2). The emancipatory potential of these technological changes can mean that previously marginalized voices have an opportunity to speak, and to be heard. In this sense, we could argue that new technologies have revolutionized how we view the world, the way we make sense of it and how we decide what really matters as 'news' (cf. Kline and Burnstein, 2005). We witness activists make 'news' such as the work done by a variety of campaigners who have got their voices heard (and this is discussed in more depth in Chapter 8). Characterizing much of the discussion around new media technologies is an underlying assumption that technological change is often intimately linked, and often taken to imply transformative social change, in this case, the news agenda is transformed, because of media technologies. But what does this communicate to us politically? In part, this focus on technology links to and reifies the 'scientization' which privileges science and technology as mechanisms which drive social change (rather than other ideological agendas). For Wajcman (1991), this is an inherently masculine process, and so we now turn to consider how gendered power relations may be reconstituted through news construction.

The gendering of news

We may tend to think of news as gender neutral, but once we start to unpack how news is constructed, we could argue that there is an intersection of dominant interests represented, and exploring this helps us to make sense of ways in which power circulates and operates. For example, if we are looking at how news is constructed in mainstream media contexts, we tend to see news coalesce around a general three-fold structure. The first of which is the 'news' which covers events deemed to be newsworthy (in accordance with the news values outlined above). A second section in many newspapers is the 'business' or financial news. Indeed, the BBC's flagship, 'agenda-setting' news programme *Today* devotes the first part of its programming each day to business news. In this sense, we see the news agenda privilege capital, its acquisition and material effects. In essence, through the news agenda, capital gets its own 'advertising' spot, and we could argue that this structure reinforces and communicates to us, the primacy of capital as a way in which our society operates. Finally, most press and broadcast news bulletins end with sports coverage. What is important to observe here, however, is this isn't general sports coverage; this is largely 'male' sports coverage. Sports news is gendered through 'othering', where football is taken as the norm and means 'men's football', women's football is defined by its deviation from the norm. The way women and women's interests are defined through news coverage has long been of concern to scholars in media studies literature and it is this issue that we now expand upon.

The notion of news 'values' implies the possibility of neutrality in the representation of news and the presentation of news agendas. However, as successive scholars have argued, the way news is selected and constructed is not gender blind; newsrooms themselves are highly gendered, as are the values that inform what we are presented with as news (e.g. Allan, 2010; Byerly, 2004; Carter et al., 1998; van Zoonen, 1998). As Ross and Carter observe, 'journalists' daily decisions about what is newsworthy remain firmly based on masculine news values … issues and topics traditionally seen to be particularly relevant to women tend to be pushed to the margins of the news, where the implicit assumption is that they are less important that those which interest men' (2011: 1148). In this way, we see gendered relations played out; the construction of news is not value free. Rather it reinforces existing political relations, communicating to us that it is male interests that matter in the world 'out there'. Van Zoonen (1998: 36) sets out a typology of how we might identify the gendering of news stories, where topics such as politics, crime and economics are seen as reflecting a masculine agenda and are prominent in news coverage; they adhere to the 'objective' rationality attached to the notion of masculinity. Conversely, the feminine is 'othered' and presented in contrast to the masculine news agenda. Feminized news is assumed to be 'soft' emotive news.

Drawing our attention to how news is gendered helps us reflect on how this comes to inform the 'news values' that inform the journalists' selection of news; masculine norms dominate the 'professional' selection of news. This structures the kind of news that is deemed to be of interest and selected in alignment with dominant news 'values'; but if those values are masculinized, then it becomes somewhat inevitable that news reflects male interests. As Ross and Carter (2011) argue, not only does this way of constructing news marginalize women and underrepresent their contribution to social, economic and cultural life but it also contributes to the notion that women are second-class citizens.

In the 1970s, Tuchman et al. argued that women were neither seen nor heard on the news agenda; in this way women were 'symbolically annihilated' (1978). While the news landscape has changed somewhat, as Ross and Carter argue, women's inclusion in the news agenda, as subjects, newsmakers and producers, is still significantly below that of men (2011). They base their claims on findings from the Global Media Monitoring Project. This monitoring project began in 1995 and takes a snapshot of global news coverage once every five years. Their (WAC, 2010) report highlighted that women appeared in only 26% of news stories (globally, across mainstream media); 37% of reporters are women, and men dominate in the coverage of 'hard news' such as politics (67%) and the economy (60%). The descriptive statistics point us to one of the ways dominant interests may be reproduced. Where the dominance of men in an organization or institution means that a single worldview comes to dominate, this is also referred to as 'hegemonic masculinity' (Connell, 1987). This conceptualization highlights how this particular kind of masculinity is the dominant 'norm' and the consequences thereof. Questions or alternative representations become positioned as 'other', peculiar, unusual, notable and demarked as other in their labelling. For example, news coverage may refer to an MP (meaning male MP as the norm), and use the term 'female MP' representing the aberrant other (O'Neill and Savigny, 2014). One of the broader conclusions drawn from this research is that although there have been slight improvements in women's visibility in news in relation to men, this still constitutes an increase of 0.5% per year, and as Macharia commented (2010: 1) 'at this rate it will take 43 years... to achieve gender parity in mainstream news'.

In formal politics, it has been empirically documented that men are twice as likely to receive news coverage as women (Ross, 2007; O'Neill and Savigny, 2014). And if, as Kim and Weaver (2003) argue, we reflect on whose opinion counts as 'expert', who is invited on to legitimate a story, then this reminds us whose views are regarded as legitimate; where white, middle-class, middle-aged professional males are predominantly called upon (Armstrong, 2004; Ross, 2007, 2010). This matters because as Ross argues 'if what we see and read are men's voices, men's perspectives, men's news [then] women continue to be framed as passive observers rather than active citizens' (Ross, 2011: 19). But it is not only the absence or presence of women as news makers, subjects or producers that matters, where women are judged in relation to those who have the power to influence the public agenda, but the language we use, the discourses that circulate in how we talk about women also matter. 'Truth' and 'objectivity' are key features of a journalist's professionalism, although the focus is often on whether it is possible for the news reporter to 'reflect' a social reality. However, as Allan (1998) observes, these discourses of truth that permeate the construction of our news are highly gendered, which can lead to gender bias, rather than objectivity in reporting. Although some would argue (e.g. Harding, 1990; Nicholson, 1990) that there is no such thing as 'objectivity' and to search for that simply reinforces and legitimates patriarchal hegemony, that which counts as 'truth' is determined by those who have the capacity to define and shape what 'reality' looks like. While producers of media have agency, and this is not to deny that, we are reminded that what is communicated to us politically is informed by a set of pre-existing power relations, around capital and gender, which is reinforced in the construction of news, rather than challenged. So how can we challenge these gender norms that permeate news construction? Arguably, although the descriptive numbers of women in journalism matter, and the numbers of women in senior decision-making positions matter, these decisions and what 'counts' as news are still informed by and located in a discursive context.

The discursive context

Discourses are historically constituted bodies of knowledge and practices which shape people and social contexts. They afford power to some but not to others. Discourse is 'socially constitutive as well as socially conditioned – it constitutes situations, objects of knowledge, and the social identities of and relationships between people and groups of people. It is constitutive in the sense that it helps sustain and reproduce the social status quo, and in the sense that it contributes to transforming it' (Fairclough and Wodak, 1997: 258); so news can be both constitutive of and constructed by dominant discourses. Beck (1992) argues that as modernity progresses, we are increasingly living in a society characterized by risk and hazards which cross spatial and temporal boundaries (climate change is perhaps a pertinent example here). For Beck (1992), reflexive modernization points us to the ways not only that our underlying structures change (through science and rationalization) but there is a relationship between structures and individuals situated within those structures (agents). As structures change in the process of modernization, agents become less and less constrained by these structures. In modernization, individuals were supposed to become more and more 'free'. This choice, however, becomes constrained by other kinds of cultural traditions, informed by an adherence to 'scientism'. And here the construction of news according to 'objective standards' of truth adheres to this notion of scientism and 'enlightened rationality'. In this way scientism becomes the cultural norm of social control and restrictions upon individuals within structures. Identification is demanded by social institutions in their construction of risk and other rational 'modern frames' of social control (e.g. around sanity, sexual behaviour). But more widely, risk, for Beck, is the dominant discourse which illustrates the tensions between the crisis of modernity and industrial society, but takes the form of technological or other processes; as such technological experts come to dominate.

Risk is also intimately linked with fear. For Beck, following the nuclear accident in Chernobyl, the nature of risk fundamentally changed. Individuals themselves were no longer able to assess risks, rather the nature of risk today is characterized as global, catastrophic and beyond the possibility of individual intervention. The way discourses of fear and risk are invoked by governments has been widely discussed since the events of 9/11 and the discourse of a 'War on Terror' has been used as a mechanism to instil fear into citizens, and a means through which a whole host of legislation has been introduced to monitor the activities of individual citizens: to internally control nations. News agendas reinforce this risk by affirming political agendas which homogenize groups, 'other' them, and make them responsible for the 'risk' in contemporary societies. For example, the current UK government is introducing new regulations (as part of the Counter-Terrorism and Security Act) where teachers in schools are required to 'assess the risk' of children being drawn into extremist activities (Coughlan, 2015). Yet, as commentators observe (e.g. Francois-Cerrah, 2015), this turns teachers into Orwellian 'thought police' where government is seeking to control the population in an unprecedented manner. Here, then, the assertion of 'risk' becomes a mechanism through which fear is promoted, populations can be managed and justifiably surveilled and controlled.

Discourses of fear and risk may be a mechanism of controlling nations, and we might consider that these discourses of fear also contain a gendered component; where not only governments control their citizens, but men control women. For example, women are taught through news coverage to be alert to the 'stranger danger' that men pose, positioning women as responsible for keeping themselves safe (Stanko, 1990) rather than telling men not to commit the violence in the first place. Mediated discourse reminds women about the need to 'self-regulate' in order to avoid becoming victims of crime (Weaver, 1998: 248). Cindy Carter analyses how male sexualized violence against women has become an 'ordinary' feature of how news is constructed, which encourages readers to accept 'certain ideological justifications for male sexual violence as a typical, even inevitable feature of everyday life' (1998: 221). And we can see how male-based violence is 'normalized' in news coverage (Carter, 1998) in the assertion of dominant tropes, whereby women themselves are held responsible for how men commit violence against them. In the coverage of Irish student Karen Buckley's murder, Boyle (2015) observed that news of this event included frames about the extent to which the victim may or may not have been drinking, and details of her visit to a nightclub prior to her murder. Yet these details do not appear about the murderer – we do not know whether he had been drinking (would we as readers have been quick to attribute the blame and attribution that is implied by the detailing of a victim's behaviour?). We do not know what he was doing prior to the murder, yet implied in the framing of her whereabouts is that she was transgressing the established gender norms, of what is and isn't acceptable as a way for a woman to behave (Boyle, 2015).

We could argue that discourses of terror and fear are broader political contexts designed to keep citizens behaving as states, governments and existing power structures need them to. These discourses are played out and reinforced through news agendas, our political role as analysts of communication is to unpack and ask questions about the wider narratives that inform our news coverage. Throughout this chapter, we have been concerned about what news is, how we identify it and how people use differing technologies to redefine what news is, but we have also drawn attention to some of the things that don't change, despite advances in technology. And this, it is argued, is where politics is being communicated to us through news. The production of news is not a neutral process, and so it behooves us perhaps to think what 'good' news might look like if we are aware of the political norms and values that are being communicated to us through the above.

So to think about how we construct a different kind of news, one that challenges dominant norms and values, we might usefully ask the following questions: whose interests are being reflected in the news that is being written? How are Black and minority ethnic (BAME) groups represented in this story? Are their interests reflected, their voices heard? What assumptions are we making about wealth and capital, about those who deserve it and those who don't? What assumptions are we making about women? Are their interests reflected in this story? Are their voices heard? What assumptions are we making about the 'natural order' of how the world works? Do we accept the dichotomy between rich and poor; men and women; white and BAME; able and differently abled; Christianity and other religions? We might also ask how it is we come to define and 'other' communities and position them as threats to ourselves; what space does that leave for those in those oppositionally defined communities to identify or behave in a manner that is politically different from the broader narrative that they are situated in?

Summary

This chapter has reflected on how news is constructed and how this serves to shape the way we see the world around us. News is not something that exists 'out there' awaiting objective discovery. Rather it is the outcome of a set of social and political processes. Contestation and negotiation can be overt, such as disagreement between journalists and editors as to what a lead story may be, for example, or it may be more subtle, ideological, taking place in how news is selected, chosen. To ask political questions about how news is communicated to us is to ask questions about the power relations that underpin the context in which news is generated. It also encourages us to reflect on whose voices we hear. In the 2015 UK election, for example, research conducted at Loughborough (2015) showed that the economy dominated media coverage; yet the discourse of austerity remained unchallenged and the discussion of 88% of the cuts as a result of 'austerity measures', which directly impacted women, was largely left to activists and campaign groups such as Fawcett (2015).

The argument here is that news is intensely political, not only in the partisan bias that characterizes mainstream press coverage but in the way it reinforces existing structural power relationships (such as around gender, race and capital). This is not to suggest journalists are like zombies with little autonomy or professionalism. And indeed there are journalists who do challenge these structures: Laura Bates (gender), Reni Eddo-Lodge (structural racism), George Monbiot (capital) and Owen Jones (class) to name but a few. Technology plays and has played a role in how we can access news, and indeed, for some, technology itself has changed how news is produced. But technology cannot act without individuals, and how individuals appropriate and use technologies arguably simply reflects the same power struggle in a different technological venue. When we think about how news is communicated to us politically, and if we want a news agenda that challenges rather than reinforces existing structures of power, we might think about how news comes to be constituted, in its technological, social and political context. News is not the communication of neutral events; political choices are made in the ways news is constructed and communicated to us as citizens.

Reflection/seminar activities

What is news? Who decides what news looks like?

Write your own news blog. How have you decided what 'counts' as the news story? Whose voice have you included/excluded? Who is your story aimed at? How would you be able to make the claim your news story is 'objective'?

Select a random day's newspaper coverage. Use this table to count the number of times the following appear:

	Women of colour	White women	Men of colour	White men
Reported story about... And is each one P (positive) N (negative) or O (neutral)				
Direct quote from...				
Picture of...				

What does this tell us?

Chapter 6

How is Politics Communicated beyond the News?

Introduction

There is often a tendency to assume that politics is what happens on the news. But as Street (1997) argues, politics is also about what happens in media *beyond* the news. This chapter invites us to think about how politics may be manifest in media content that we might not immediately think of as 'political'; the communication of societal norms and values, the very meaning of politics, can take place beyond the formal institutions of the state. The recognition of the significance of popular (and more recently, celebrity) culture to the 'political' is evidenced perhaps when we see politicians behaving as celebrities, seeking some 'sparkle' as they fraternize with rock stars. At the same time, we also see TV, music and film stars seek to raise awareness around political issues and influence policy. Angelina Jolie is UN ambassador for refugee issues; Joanna Lumley raised the profile of the Gurkha Justice Campaign group; and Hugh Grant, Steve Coogan and others have used their status to challenge how contemporary journalism has been operating, heading up the UK 'Hacked Off' campaign group (making representation about how mobile phones had been hacked by journalists).

The overlap between popular culture and the activities of politics is also evident at audience, or citizen, level. For example, punk music was viewed as a means of articulating politics; and at this point in time, as Street observes, 'popular culture *was* politics' (1997: 121, original italics). Popular culture is not something that exists separately from the state or the media context that it is situated in. Rather, and the argument in this chapter, is that popular (and celebrity) culture is simply another venue for political communication to take place. In his analysis of the relationship between formal politics and popular culture, Street makes two claims: that popular culture is political activity – in its expression of political ideas – and that to understand politics we need to understand popular culture (1997: 121). In this way, we see that popular culture has become another vehicle for politicians to seek to engage those 'hard to reach voters'; while not creating their own forms of popular culture, they seek to emulate those who do. For some, this is seen as a good thing as it enables citizens to express political identities beyond those of political parties (as with the example of punk above). For others,

103

however, the overlap between popular culture and politics represents a 'dumbing down', an emptying out of the formal content of politics – so that Parliamentary politics has become nothing more than 'infotainment' (Brants, 1988).

This chapter takes as its starting point an acceptance of how popular culture has become intertwined with politics. It begins by exploring how political actors have engaged in popular culture forms and reflects on how the 'culture industry' itself plays a political role. The chapter then moves to chart the rise and consolidation of celebrity culture. In considering how popular culture matters politically, I draw on two examples. The first is a consideration of how celebrity has become increasingly significant and interlinked with the rise of reality TV; the second is to consider the gendered nature of this celebrity status and to explore some of the ways Western women are politically constructed in popular and celebrity culture.

Popular culture and the culture industry

We start from the premise that popular culture 'matters'. That is, popular culture matters because it is part of a media landscape that informs our thinking, and the way that we perceive the world. We need only to think of headlines that blame marginal music forms for teen high school shootings, or how TV soap stars are mistaken for their characters in the street, to recognize that popular culture is intimately bound up with the ways we experience our political and social lives. The ubiquity of access to mediated forms of popular culture means that popular culture is part of everyday life. And that everyday life is political, as through engagement with these cultural forms we are engaging in a form of politics. That is, culture is a site where meanings are contested and negotiated, where social norms and values are reinforced and may be challenged. So we might want to think about the boundaries? Who determines those boundaries? Are we autonomous individuals who are capable of determining what is and isn't real? Or do media and cultural industries play a key role in shaping not only our knowledge of current affairs and news events but also our leisure time?

The term culture is one of those elusive 'difficult to pin down' words. For cultural studies theorist Raymond Williams, culture is perhaps one of the most complex terms in the English language (1983: 87). But it has been used to reflect how we might define a 'whole way of life' of a social group, or groups. Crucially, however, we are reminded that this is structured by forms of representation and power (Walton, 2012: 3). Popular culture matters, first as it shapes a way of seeing the world. Second, it matters as it has also been defined as a 'site of struggle' (Brooks, 1997:

135) where issues, values and meanings are determined and contested; in this sense, power is located in this struggle.

For early cultural studies scholars, the existence of popular or mass culture was problematic: it was viewed as appealing to the lowest common denominator, and as such stunted the growth and development of the individual (Leavis and Thompson, 1933/1977). The agenda advanced by these scholars was the pursuit of literature, 'higher culture', although this view was heavily challenged as elitist (Turner, 2003). However, Leavis and Thompson laid the basis for critique of a variety of cultural forms, such as advertising and many other forms of popular culture. Almost irrespective of the debates as to the elitist agenda being advanced (or not) their work set the groundwork for the analysis of culture, and, more importantly, established the significance of culture in everyday life. Raymond Williams (1958, 1983) was a key cultural theorist who established that culture was a process. Culture, he argued, is not a fixed category; it is not a conclusion; it does not have fixed objects with universal value, rather it is complex and dynamic. This complexity of culture, as fluid and containing meaning and negotiation of that meaning, rather than a fixity of meaning, reminds us that culture is thus intensely political: we need to ask whose and what interests are reflected in the meaning that culture creates, how is this negotiated, how does consensus emerge? Who decides which values society establishes as 'norms'? These questions about how power operates within popular culture encourage us to reflect not only on the political nature of this process but what it is that is being communicated to us (and our responses to those forms of communication).

For Adorno and Horkheimer, this contestation of power relationships in and through culture was the manifestation of elite-level political control. Here mass entertainment and mass culture culminated in a 'culture industry' the effects of which were to pacify the exploited masses through consumption of mindless entertainment (Adorno and Horkheimer, 1947/1972: 142). Where mass entertainment became the 'opium of the masses' this meant that exploitation in the workforce was possible as workers were dulled to their economic inferiority (subordination), and rendered passive to challenge it through their material, economic and intellectual impoverishment. This was exacerbated through the mass 'culture industry'. And while aware of the critiques of Leavis's emphasis on literature and 'authentic' art; Adorno did see high culture (such as literature) as a way to have genuine transformative potential: education and exposure to this kind of culture could stimulate intellectual and aesthetic pleasure and transformation. For Adorno, it was great art (in whatever form that takes) which could awaken the masses and encourage them to rebel against their exploitation. While this work has been criticized for assuming a passivity among the masses (that they are simply dupes of a system), Adorno and Horkheimer offered routes to emancipation and transformation. Culture was a source of oppression, but in its 'higher' form provided the source of enlightenment which would enable the masses to recognize their exploitation. The transformative potential of high culture would give them the impetus to rebel, to overthrow the exploitative system in which they were trapped. To suggest that this is possible or not perhaps denies the complexity of how culture operates, but yet also reinforces the notion that culture is and can be incredibly powerful.

While Adorno and Horkheimer were writing during the Nazi era, their words have been somewhat prophetic for political actors who increasingly acknowledge the significance of culture as a mechanism through which the masses can be exploited for their own purposes. The way popular culture has been embraced within formal politics has been widely documented by scholars such as Street (1997); Drake and Higgins (2012); van Zoonen (2006) and Cardo (2014). However, they also chart something slightly different in their discussion of the emergence of a celebrity culture. While popular culture is by its nature focused on the populous, the popular, what reaches wide audiences, celebrity culture, is much more focused on the celebrity individual. Arguably this emphasis on the individual celebrity is part of an entrenchment of the neoliberal celebration of the individual; and these two themes will form the backdrop of the discussion which follows.

Elite politicians, popular and celebrity culture

In formal politics, we can increasingly see politicians acknowledge the importance of culture in everyday life – no longer do politicians simply assume the media will come to them (as the Attlee quote suggests in Chapter 4), nor do they assume it is sufficient to stand on formal policy platforms alone. The engagement with politicians in popular culture has been widely documented. Indeed this has taken the form of politicians engaging in popular culture, but in a particular way. Politicians are not engaging in all forms of popular culture, rather they have accepted the emergence and growth of celebrity culture. In seeking to engage with popular culture, politicians are not producing popular culture, rather they are appropriating the symbolism, and seeking the status of celebrity in a bid to attract voters. We can think of many such examples, such as Bill Clinton playing the saxophone, Tony Blair posing with a guitar and appearing on *Richard and Judy*, Obama dancing on *Ellen* and Aretha Franklin, Stevie Wonder and Beyoncé performing at his inauguration, David Cameron appearing with One Direction in the Comic Relief video. Notably, former film and TV stars have become politicians (e.g.

Ronald Reagan, Arnold Schwarzenegger and Glenda Jackson). As Street (2004) argues, we can cast the notion of celebrity politics in one of two ways – either the politician seeking to behave as a celebrity to get his/her message across; or the celebrity who seeks to use their status to exercise political influence. This explicit acknowledgement that popular culture matters to people's lives is taken on board and plays an unprecedented role in formal politics.

As Street observes there is an 'implicit assumption that "reaching" potential supporters entail[s] understanding their cultural lives and adopting the methods of communication that marked those lives' (2012: 347). As marketing methods are increasingly adopted in electioneering practice (see Chapter 4), connection through forms of popular culture become another weapon in the (permanent) campaign armoury. Research has demonstrated that the more engaged with celebrity culture audiences are, the less likely they are to engage in formal politics (Couldry and Markham, 2007); for van Zoonen (2005), however, entertainment media and blurring the boundaries between formal politics and popular culture can be a mechanism for rejuvenating politics, a way to re-engage voters and citizens, increasing their opportunities for political knowledge and participation. TV programmes such as *Big Brother* encourage a connection between voting and participation (Cardo, 2011a), and where 'ordinary' people are fictionalized as having the capacity to stand for office (Cardo, 2011b), it can happen to you is the message that is sent. Underlying this concern with popular culture, more recently we have seen the increasing celebration of the celebrity, and so one of the foci in this chapter is the way the idea of celebrity communicates a particular set of complex and nuanced political values to us, as audiences and citizens.

The celebrity is a 'strategically important figure', offering a model of personal success, reinforcing the idea of individual achievement that is attainable by all (Nunn and Biressi, 2010: 49). There is an aspirational celebration of the neoliberal individual for whom anything is possible. Commodified meritocracy prevails in this cultural context, and the celebrity is reified. For Marshall, the cultural conditions which facilitate this 'expansion of celebrity status' is the reliance on both capitalism and the 'democratizing sentiments' associated with the perceptions of an accessible culture (Marshall, 1997: 25–26). While popular culture, and its derivative, celebrity culture, suggest mass audiences, the notion of celebrity focuses our attention, very much consistent with dominant neoliberal tropes, on the 'freedom' of the individual and denying associated structural constraints (such as race, gender and class). The term celebrity 'derives from the fall of the gods, and the rise of democratic governments and secular societies' (Rojek, 2001: 1). Indeed, Marshall takes this further and highlights how celebrity is not only tied to the rise of democratic societies and a focus on the personal in public life, but crucially he recognizes how celebrity is adopted as a mechanism 'to contain the power of the mass in those democracies' (Marshall, 1997: 241; see also Farrell, 2013). For Marshall the celebrity is both an embodiment of the industrial/institutional setting that they are situated in and the expression of the audience that attaches meaning to that figure (1997: 185). To understand the effectiveness of the celebrity we thus need an awareness of these two interlocking features: the cultural setting and the affective reaction of the audience. This cultural setting, as has been noted, is not value free, however, and reflects the dominant norms and values of the society. But we increasingly witness how both identity and individuality are conceptually bound up in the notion of celebrity, which links more broadly to the shift in narratives from class-based politics to identity politics (Fraser, 1985). Marshall argues in contrast to formal politics, which conducted in a language of rationality; celebrity communication relies on emotion and affect. For the media industry, the intention is to turn cultural capital into economic capital (Marshall, 1997: 189), and the commodification of celebrity is a key mechanism through which celebrity status becomes reinvented, reinforced and embedded. Celebrity affect is encouraged and promotional products and spins offs are thus available to an emotionally connected consumer. In TV shows, the celebrity is presented as originating from the audience (Marshall, 1997: 190), which engenders the illusion that we as audiences can be like celebrities (and this is discussed below with reference to reality TV).

To be able to connect emotionally with audiences is a powerful resource for politicians in an era where traditional partisan identities are no longer fixed. Existing celebrities have 'cultural capital' and it could be argued that it becomes in politicians' interests to capitalize on this, not for the commercial gain of the culture industry but for the electoral benefits that may follow. We also see celebrities such as Bono and Geldof use their fame and star status to encourage politicians to change development policies and to mobilize audiences to rectify governments' failings. Indeed, the failings of governments' structural approaches towards many of the world's major inequalities, it has been argued, has led us to a new form of 'conscience capitalism' (Farrell, 2014) where audiences and citizens are responsible for making up the economic failings of the state. Here again, the individual is privileged as responsible as the state is rolled back.

Marshall suggests that the way celebrities work across the culture industry (e.g. pop stars making TV commercials; footballers in films) functions politically as this serves to contain and restrain what could be volatile affective power within the audience. In states of fluid citizen and audience identities, celebrities represent a point of attachment for audiences, and they are kept stable through consumption. For example, the celebrity endorsement of products is designed to provide an affective link with consumers and fans of the celebrity, bringing the two together to create meaning for a particular group – for example, Kylie's advertising of Evian water creates a link to the product and a connection with fans who may not previously have bought the product. We can see similar in the range of perfumes and aftershaves, for example, Britney's *Fantasy* and *Homme* by David Beckham. Here the use of Beckham provides men with 'permission' to take an interest in their appearance. However, their identity and individuality is expressed through consumer products (Pringle, 2004). Here what we see is celebrities perform the expression of ideologies of consumerism connected to the individual (Marshal, 1997: 247). To emphasize the individual and particular discourses of what 'success' looks like in the elevation of the celebrity binds us to consumption as expression and serves to embed the individualism of neoliberalism. As Rojek notes, 'Capitalist organization requires individuals to be both desiring objects and objects of desire ... Celebrity culture has emerged as a central mechanism in structuring the market of human sentiments' (2001: 14). And this has been incredibly prolific over the last decade as celebrity culture is 'one of the growth industries' (Turner, 2010).

This wider, politically charged cultural context matters, as it is embedded through the behaviours of elite actors, and amplified as significant through the media we consume. As celebrity news increasingly dominates the broadcast and print media agenda and is pervasive on social media (Turner, 2010), so we are disciplined to reflect on how we should behave. As has been noted earlier, media scholars debate the direct effects that media have on us, but the argument here is that media make up part of a landscape in which dominant norms and values are circulated, and serve to regulate our behaviour. And it is perhaps useful here to situate the rise and dominance of celebrity culture within the work of Michel Foucault.

Disciplining audiences in celebrity culture

Foucault's work explored how the rise of the modern state was linked to discourses of regulation and control in various aspects of life (such as sexuality [1976], madness [1961] and punishment [1975]) and it is the way we internalize those discourses and self-regulate that is of particular interest here. Foucault argued that: 'each society has its regime of truth, its "general politics" of truth: that is, the types of discourse which it accepts and makes function as true ... the techniques and procedures accorded value in the acquisition of truth: of those who are charged with saying what counts as true' (Foucault, 1980: 131).

In this sense, power is exercised through these truth regimes, through discourses. The state uses knowledge to exercise power over its subjects. While Foucault's attention was focused on the modern state and how power was distributed and exercised, this did not account for the layer of media which sits between state and its subjects. And so, if we think that media provide a key site of knowledge for us, about what does and does not matter within a society, then we can start to unpack how power is exercised. The 'politics of truth' in popular culture determine that celebrity status is something to be valued. But power for Foucault, was not necessarily top down – it was something that was constituted and reconstituted through people. In this sense, subjects are coerced in subtle ways – people are disciplined to self-regulate. This is similar to Althusser's notion that subjects of ideology accept their subjection because they are under the illusion they are 'free' and can perform 'the gestures and actions' of their subjection without coercion (Althusser, 1971: 182). Back to Adorno and Horkheimer – popular culture, and in this case celebrity culture, provides an 'illusion of freedom'; it is constructed to contain emancipatory potential while simultaneously facilitating the self-regulation of the individual. So how does the state produce self-regulating citizens? We will return to this issue below as we explore the rise of the cult of celebrity through reality TV.

Reality TV and celebrity culture

While politicians are engaging in a form of popular culture, they are drawing on the dominant culture which populates popular culture: celebrity status. Intertwined with the notion that politicians as celebrities can reach people's lives is an attempt to connect with the aspiration of celebrity status of 'normal' people (discussed in more detail below). Celebrities in this way 'express an ideology of heroic individualism, upward mobility and choice in social conditions wherein standardization, monotony and routine prevail' (Rojek, 2001: 33); celebrities can therefore be a mechanism of exploiting and subduing the masses. But not only can celebrities and popular culture function to exploit the masses, or at least keep them amused, for Debord, this 'culture of signs' functioned to encourage the masses into imitative consumption (1967). It is not enough to aspire to celebrity status; we must consume to be like them too. Like van Zoonen (2005), Curran (2010) also adopts a more positive approach and argues that entertainment media, and popular culture, can play a democratic function: in helping citizens understand where they 'fit in society'; a way to debate moral and social values; and can reaffirm our norms that govern our common social process. However, what all accounts point us towards is the notion that celebrities and popular culture are intimately bound up with the public as audiences, and personalities from public life.

This facilitates, as Marshall (1997) notes, the wielding of considerable power. Foucauldian governmentality is achieved through providing aspirational role models and morality stories and/or escapism that reconcile ordinary individuals to their subordination; order and compliance are reproduced (Rojek, 2001: 37). And luckily (?) there have been changes in how TV content is produced which fits neatly into this evolving context. One area of major change in TV production has been the growth of reality TV programmes, such as *Big Brother, Fame Academy* and *Britain's Got Talent.* These programmes rest on the notion that 'ordinary' people want to become celebrities; they aspire to public status and recognition. Indeed a YouGov survey conducted in Britain and Australia revealed that young people increasingly have fame as a primary future goal (Cassidy, 2006). Reality TV links back to the idea that individuals can be recognized, have their voice heard, and ultimately it offers the opportunity for celebrity status to be achieved.

Following Foucault, we might well see celebrity culture as a mechanism of self-regulation. Foucault argued that the state was able to effect self-regulation through disciplinary mechanisms, and drew on the work of Bentham's panoptican prison design, which was comprised of a central watchtower visible at all times to the prisoners whose cells were positioned in a circle around the tower. In this way the prisoners were always visible to the guards, although the guards were not visible to the prisoners. Control was maintained because irrespective of whether they were being watched, the prisoners thought that the guards were there and so behaved as though they were being watched; the prisoners regulated themselves rather than being coerced by violence, for example. For Foucault, it was this notion of self-regulation that was achievable through the idea of being watched. Surveillance then was a mechanism of ensuring nonviolent control – and this could be extended to all aspects of life, not just prison. Workers could become self-regulated in this way; the recording of phone conversations in call centres, the monitoring of bathroom breaks, of emails and computer usage. Employees may not know when this happens, but the knowledge that this is possible serves to regulate their behaviour. Perhaps the most common contemporary example of how we are regulated in society is through the expansion of the use of CCTV cameras. It doesn't matter whether they are switched on or not; people behave as though they are and self-regulate accordingly. This attributes coercive power to technology, but perhaps we should consider more carefully how it is used. One way to think about how we are now disciplined to self-regulate and internalize the desire for celebrity status is through reality TV.

Reality TV provides 'ordinary' people with the opportunity to achieve varying degrees of fleeting celebrity status, through their own skills in the kitchen (*MasterChef; Come Dine with Me*) or in the work environment (*The Apprentice*), through the capacity to entertain (*Britain's Got*

Talent; *Pop Idol*) or simply through being themselves (*Big Brother*), or improving themselves (*How to Look Good Naked*), reality TV has become ubiquitous. Cheap to make and a consequence in part of the out-sourcing and deregulation of media, reality TV functions to normalize a particular kind of neoliberal individualism (Couldry, 2010: 79). Reality TV has also been positively viewed as intensely political in that it fulfils claims for recognition that people may not be able to express elsewhere (Coleman, 2003), although the argument here is that there are a set of structural conditions (race, gender and class, for example) inscribed into media discourses which limit what is and isn't possible for an individual to achieve (this will be returned to below, when we explore how gender is constructed through mediated popular and celebrity culture).

There are also wider political questions and concerns that underpin the move towards celebrity culture, and while the focus tends to be on those who currently comprise celebrity culture, what about the audi-ences who seek to be part of celebrity culture, or whose voices we don't hear; or the 'wannabes' of celebrity culture? The first component is the way celebrity culture is pernicious in the media that we consume, it is not simply the preserve of politicians and celebrities, rather celebrity has become a way of life, a mechanism of self-regulation. But to assume that celebrity status can be afforded only through traditional power struc-tures is being increasingly challenged through contemporary media and culture. Celebrity status is conferred by what? Media attention. There is a tendency to assume a particular 'way' of celebrity status. We can list celebrities who are famous for not doing anything in their own right – Kim Kardashian, Liz Hurley, Coleen Rooney – what these people share in common is that they tend to be photogenic women conforming to a particular stereotype as to what it means to be a woman. And celebrity status is ever more achievable through new media technologies provid-ing platforms such as Facebook, YouTube and Twitter where instant celebrity status can be achieved, however fleeting, if your selfie or video goes viral; in this way we monitor our own behaviour in a bid for celeb-rity status (see also Senft, 2008).

The darker side of celebrity status

If celebrity status is about being recognized, having your name known, then the flip side of this fame is notoriety (Rojek, 2001). As we self-regulate and internalize the desire for fame and recognition, then there is a darker side. Less discussed are the more pernicious effects or con-sequences of celebrity culture. Internalizing the values of fame, the desire for publicity and recognition also incurs more pernicious out-comes. The Columbine high school shootings on 20 April 1999 are part of a Western common historical knowledge. At the time, the motiva-tions of the gunmen were unknown, and variously attributed to being bullied, musical tastes, although nothing was ever proven. Today, social media allow people to post videos and writings claiming their intent. Anders Breivik's killing spree of 69 people in Utøya gained himself and his 'cause' notoriety, and a cult following across the internet. The Lufthansa co-pilot who brought down the plane, killing all 150 people on board, had reportedly told his girlfriend 'One day I will do something that will change the whole system, and then all will know my name and remember it' (Knight, Harding and Willsher, 2015). As Rojek observes, 'if the desire to "be someone" is not achieved by "normal" means, some individuals may have a compelling propensity to use violence as a means of achieving fame through notoriety' (2001: 146). The intention here is not to offer psychoanalytic explanations for individual behaviour, but rather point to a social and cultural context, where celebrity status is something which becomes privileged as a norm and value, 'a widely desired characteristic of modern life' (Rojek, 2001: 148) binding us together, the end is public recognition and the means are a secondary consideration.

The political representation of gender in popular and celebrity culture

When we explore the notion of celebrity, as with other areas, there tends to be an assumption of gender neutrality: that the notion of celebrity is applicable equally to all genders. As has been noted above, culture is fluid, recreated through interactions. But how we define what celebrity status looks like is imbued with a set of pre-existing structural conditions. These structural conditions are located in ideas around gender, race, class, sexuality, physical ability, mental health and religion. There are a set of norms which are assumed and underpin how contemporary celebrity is constructed and valued. The following focuses on just one aspect of these structural features: gender.

In her groundbreaking work, van Zoonen (1994) points us towards how the political economy of the media industry plays a key role in structuring how women are represented in the media. Exploring how media content is produced enables us to reflect on the notion that the dominance of men in the cultural industries is reflected in how media content is produced. Here we see media and cultural industries exhibiting 'hegemonic masculinity' (cf. Connell, 1987) where the overrepresentation of men in production results in male-oriented output. One of the outcomes of this is that cultural 'products' are produced by men, with male audiences in mind. In this way, the idea of what a celebrity looks like is not gender neutral. Rather it is constructed according to a masculine norm. An important author who unpacked the power relations which underpinned women's representation in the media was Laura

Mulvey. In her essay, she explored how 'the unconscious of patriarchal society' (1975: 6) was (re)asserted through cinematic form. Film stars are exemplars of the 'celebrity status': wealthy, glamorous, famous, living apparently beautiful lives which are within our reach. The celebrity film star plays out and reinforces gender roles: women are associated with the body; men with the mind (Rowe, 2011: 13).

Using psychoanalytic theory, Mulvey argued that 'Woman then stands in patriarchal culture as signifier for the male other, bound by a symbolic order in which man can live out his phantasies and obsessions through linguistic command by imposing them on the silent image of woman still tied to her place as bearer of meaning, not maker of meaning' (1975: 6). That is, women do not exist in their own right, nor have roles as meaning makers in their own right, rather they exist for the purpose of the male protagonist and viewer. Women are 'othered' and rendered as adjuncts and objects, rather than subjects in their own right. As such, cinema functions to render the male an active subject, the female a passive object, and she observes that 'the determining male gaze projects its phantasy on to the female form which is styled accordingly' (1975: 10). Women are looked at and displayed; they function as objects of male desire, motivation; she inspires love and fear, but at all times this is for the male protagonist and the (assumed male) audience. She does not appear in her own right, nor express her own interests and desires, beyond that which are required for the male protagonist and male spectator. Moreover, this form of representation serves to encode gendered power relations into Hollywood films, as Mulvey argues (1992: 160): 'mainstream film coded the erotic into the language of the dominant patriarchal order'. In this sense, women are not presented as they 'really are', rather they are presented as dominant interests want to see them.

The idea of the 'male gaze' can be seen across a variety of media content, not just cinema, and a tranche of subsequent media analysis has pointed to how women have been repeatedly subject to the 'male gaze' from newspapers, to TV programming, to advertising (e.g. van Zoonen, 1997; Gill, 2007; Carter, 1998). The notion of the male gaze was popularized in the comic *Dykes to Watch Out For* (Bechdel, 1985) and the Bechdel test was developed as a simple model of establishing the role of women in films. It has three very simple rules for a film to pass:

1. It has to have at least two [named] women in it
2. Who talk to each other
3. About something besides a man.

A website (the bechdeltest.com) has been established to track the number of films that pass the test. In their database at the time of writing they had 5,856 films. Of this, 3,378 (57.7%) passed all three tests;

598 (10.2%) passed two tests; 1,282 (21.9%) passed one test; and 598 (10.2%) passed no tests at all (Bechdeltest.com, 2015). If films cannot pass this basic test, what does this communicate to us about how power is operating? In this sense, women are denied agency, interests in their own right, if they serve as objects for male protagonists to act out their fantasies, desires and heroism rather than reflect the diversity of interests and experiences of women.

Whereas in the time of Mulvey's writing, women were objects of male heterosexual desire, increasingly sexual violence is becoming a 'norm' as a motivator of male behaviour. The male protagonist has to avenge the rape of his wife/daughter/partner/sister ... Sexual violence has become so common as a trope that even where women protagonists exist, such as in the video game/film *Tomb Raider*, the backstory now for Lara Croft is that her strength is derived from attempted rape (Hamilton, 2012). Projansky offers an analysis of how rape is increasingly commonplace in popular film and TV and often used as the site whereby rape, or the threat of rape, is the trigger that 'transforms' the woman into a powerful and independent person (2001: 100). The increasing glamorization of sexual violence against women performs a communicative function as a narrative of masculine control. Sexual violence is a mechanism through which a woman derives her strength or a motivation for revenge for the male protagonist. In *The Equality Illusion*, Kat Banyard (2010) details how sexual violence has become the normalized 'go to' way of having sex on the internet. And this is reinforced throughout other popular culture forms, made by mainstream media and through user-generated content uploaded to social media sites. Celebrity notoriety (Rojek, 2001) is achieved through the uploading of videos that go viral. The harrowing Stubenville rape video went viral (Penny, 2013) and in the notoriety gained from it, we see the transformation of celebrity culture into 'rape' culture.

Popular culture, celebrity and postfeminism

Beyond the violent ways in which we are encouraged to think about the position of women in the contemporary context, it is also useful to explore women's rejection of their secondary status in our societies and how popular culture has responded to the demands placed upon it through feminisms (the plural is used to acknowledge a variety of approaches within feminism), and how mediated culture seeks to discredit the advances of women's movements. In her widely cited essay, McRobbie (2004) discussed how popular culture has served to repudiate the advances made by feminism as a political movement. In this way, popular culture serves as a site where power relations are contested and negotiated; and for feminisms a fundamental power relationship that is being challenged is patriarchal. But mediated popular culture has responded to the challenges posed by feminisms. As McRobbie (2004) observes, contemporary popular culture serves to challenge the political acceptability of feminism – presenting us with the notion that we live in a 'postfeminist' era, where we are encouraged to ironically engage in sexism, as feminism is presented to us as having achieved its goals. In mediated popular culture we have witnessed a 'backlash' against feminism (Faludi, 1991); the female celebrity displays her agency and empowerment, which are dependent upon her bodily capital, sexual skills and sexual subjectivity (Gill, 2008). These gendered analyses enable us to reflect on the way in which they are cultural and structurally positioned by the 'sexiness' of their bodies: external criteria defined through 'hegemonically masculine' (Connell, 1987) structures of popular cultural production. Contemporary criteria dictate a prevalence of women who are young, white, thin and blond as the mainstay of what a female 'should' look like. There has been a range of literature which has charted how women and girls are increasingly sexualized through forms of popular culture. Kat Banyard (2010) details how the sex industry now plays such a prominent role in the high street, in a wide range of cultural forms, that it now defines what we think of as women's roles in society, as well as what they should look like. Not only has this changed how women are represented in popular culture formats but the political agenda that women have fought for, Banyard argues, has been stolen by capitalism and feminism is being sold back to us through the porn industry, through, for example, the proliferation of playboy motifs and products, and women's willingness to engage in their own commercialization as sexualized objects. There has been a range of academic literature which has charted the increasing 'pornification' of popular culture (Levy, 2005). Agency and empowerment become reduced to a woman's capacity for sexual expression. And indeed, so successfully has this agenda become embedded that as McRobbie (2004) observes, the absence of objection to this kind of sexualization has become a condition of contemporary female freedom (2004: 260). Women, it seems, are not allowed to object to 'ironic' sexism or as Douglas argues 'enlightened sexism' – the irony being the narrative of feminism is rejected so that media producers are able to use semi-naked women to 'sell' TV programmes and to become celebrities within those TV programmes. The contemporary neoliberal capitalist project requires not only that we, as audiences, consume products but that we make ourselves the products; women are positioned as sexual commercial commodities – in the name of individual freedom. Women have choices, but these choices are culturally restricted; women are encouraged to make the 'right' choice, through the use of their bodies, except they are a particular kind of body. But Black, bigger than size zero, over 21? Not so much choice there. Relations of power are communicated, made and remade through these cultural forms. For many feminist scholars, the body is the site where politics played out (e.g. Butler, 1990; Haraway, 1991; Phipps, 2014; Spivak, 1988), power is dispersed but consolidated through discourses, where media and cultural texts 'interpellate': they produce women into being.

Popular culture is not monolithic and contains tensions, and there have been challenges, and indeed there is a history of TV programmes where female characters are the key protagonists (such as *The Golden Girls*, *Kate and Allie*) and have functioned to 'address the agenda that feminism has made public about the contradictory demands on women' (Brundson, 1997: 34). And we can point to a rise of programming where women are treated as a rise of programming where women are treated as subjects, rather than objects. In comics, Marvel has recently made Thor a female character and produced the superhero Jessica Jones; the most recent *Mad Max* movie had strong links to feminist history (although it is worth noting the backlashes to this in some predominantly male online communities). That we can point to these exceptions arguably reinforces the notion that much of the popular visual culture that we consume is predominantly communicating to us the significance and dominance of the white heterosexual male.

So how do we ask political questions about what is taking place in popular and celebrity culture? In order to do so, we need to unpack what is taking place. Not only do we need to understand how celebrity culture is produced and presented to us through a variety of media forms but we need to understand our position in the consumption of such culture. Once we start to unpack what is taking place in popular and celebrity culture, we can start to expose the underlying power relationships, how power is contested, negotiated, and consent produced. Through representations of gender in popular culture we see how women are defined in opposition, as the 'other' of men. If we want to challenge this binary structure, we might draw on the work, for example, of Derrida, who highlights how the privileging of one term over another reinforces existing power relations. To deconstruct this opposition will enable the 'overthrow of the hierarchy' but without allowing the subordinate to dominate (Derrida, 1972/1987). Deconstruction therefore undermines systems of meaning through challenging them and enabling us to understand how cultural systems of meaning and value production privilege certain individuals and groups (e.g. races, classes, genders, sexualities) over others. In Stuart Hall's deconstruction of 'The Popular' (1981), he argued that popular and high culture were not free from politics as they are culturally contested, and interdependent and reliant upon each other for their definition. Maintaining high culture depends on the very thing it excludes – popular culture. And so with gendered divisions, to be a man, or to be male, relies on excluding what it means to be female. Butler (1990) highlights how gender and sexuality are 'performed', rather than a 'natural' consequence of biology. Once we start to deconstruct how popular and celebrity culture are presented to us and the binaries that they are reliant upon – for example heterosexuality v homosexuality, male v female – not only can we establish where power relationships are taking place but we can also reflect on how these power relationships are communicated to us.

Perhaps one way to deconstruct and expose these binary oppositions is through work that has been done on humour. Here we are invited to reflect, for example, on the way racist jokes are contingent upon race: once the race element is reversed or re-written, the 'joke' doesn't work, the racist component is exposed (cf. deSousa, 1987). And so in popular and celebrity culture, if we reverse the way women are represented, we can start to expose the gendered opposition upon which existing systems are reliant. So if we reverse, for example, female and male roles...do they still work? Would it be possible to see James Bond or Doctor Who as a woman? Why don't we talk about the appearance of male politicians in the ways that we might focus attention on female MPs' shoes, for example? Can we imagine a front-page media headline that asks whether David Cameron has had Botox? Or observes that George Osborne looked svelte in his evening suit? These ideas might sound ridiculous, yet perhaps in this we expose just how deep-rooted are our assumptions about gender and the reliance of one upon the other.

Summary

Throughout this chapter, we have explored the relationship between formal politics and popular culture, and then how culture itself is highly politicized. What we see is the way that culture is intertwined with all aspects of our political lives, which means that culture, and the particular focus here is on popular culture, has become appropriated by people and within systems of ideas, yet this culture also forms the site of challenge. Politicians may take to acting as though they are celebrities, and celebrities may seek to wield formal political influence. Or indeed encourage audiences and citizens not to engage, as the high-profile comedian Russell Brand recently encouraged UK citizens not to vote. Celebrity culture embodies a set of norms and values: aspirational neoliberal individualism is engendered, encouraging the populace it is possible to become famous, however fleetingly, and in whatever way. Simultaneously, we are encouraged to consume, which sustains our economic systems. Gendered relations are reinforced which sustains our patriarchal systems. If we think about how we self-regulate and discipline ourselves in this process, we can see how we internalize a governmentality that facilities stability of the social order. This chapter has sought to reflect on how the communication of popular and celebrity culture is highly political – sites where existing power relations are negotiated and contested in the struggle for consensus and consent are also sites where wider politics about gender, consumption and our identities beyond those connected to political parties are communicated and constructed.

Reflection/seminar activities

If you were a celebrity, who would you be and why? What gives this person their celebrity status? How is 'success' defined by them, and for them?

Giving reasons for your decisions, sort the following into high or popular culture:

Rammstein; Banksy; Mona Lisa; Harry Potter and the Chamber of Secrets; War and Peace; Pavarotti; Lamb of God; Kate Moss @ Topshop; Versace; Opera; Lloyd Webber musicals.

Apply the Bechdel test (below) to your entertainment viewing for seven days:

1. It has to have at least two [named] women in it
2. Who talk to each other
3. About something besides a man.

How many programmes and/or films pass? How many fail?

Chapter 7

How is Politics Communicated beyond the Nation State?

Introduction

Perhaps the ultimate form of political communication by nation states as political actors is that of the declaration of war, which is a definitive act of 'persuasion' and communication: using hostile means to achieve political goals. Governments use a variety of techniques to communicate political messages to opponents, to citizens and to military audiences. Media play a crucial role in how war is framed to citizens at home; once war was declared on Iraq, for example, UK national newspapers played a generally supportive role calling on public support for 'our boys', personalizing the war agenda onto the soldiers who were fighting, drawing attention away from government policy. Media framing, sympathetic to the actions of the government of the day, is crucial in the battle for 'hearts and minds'. One of the most poignant moments towards the end of the Vietnam War was Nick Ut's communication of the atrocities being suffered by civilians in his photograph of a small girl fleeing a napalm attack in her village. This picture was widely credited with swaying public opinion against the war; military and political strategists learned the lessons of the need to ensure public support for later acts of warfare and crucially the need to get supportive media framing.

For Clausewitz, war is another form of politics; for Sun Tzu the most effective military renders physical battles unnecessary and is able to achieve goals without protracted war (Caleb, 2000: 79). Modern warfare includes the need for the 'winning of hearts and minds' – persuasion is a key element of this. As such, media have a vital role to play in providing information and the presenting (or re-presenting) of war to the public, whose opinion is crucial in legitimating support for government intervention. This chapter explores some of the ways war, and its consequences, is communicated to us, and what this means politically. The chapter begins with an overview of what we mean by war, and then moves on to explore some of the more practical aspects of how journalists provide coverage of war. We then move to reflect on the role of popular culture in shoring up public support for such interventions, and reflect on Baudrillard's claim about the extent to which war is now so mediated, he argued, that 'the Gulf War did not take place'. Finally the chapter reflects on how terrorism has become a routine, normalized, depoliticized part of our daily mediated discourses.

War

The term 'war' has become frequently used in national discourses. Politicians declare a 'war' on benefits cheats; we have recently seen the 'War on Terror' and war is declared on cancer, on poverty and many other aspects of social life. The term has become so frequently employed that there is a danger of it becoming meaningless. For Clausewitz, a historical referent for the theorizing and discussion of the nature of war, war is both a political act and a political instrument; it starts from a political condition and occurs because of political motives (1874; 22). In perhaps one of his most famous quotes he argues that 'war is a mere continuation of policy by other means' (Clausewitz, 22). This suggests a somewhat sanitized notion of war as simply another mechanism available to policy makers, and it is notable perhaps how far this sanitization has come to form part of our wider mediated discourses of war. Yet as Clausewitz also observes, war 'is an act of violence intended to compel our opponent to fulfill our will' (1874: 14). While violence is something that the establishment of the state was intended to protect individuals from inflicting upon each other (Hobbes, 1651/2014), political theory draws our attention to states as having legitimacy in the use of force and violence, against other states. This is also supported through a variety of instruments in international law. Yet this overt violence remains largely hidden from us, as citizens and mediated audiences, where we are presented with more sanitized victories and successes, combined with a simultaneous 'othering' political discourse, that justify 'our' war efforts.

There has been a range of literature which has sought to explore how there are attempts to manipulate public opinion in favour of supporting war efforts through techniques of propaganda (which are not dissimilar to the strategies of 'spin' deployed by politicians as discussed in Chapter 4). If legitimacy is derived through public support, then it is logical that the public are also required to support the 'war effort' (and as noted in Chapter 4, and as seen in the two World Wars, propaganda is a key means of shoring up public support). For example, powerful imagery of the events of September 11, 2001, was shown and reshown on Western TV channels and provided elites with a visual justification for the foreign policy decisions taken by Bush and Blair in their decisions to invade Afghanistan and then Iraq. A major way in which Western publics were encouraged to support the war was through the continual coverage, made available through the 24-hour news channels, as technology enabled us to witness events as they unfolded. However, as Hoskins (2004) suggests, the demand for immediacy overrode the demand for accuracy or content. Bush's speeches initially referred to acts of terrorism, but within days referred to acts of war being waged upon America. Crucially, these speeches were linked with these evocative images with the aim of embedding the conflation of political objectives with the tragic events played out in media agendas.

What is perhaps less discussed in war coverage is how it is often conceived of in very masculine ways, and is predominantly a masculine pursuit; largely enacted by men, decided upon by men, and conducted broadly in their interests. If women are underrepresented in legislatures, militaries are overwhelmingly dominated by men. Ninety-seven percent of uniformed soldiers are male (Goldstein, 2004: 107). And in only six of the world's states do women constitute 5% of the armed forces. Margaret Mead observed how war was ultimately a male pursuit, culturally gendered and, as a result, to make sense of it we need to 'pay particular attention…to the need of young males to validate their strength and courage, and to…the conspicuous unwillingness of human societies to arm women' (1967: 236). This is not only about numbers of men involved in the decisions that lead to war, and conduct it but also the cultural climate which supports masculine interests, and this has consequences. This domination of masculine interests thus means that women's interests become obscured, marginalized and sacrificed to the 'war effort'. The way war is conducted thus serves to reflect and reinforce masculine hegemonies. As Weaver-Hightower observes in the US response to the events of September 11, 2001, these codes were evident through the discourses of political elites where 'refusals to conduct diplomacy with a sovereign state under threat of war are examples of particularly masculine posturing. Violence before discussion…fits the pattern of hegemonic masculinity in the Western world' (cited in Mac An Ghail and Haywood, 2007: 203). And while I am not seeking to essentialize here, and recognize that there is not an homogeneity among either men or women, this does raise the question, would war exist in the form that it does if the gendered numbers in the military and in legislatures across the world were reversed?

Not only does gendering shape the conduct of war, but analyses of the mediation of war coverage tend to be presented without distinction or recognition of gender, speaking in 'gender neutral' terms, which suggests that this mediated process is, at an ontological level, free from gender concerns. There has been much literature in international relations which acknowledges the gendered nature of the conduct of warfare (cf. Steans, 1998; Goldstein, 2001) yet this has yet to cross into the realm of mediated political communication. The argument here is that the processes of war and the way they are communicated to us are political not only in the way that we are positioned in relation to existing structures of political power, but that those structures are gendered, and so in what follows the aim is also to argue that gender is constitutive of the processes by which war is mediated and a process of political communication. In order to 'bring gender' back into analyses, we need to understand the differential ways in which war and its mediation has differential effects for men and women.

War reporting

The way that we in the West find out about war, as a means of communicating international politics, is largely through media sources (of course this is not true globally for those unfortunate enough to live in conflict zones). As Lewis et al. note, 'the use of information as a weapon is becoming a dominant feature of modern warfare' (2006: 16–17). There has been detailed research about how media relay news of battle-grounds, 'victories', and how media produce and describe this matters. For example, the 2003 invasion of Iraq saw the phrase 'collateral damage', to mean civilian deaths through Western acts, come into common usage. This sanitizing of the deaths that our governments were inflicting on innocent civilians in the name of a policy agenda was shored up and reinforced through mediated discourses, although this was not without reflection, and journalists themselves have demonstrated an awareness that audiences may become sceptical if there is too much sanitization in television news pictorial coverage (Higgins and Smith, 2013: 28).

During, the Falklands Conflict in 1982, the UK government understood the importance of placing journalists alongside the military in order to produce more 'sympathetic' reporting (Miller, 2004). The Gulf War in 1990 saw extensive engagement by the government in media management strategies, which reminds us that 'spin' is something operationalized not only at election times, but is an essential element of governmental communication. In coverage of the 2003 Iraq War, we witnessed a further consolidation of the journalist/military relationship. Journalists were 'embedded' within military operations facilitating instant access to news, but this also provided a site where 'information systems talk to and work with each other' (Miller, 2004). In this way, we see journalists embedded with combat troops, military PR, and governmental PR working together to create news coverage. It is somewhat logical to assume that journalists embedded in military contexts, reliant on the military for their safety, will be directed by military in the identification of news; rather than independent reporting, we witness the 'integration of the media into the war machine' (Lewis et al., 2006: 20). Indeed, with respect to the Iraq War starting in 2003, we see governmental media and communications strategies carefully crafted by those skilled in presentation and perception management (Lewis et al., 2006: 23). The prevalence of elite-level views of the war (as opposed to the human costs) was reinforced not only through the careful management of communications of PR in government and the military but through the embedding of journalists 'in the battlefields'. For example, over 600 US journalists were embedded in US-dominated forces (Hoskins, 2004: 57). That is a lot of news coverage. But as Hoskins observes, this embedding seemed to shrink not only the physical distance of journalists from the war itself but also critical journalistic distance. Lewis et al.'s (2006) study suggests a greater complexity than may appear at first sight. While they detail how government news strategies were devised assuming military personnel directing access, some journalists themselves maintained their surprise at the degrees of access they were afforded, while others detailed their constant juggling act of trying to maintain journalistic distance while not upsetting the military (Lewis et al., 2006: 85–6). Professionals were also recruited to manage and advise on media strategies, and advertising and PR consultants were also brought in. Charlotte Beers, one of the most powerful figures in the advertising industry, was brought in to lead the work of the State Department. In 2001 in the US, the Pentagon's Office of Strategic Influence was formed (which latterly became the Office of Global Communication) with an explicit emphasis on 'information warfare', with government officials being dispatched to areas of 'media interest' to 'advise' journalists on government policy. This careful management and presentation of the news agenda meant, as a government official noted, 'The American people won because they got to see how well-trained, how well-equipped and how well-led their US military is ...' (cited in Hoskins, 2004: 61). In this sense, the embedding of journalists with the military meant that elite views were reinforced through their representation rather than, for example, the human costs of war for the civilians involved who lost their lives, homes, families and communities.

While the nature of journalism had changed, this was also situated in a context of changing technologies, and increasing availability of news about war. Proponents of technological change in the coverage of war might suggest that the rise of 24-hours news, the proliferation of advanced technology used for gathering news, the internet and the growth of transnational news organizations led to greater pluralization. From this perspective, this would suggest an increased 'fourth estate' role for the media, greater adversary, and increased opportunities to challenge elites and hold them to account. This also enables the public to have a deeper understanding of war. However, critics have argued that 24-hour news coverage has led to the emergence of 'war porn':

the relentless broadcast of images without context or analysis (Welch, 2005:iv). Jack Straw suggests that too much 'reality' can have a detrimental effect on public morale (cited in Welch, 2005: iv–x). Not only was public morale shored up by the imagery used but also in wider discourses and language; what and how we do talk about war matters because of the way we talk about it, and then which aspects we don't talk about. While journalists were embedded with military and across the board officials were seeking to manage news coverage favourably of the Iraq War, we were less likely to see discussion of those economic interests who benefited. Unusually, the *Guardian* did run a story which highlighted the role of private security firms in enabling political elites to achieve their objectives. These companies had become so integrated and essential for the war effort that they were described as 'the second biggest contributor to coalition forces in Iraq after the Pentagon' (Traynor, 2003). Yet there was very little discussion of the prominent role that private security companies were playing, or how economic interests were benefiting from the war effort. Indeed, a study from the PEW Centre for Journalism (2007) shows that in a four-year period (2003–2007) in analysis of over 100,000 stories, they found only 248 dealing in some way with the topic of Private Security Companies. As Baudrillard observes, 'Iraq [was] being rebuilt even before it [had] been destroyed' (1995: 52).

We are also encouraged not to reflect on the gendered relations that are being played out through coverage of warfare. Hegemonic masculinity is reinforced through newsrooms, and, as Ross argues, women are 'most noticeable in the news media by their conspicuous absence or at least spectacular marginalization' (2005: 287). In the coverage of war, this leads to the asking of questions about women's interests, for example where have the women's voices been in opposition to the reinstatement of the Taliban in Afghanistan (Ross, 2005: 268)? In war coverage, what we see is news constructed around a masculinized agenda; images of male soldiers dominate. When we do see women feature, this is either as victims, or if they are engaged in acts of warfare or retaliation, we see the expression of shock that women could engage in these kinds of activities. For example, the use of the term 'female' suicide bomber is used to denote aberration, where a woman deviants from her femininity, rather than in terms of her religion or beliefs as is used to describe male suicide bombers (Naylor, 2001; Carter and Weaver, 2003). Notably, such construction encourages us to view and to question aberrations of gender, rather than the horrors of war. Discourse and language are again a significant part of the news agenda in helping us 'make sense' of the war that is taking place, and signalling to us as audiences appropriate responses. Consider the phrase 'humanitarian warfare'; this was first used in the Kosovo conflict – used to imply that no one (from our side) gets hurt (see also Lule, 2004); collateral damage has been used as a synonym for civilian deaths, itself a term deemed too unpalatable for audiences who are required by political elites to maintain popular support. But the ways we talk about war, the language that is used to sanitize it, raises a broader political question: how far does this serve to legitimate war as an acceptable method of conducting politics? Moreover, let us not forget the economic beneficiaries and the significance and importance of the arms industries to gross domestic products; the United States, United Kingdom, France, Russia and China are the largest arms exporters in the world, responsible for nearly 80% of international arms trade (Stohl and Grillot, 2009: 3). And for the period 2001–2011, the average for world military expenditure was between $1.41 and $1.80 trillion (WMEAT, 2014: 3). Is it surprising then that such expenditure remains largely undiscussed in national media contexts (cf. Lewis, 2008)?

We might also note that war coverage tends to be about those conducting war rather than the recipients of war and its effects. When war is documented, one set of communications strategies is linked to masculine strength; military power equals political success. Yet what is less commonly and routinely reported in media coverage of war is the experiences of women, who at a domestic level in conflict zones are likely to suffer disproportionately to men. 'We have documented ... systematic sexual violence, committed by the Burmese military as a weapon of war in the ongoing conflict ... where women are raped ... in order to terrorize the women, and the local community, morally, psychologically, and also physically' (Nang Charm Tong, Burma, 2006, cited in Shephard, 2008). This is also a form of communicating politics; individual level violence against women is a widely acknowledged weapon of warfare, a means to systematically undermine troops' morale, destroy villages, homes, communities and ultimately opposition. Rape has become an orchestrated tool of contemporary combat as a means to destroy morale and to physically rebuild communities in the image of the regime (with women being raped with the aim of creating new generations of regime - sympathetic citizens). As Brownmiller observes, 'In one act of aggression, the collective spirit of women and of the nation is broken, leaving a reminder long after the troops depart. And if she survives the assault, what does the victim of wartime rape become to her people? Evidence of the enemy's bestiality. Symbol of her nation's defeat. A pariah. Damaged property. A pawn in the subtle wars of international propaganda' (ND; 2). According to Amnesty International, rape has been used as a weapon in recent and ongoing conflicts in places such as Colombia, Iraq, Sudan, Chechnya, Nepal and Afghanistan. Yet the coverage of this issue in mainstream media remains limited and marginal. We might ask what is being communicated here. Why are we more likely to see the 'victories' of decimated cities than the damage being done to women in conflict zones?

Popular culture and war

While less often discussed, popular culture plays a significant role in mediated constructions of war. Audiences are positioned as spectators, watching 'virtual war' coverage which resembles a TV programme/film or computer game rather than reality: in this way we gain only a superficial coverage and knowledge of war. As Taylor notes, the 'most effective propaganda is that which is conducted hand in hand with policy' (2002: 440); but it is not only that propaganda is grounded in existing policy but how mediation of that propaganda takes place that is of interest here. While the focus in the literature is largely upon news, that is not to deny the contribution and role of popular culture in shoring up support for and sanitizing war, and it plays a significant role in shaping the cultural context through which we are sensitized and desensitized to the atrocities of war.

War and Film. Goebbels, widely recognized as probably one of the most effective propagandists of the last century, made much of the use of film as a mechanism to shore up support among the German people for the Nazi agenda. For example, Leni Riefenstahl's *Triumph of The Will* became a powerful vehicle of Nazi propaganda, showing Nazi Germany as a super-organized, highly efficient state, at a time when the country was in severe economic crisis. The effectiveness of film as a mechanism for shoring up public support for war is not restricted to Nazi Germany, nor only a thing of historic eras. Hollywood has a history of selling movie tickets in record numbers during wartime, and lending 'star power' to recruitment drives (Carruthers, 2011: 3) to the extent that in World War II, Hollywood secured for itself a protected 'war industry status'. Not only did this mean a prodigious output of films during World War II but this consolidated a rotation of staff between the film industry and the military, whereby talented directors would help with instructional films and documentaries for the military. And as Carruthers observes, this was clearly an effective model; following the attacks on the Twin Towers on September 11, 2001, Hollywood executives were called to the White House to discuss how studios could contribute to the 'War on Terror' (2011: 3). There followed a raft of films, shoring up psychological support, from the perspective of those engaging in the 'just' war at policy level in Afghanistan or encouraging empathy through psychological depictions of individual soldiers in Iraq (e.g. *The Hurt Locker*), muscle-bound masculinity a popular trope in film making (Connell, 1993: 598). The 'War on Terror' has been a key theme in Hollywood movies, which have played their role in 'normalizing' the authority of the CIA, for example, and marginalizing the historical conditions which have given rise to conflicts the United States is engaged in (Boyd-Barrett, et al., 2012). The proliferation of CIA-based films has served to 'normalize' spying and covert operations, while working ideologically in favour of US foreign policy (Boyd-Barrett et al., 2012: 131). War films being an essential feature of winning the 'battle for hearts and minds' as propaganda films and escapist cinema provide a mechanism for maintaining morale of both citizens and the military (Fox, 2007).

War and Video Games. In the US, video games are estimated to bring in a similar revenue to box office receipts (Goldstein, 2001), and games such as *Theatre of War*, *Gears of War* and *Call of Duty* and many other similar titles can provide a training ground and, again, play a role in sanitizing warfare. As Grossman has observed, 'combat training' takes place where there is 'no real sanction for firing at the wrong targets' and good marksmanship is encouraged, where in some cases 'you actually hold a weapon in your hand and fire it at human shaped targets on the screen' (1995: 299–305). High levels of masculine aggression are encouraged (e.g. Kielser et al., 1985; Dietz, 1998), aggression necessary for the conduct and fulfilment of warfare. Eighty per cent of video games, in Dietz's (1998) research, were found to be specifically violent, with 21% of those played containing violence directed at women. Not only is killing and extreme violence 'normalized' in this way, but collaboration with the games industry by the military has proved a fertile training ground for new recruits. An email from Microsoft spokesman David Dennis stated that the army

> has multiple avenues to pursue building simulations. They can team up with a professional Xbox 360 publisher and development studio that have the expertise to assist them with development of a complex simulation. In fact, the Army has successfully done this in the past by working with publishers such as Ubisoft ('America's Army') and THQ ('Full Spectrum Warrior'). (cited in Peck, 2010)

There are benefits to the military for collaboration with the games industry. In 2010, 61% of US aircraft were unmanned (Brooks, 2012). With insufficient numbers of pilots to fly planes, unmanned drones have become a recent technological development, but part of their success hinges on how the operators no longer need to be qualified pilots. Rather, if regular soldiers 'can operate a video game as well as they can use a rifle – and that is now part of the entry test – they can fly a drone, and use that to kill people, too' (Brooks, 2012). Not only do video games 'normalize' the killing of others but they also provide a technological basis from which future recruits come ready trained, as we see that control technology in military contexts is becoming ever more similar to that used in video games. For example, a recent recruitment advert for the British army depicted a soldier using an (unbranded) Xbox controlled to fly a drone over a troop of soldiers (Brooks, 2012); and some have expressed shock that journalists embedded with the US military have compared their experience to a video game (Power, 2007: 71). Yet this is unsurprising as the United States has a history of collaborating with the games industry. In the 1980s, the Pentagon worked with Atari to develop *Battlezone*, an arcade game, as a flight simulator for pilots (power, 2007: 276). And as Miller observes, today there are numerous journals and institutes on games linked to the Pentagon whose role is to 'test and augment the recruiting and training potential of games to ideologize, hire and instruct the population' (2012: 107). According to the Pentagon *Full Spectrum Warrior* was the 'game that captured Saddam': those who found Saddam Hussein had been trained on this game (Miller, 2012: 109).

Music. In *Othello*, Shakespeare tells us of 'the spirit stirring drum, the ear piercing fife, The Royal banner, and all quality, Pride, pomp, and circumstance of glorious war!' and music has been an integral part of psychological warfare and as a means of communication. In World War II, Goebbels used Wagner operas as powerful metaphors and symbols of prestige for the Nazi regime (Trotter, 2005) while Edward Elgar's *Piano Quintet* was an allegory of the madness of war (Isserlis, 2013), and in more contemporary circumstances Green Day's 'American Idiot' articulated a powerful anti-war sentiment. The significance of music and its relationship with warfare is perhaps nowhere more clearly articulated than in the 2001 memo from Clear Channel, distributed in the United States to its 1,200 radio stations, with an extensive list of 'lyrically questionable songs' that stations 'may wish not to play' following the events of 9/11. This list included a range of songs, from Black Sabbath's 'War Pigs', to Petula Clark's 'A Sign of the Times' to John Lennon's 'Imagine', which were deemed liable to upset people at an emotionally volatile time. Music has not only been used to galvanize or manage populations, but it has also been used as an instrument of torture. In Guantanamo Bay, Metallica's 'Enter Sandman' was just one of many songs blasted at excessive volume as part of pscyh-ops operations, and was an effective instrument as 'One Guantánamo interrogator blithely estimated that it would take about four days to "break" someone, if the interrogation sessions were interspersed with strobe lights and loud music' (Stafford Smith, 2008). There is a long history of music's relationship with politics and the censoring of music for 'political' reasons (Street, 2012) and music, like other forms of popular culture, plays an important role in how political actors communicate with the citizens of states in times of war.

War as a media non-event?

Images of war have become part of our daily news. From the genocide in Rwanda, to Bosnia and Sarajevo (see discussion about the CNN effect in Chapter 5) we are now regularly seeing media coverage of wars which are 'ours' and are deemed 'just' and those which happen at a distance. For Hoskins, this suggests the legitimization of war as an acceptable means for nation states and governments to 'settle scores' (2004: 10). As Hoskins observes, the televising of the Iraq War was historically unique and this mediation 'fundamentally disconnected the machinery of warfare from the bloody consequences of its use' (Hoskins, 2004: 10). The televising of war, the visual impact of seeing 'first-hand' the effects of foreign policy, represents a fundamental shift in the nature of contemporary warfare.

In a compelling and challenging essay, Baudrillard argues that 'the Gulf War Did Not Take Place'. While this might seem a remarkable claim on the surface, given that many of us did see it being played out on TV screens, Baudrillard points us to the powerful role that media have played in fundamentally reshaping how we understand warfare; and through media 'the war ... watches itself in a mirror: am I pretty enough, am I spectacular enough, am I sophisticated enough to make an entry on to the historical stage?' (1991: 32). Not only this, but the nature of warfare has changed with available technologies, which means that militaries no longer need to meet their enemies: the enemy is 'annihilat[ed]... at a distance' (1991: 43); the vast use of airpower meant that the Iraqi army was not directly engaged with. We do not hear of Iraqi deaths and in these senses 'real war' did not take place. War becomes a technological relationship; the simulation of real communication (Merrin, 2005: 84). Media play a critical role, as a supporting cast for political elites, in creating for us an illusion of war, as we are distanced, rendered passive spectators. Media attempt to present conflict in 'real time' reinforcing the simulacra of the war, and serve to further distance us, as citizens and audiences, from the event itself. It is conducted as a 'clean' war where we do not see the victims. In these ways, for Baudrillard, the Gulf War was a non-war; won before it was begun; was not war by conventional means; and was mediated to the extent that we were not able to tell the difference between reality and its simulation, a media non-event. In this way, Baudrillard substantiates his claim that the Gulf War, war by conventional means, did not happen.

Clearly there is not the intent to deny the vast (and much less discussed in Western media) loss of Iraqi lives. However, Baudrillard questions the 'reality' of the war, and reminds us of how Hollywood scripts have preceded and become intertwined with 'the real'. The events of 9/11 – planes crashing into the Twin Towers – could have been a scene from a Hollywood movie and in this sense Hollywood has already preceded the 'real'. Carefully choreographed mediated responses mean that the media perform to a script already written, constructing the war in the way we have already seen it depicted in films and on TV, rather than showing us what is 'really' taking place. In this way, Baudrillard (1994) highlights how we don't see war, rather simulacra of war. Media products and imagery are constantly reproduced where they take on meaning because of earlier media products and imagery. It is not possible to distinguish between the 'real' and the representation of the 'real' and so we live in a world of hyper reality, where media representations create a world for us that feels more real than 'reality'.

Terrorism and media

Thus far, the focus has been on the way elites enact war, and how this is communicated to us. The Iraq War was justified through reference to terrorism. Actions of terrorists are a central feature of our daily news agendas. While war might be the ultimate form of communication for political elites and states as actors, terrorism is perhaps the ultimate form of political communication of citizens to elite actors. For Weaver-Hightower (2003), terrorists are those groups whom nation states define as dangerous; but their existence is only possible because of the meanings and values held by nation states, and terrorists are 'othered' by their contestation of these values. In this way, the construction of 'terrorists' becomes a useful shorthand to reinforce national identities. In this sense, when thinking about terrorism as a means of communicating politics globally, it is useful to reflect on the norms that underpin our definitions of terrorism in the first place. States and political elites define who 'counts' as terrorists. States themselves claim the legitimate use of violence in the act of war, underpinned by international law. However, as Chomsky argues, the terrorism of the weak against the powerful, cannot be addressed without dealing with 'the unmentionable but far more extreme terrorism of the powerful against the weak' (Chomsky, 2003: 7), and what seems to be largely absent in much media coverage of terrorist activities is a willingness to discuss the conditions that have led to these events in the first instance. The failure to contextualize the historical, colonial, economic and political decisions that have led to actions of terrorists is a continual feature of media coverage of terrorist activity.

At present the current legal definition of terrorism is incredibly broad and involves a 'heavy reliance [being]... placed on the wise exercise of discretions by Ministers, prosecutors and police' (Anderson, 2014). In scholarly literature, the contested nature of the term is widely noted and there is clearly difficulty in delineating the boundaries between terrorism and other forms of political violence (Crenshaw, 1995). An example of the difficulties in definition can be illustrated perhaps with reference to the case of David Miranda. He is a journalist who was thought to be carrying leaked documents from whistleblower Ed Snowden. Intelligence agencies sought his arrest on the grounds that 'Disclosure [of the Snowden files], or threat of disclosure, is designed to influence a government, and is made for the purpose of promoting a political or ideological cause. This therefore falls within the definition of terrorism and as such we request that the subject is examined under Schedule 7' (cited in Harris, 2014). In this instance, as Harris wryly observes (2014), the publication of *words* was deemed to constitute an act of terrorism.

As Chomsky notes, terrorism in the public mind is seen as something 'which targets civilian populations or democratic governments' (2008: 4) and yet as with other perceptions, this view is not created in a vacuum. Rather as Jackson argues 'through a carefully constructed discourse, officials have created a whole new social reality where terrorism threatens to destroy everything that people hold dear – their lives, their democracy, their freedom, their way of life, their civilization' (2005: 1–2), and this discourse is one which has served elites well as legislation is brought in to control and enact surveillance over populations (cf. Barnard-Wills, 2012). Moreover, the discourse of terrorism serves to legitimate government decisions to commit public resources to military spending (as above). This discourse of terrorism also normalizes and institutionalizes war as a mechanism of conducting politics. This necessitates, for elites, the 'construction of a whole new language, or ... public narrative, that manufactures approval while simultaneously suppressing individual doubts and wider political protest' (Jackson, 2005: 1). This discourse is mediated and government officials hold large sway over what is reported, as media defer to them to define, to describe, to shape and frame how terrorism is discussed. But it is not only the use of words but also imagery that matters. Following the aftermath of September 11, 2001, American news media framed coverage in a style akin to a Hollywood blockbuster with banners on news channels reading, for example, 'America Strikes Back' and 'America Under Attack (Jackson, 2005: 167). This conflation of news and popular culture is part of a wider process of normalizing our responses to actions of political elites. So effective has this discourse been that as Castells argues, 'the war on terror and its associated images and themes, (al-Qaeda, Afghanistan, the

Iraq War, radical Islamism, Muslims in general) constructed a network of associations in people's minds. They activated the deepest emotion in the human mind: the fear of death' (2009: 169). Media have been complicit in this activation, this discourse, with little questioning and indeed little acknowledgement that the vast majority of the world's Muslims have nothing to do with terrorism, and have suffered considerably as a consequence of the misery that the 'War on Terror' has wreaked upon the Islamic world (Freedman and Thussu, 2012: 3).

As such, to ask political questions about how terrorism is communicated to us is to ask how discourses of 'others' are used to normalize and naturalize opposition to 'an enemy' useful in the justification of elite political actions. We might ask how mediated political discourses frame the terror threat. Moreover, media discourses have served to repress the 'political' nature of contemporary political violence, denying political motives (Stohl, 2008), and a journalism which focuses on *'what* was done, not *why'* (Berkowitz, 2007: 178, cited in Lewis et al., 2012: 17). In this way we see the 'repression' of the political in discussions about contemporary terrorism (Lewis, et al., 2009). The failure of attempts to understand what is driving terrorism is combined with an increasing focus on British Muslims in the media (Whitaker, 2002). And as the work of Lewis et al. shows, since 9/11, this increased coverage falls around two broad tropes: the 'War on Terror'; and 'controversial' cultural and religious issues. This framing and conflation of Muslims with terrorism serves to play a central role in the way 'terror' has been used as a mechanism to normalize, culturalize and mobilize anti-Muslim sentiment in Britain (Khiabany and Williamson, 2012). They argue that although anti-Muslim racism predates 9/11 this cultural predisposition has become widely reanimated, where Islam is completely redefined in cultural terms, those cultural terms being 'us' versus 'them' where Muslims are othered and Islamic culture is set in opposition to Western culture (Khiabany and Williamson, 2012: 138). Crucially, what this positioning serves to do is not only to 'justify' wars abroad but also to terrorize sections of Western national populations by depicting them as belonging to a culture of violence. In the United Kingdom, the depiction is of a 'culture of violence' in opposition to 'British culture'. This discourse is shored up not only through media outlets but through the words and actions of politicians (Khiabany and Williamson, 2012: 141), where terror suspects in the British media are subject to high degrees of demonization and selective interpretations of the law (Banakar, 2010; Kundnani, 2009). This demonization has meant that the way in which the 'War on Terror' has been culturally conducted means that this has become a way of life, rather than about the preservation of a way of life (Khiabany and Williamson, 2012: 147).

In asking political questions about what is communicated to us in relation to terrorism, we need to ask what is normalized; what remains undiscussed and unexplored. Not only are we failing to ask historical and contextual questions about the reasons why terrorism is a common feature of contemporary society, but we are also failing to acknowledge, or ask questions about why women are taking part in such actions. Women's participation in terrorism, according to Sjoberg and Gentry (2011; 228), is increasing and becoming more visible in media coverage. Although they argue that media conform to a narrative which still presents women as having the capacity to become bombers only if they are dominated by men, rather than seeking to explore the political reasons for their actions (Sjoberg et al., 2011: 2–3) or indeed the personal reasons. As Bloom stresses 'what is incredibly compelling about delving in to how and why women become suicide bombers is that so many of these women have been raped or sexually abused in the previous conflict either by representatives of the state or by the insurgents themselves' (2005: 125). These levels of brutality as a driving mechanism are part of a discourse which does not take place in Western mainstream media. To ask political questions here is to ask, why do we not talk about this?

Summary

The aim of this chapter has been to think about just some of the ways Western states communicate politically and responses to that communication. In so doing we have explored how war is covered through media, and how war can become depoliticized in mediated discourse. A focus on the actions of political elites, justifying their aims, shoring up public support, means that the broader political questions about why war is necessary, or indeed the wider aims of a war, remain unanswered. To ask questions about how war is communicated to us necessitates our reflection on how war and its causes may be depoliticized through absence of discussion. How cultural support for war is shored up through political discourse, popular culture and the racializing of 'others' has also been a key area of reflection.

Baudrillard draws our attention to how mediated discourses no longer reflect reality, rather we are situated in a hyper reality, media interpretations of events precede our understanding of 'real' events to the extent we can no longer be sure what is really 'real'. And maybe nothing is more significant than his refection on the way contemporary warfare is conducted in a manner cognizant with media imagery, rather than conventional warfare.

Reflection/seminar activities

Find a media image depicting war, and one depicting terrorism. What are we invited to 'feel' and to witness? How might these images be considered political?

Why is public support for war important, and how is it achieved?

How many wars are taking place right now? How many are reported in media that you consume?

How are 'enemies' defined? And how are men and women described in this context?

How many successful prosecutions have there been against the use of rape as a weapon of warfare?

Looking at the news you have consumed today, how are Muslims referred to? Are they included or excluded? Part of a national community or 'othered'?

Chapter 8

How do Citizens Communicate Politically?

Introduction

Much of this book has been concerned with how media and politics communicate with each other and to audiences and citizens. News media, for example, are seen to provide a voice for the people (according to liberal theory). In newspapers and other media, citizens speak (cf. Lewis et al., 2005) and articulate political viewpoints. As has been discussed throughout, however, this voice is mediated, and so often when we see citizens communicating with elites, this tends to be on terms already defined by elites (such as in the framing of what 'counts' as news, and the decisions about who gets to speak). Much of the literature within political communication assumes that the communication process is 'top down' – from elites to masses. In this sense we might think that citizens have very little autonomy; it is not of their choosing how they get to communicate their political views, experiences and ideas. The aim of this chapter is to unpack how citizens are given, or may claim, a political voice, and how they choose to use it or not. In looking at how citizens can communicate through the actions that are deemed 'legitimate' in democratic theory, we begin by touching on issues of representation and participation. These forms of political communication often tend to deny the role of media in the process, so we then turn to look at new media technologies as a site where citizens have been more active than democratic theory may have provided for. Underlying this is a discussion about the loss of connection with political elites around identity; political identity construction and its communication used to be the preserve of partisan loyalties, communicated to elites in the form of votes. As partisan loyalties and links have declined, the chapter explores how citizens express their identities and how these are communicated to those with power. Finally we turn to think about resistance as a form of political communication.

Civic participation

When we think of how citizens communicate politically, we might initially think of how people vote. The vote has been a key mechanism through which citizens communicate with political elites and the history of political thought is replete with the tensions between the attempts of rulers to manage citizens and mechanisms through which people may hold those with power to account. One of the most fundamental ways people are able to express their preferences to political elites is through the casting of a ballot, and this has its roots in Ancient Greek conceptions of democracy.

Historically, the vote was given to all those who were deemed eligible to participate in public life – in Ancient Greece, this excluded women, slaves and immigrants (Aristotle, 2002), and so only approximately one-third of the population were counted as full citizens and eligible to vote. While gradually full male suffrage was achieved, it was not until much later that the same has been true for women. The battle for women's votes has been hard fought and was only fully realized in the United Kingdom in 1928, and despite the 1948 UN Declaration of Human Rights (article 21), which stated *The will of the people shall be the basis of the authority of government; this will shall be expressed in periodic and genuine elections which shall be by universal and equal suffrage and shall be held by secret vote or by equivalent free voting procedures*, many countries across the world took years to introduce full suffrage for women (for example, it wasn't until 1971 that Switzerland introduced full suffrage at federal level) and in 2011 it was announced that women in Saudi Arabia would be allowed to vote in the 2015 elections (Stewart, 2011). This reminds us perhaps that citizenship has been historically gendered, located in the masculine domain of the public sphere as opposed to the feminized realm of the private. In this way, we see gender defining the possibilities of political participation; reminding us of the gendered nature of democracy. Indeed, as Hutchinson argues, as long as there remain inequalities between men and women that prevent 'full and proportionately equal forms of participation' then 'new participatory democratic models will fail' (2002: 721).

Representation is embedded in Western democracies (Lijphart, 1984), and in theory is essential for putting into practice the notion of 'government by the people' (Beetham, 1992: 41), so to make sense of representation, and to think about how citizens make their voices heard, how citizens communicate politically, we need to understand what is meant by representation. Traditionally, representation has been restricted to how MPs speak for citizens and there is debate within the literature about the meaning of the term representation. For Edmund Burke, MPs were 'trustees' who were assumed to be reliable to act in the interest of the 'public' good rather than their own interests or the short-term interests of their constituents. However, more recent discussions about representation raise questions about the extent to which it is possible to represent a diversity of interests in the legislature. For example, we might ask if a legislature is dominated by white middle-class men, is it possible for them to represent the interests of those who do not fall into these categories? Indeed, there has been much work conducted about how increasing the descriptive numbers of women in legislatures, can lead to an increase in the substantive representation of women's interests in the policy process (e.g. McKay, 2007; Wängnerud, 2009). However, this may suggest that it is only possible for women to act in women's interests, and Childs and Krook (2009) offer a more complex analysis which suggests increasing the number of women in legislatures provides the opportunity for anyone to act in the substantive interests of women. And we could extend this assumption to other structurally disadvantaged groups; the greater their numbers in office, the greater the opportunity to open discussion space, so that action is possible in the interests of marginalized groups, by any strategic political actor.

Representation and participation are central in political theory to the lifeblood of vibrant democracy, yet successive scholars have charted the demise of citizens' willingness to engage in contemporary political processes, and titles such as *Why Americans Mistrust Government* (Nye et al., 1997), *Democracy at Risk* (Macedo et al., 2005) and *Why We Hate Politics* (Hay, 2007) seek to make sense of the causes of this decline. These studies are largely linked to the decline in citizens, voting behaviour which rests on the assumption that voting is the ultimate form of political action and communication with elites. In *Bowling Alone*, Putnam (2000) argues that the media are to blame for wider civic disengagement and political disillusionment – people would rather watch TV than collectively engage in the political process. Dalton (2006) challenges some of this literature and he argues that although there have been declines in voting behaviour in the 1980s and 1990s, this trend has reversed slightly in the 2000s. Much of this, however, assumes that voting is the ultimate form of political participation, and ultimately how the public communicate their political wishes to elite actors. Dalton argues that far from becoming disengaged with the political process, citizens are simply changing the way that they participate and communicate politically, as he finds that people are much more likely to take part in campaigning, get involved with civic groups, protest and sign petitions than in previous decades (2006: 9). Democratic theory draws our attention to the numerous ways in which, in theory, citizens can communicate with elites, beyond the vote, and these include individual methods, such as letter writing, to collective means such as organized rallies, marches, speeches and pressure groups.

Pressure groups may be legitimated in the political system and again provide a mechanism whereby organized interests can communicate with elite actors about their political preferences. In a pluralist system of government, a pressure group is viewed as an important feature of a democracy; these groups do not seek power or office, but rather do seek to influence those who have the authority and resources to make political decisions (Richardson, 1993). High-profile organizations such as Amnesty International can have profound influence on decision makers and coordinate and communicate effectively citizen's voices and discontent around the issue of human rights (see Hopgood, 2013). However, this is not to suggest that the organization of a pressure group will guarantee that citizens' voices are heard within government. Maloney et al. (1994) distinguish between groups which have privileged access to government and 'insider' status in terms of having a seat at the decision-making table, and outsider groups who have little access to power but lobby from outside the decision-making process. While we tend to think of pressure groups as having open public membership and connect their status to the size of the membership, we might also think of other forms of interest group representation.

The arms industry provides us with one example of a pressure group who have successfully been integrated into decision-making circles (Hartley, 2007). The term military-industrial-political complex highlights how some particular interests have been successfully organized into government, without citizen membership or indeed opportunities for citizens to express or communicate their views on non-representative organizations to be so closely connected with the 'corridors of power' yet we see limited discussion as to the extent of this influence in the pages of our media (cf. Lewis, 2001). The Israel lobby also forms a powerful group whose influence is not made up by citizen membership and indeed whose voice remains largely unchallenged in the mainstream media. Indeed, scholars Mearsheimer and Walt wrote an article in 2006 detailing the existence of a well-organized, well-funded, political lobby group in support of Israel. This article was deemed too controversial to be published in *The Atlantic,* but was latterly published in the *London Review of Books.* So while in democratic theory interest groups provide a forum for citizens to communicate politically with elites, we also find that economic interests can occupy a privileged position in the policy process (Lindblom, 1977). How media choose to frame and discuss this privileged position (or not) is also of concern here but in this sense, the way that media do frame protest and citizen engagement is perhaps worthy of particular note, as media coverage often serves to remind us what are and are not seen as legitimate areas of political engagement. Thus far we have discussed how citizens communicate politically with governments as something which is structured in a top-down way, that is, it is elite definitions of political systems which determine how and where communication with political elites takes place. However, there are other ways in which citizens may communicate and we briefly explore two of them.

Civil disobedience

Hoffman and Graham argue that civil disobedience is the objection to, and the non-violent breaking of, the law on moral grounds. Here civilians, citizens, minorities or the masses have legitimate ways to communicate political grievances to elite actors. In 1981, women set off to stage a peaceful protest on Greenham Common – the site where cruise missiles were due to be situated. There followed numerous arrests, but these women sent a powerful political message about their objection to the work that was being carried out by contractors on behalf of the UK government. This peaceful protest has been conceived of as civil disobedience (Hoffman and Graham, 2006) yet we could argue this was also a powerful form of political communication. Here members of the public were communicating their wishes and preferences to political elites, but this was mediated through the ways the media chose to frame what took place. The challenge was in the representation of 'ordinary' women, those not normally involved in mediated public action – this was about women leaving the 'private' sphere and engaging in the public sphere, femininity challenging the masculinity of the space where nuclear weapons were located. Disrupting the boundaries between 'ordinary life' and the world in which nuclear weapons exist (Wilson, 1992), private life disrupted public (masculine) space. Interestingly, however, local media reactions depicted the women to be cruel to children, sexually deviant, smelly and filthy (Cresswell, 1996; Young, 1990), and media were a significant site of conflict (Young, 1990) and as Couldry observes, 'the vilification in much of the mainstream media of the women who opposed the British state at Greenham has political implications in itself' (Couldry, 1999: 339). While the Greenham women organized their own informal media campaigns, it was notable that latterly, their voices were marginalized in the mainstream media, and rendered silent (Couldry, 1999). In this way, we witness mainstream media play a significant legitimizing voice in what counts as political voice, political activism. The Greenham Common women were first rendered deviant, then marginalized and their political voice silenced in mainstream media discourses.

When we think about how media frame what counts as legitimate political communication from citizens, we might also turn our attention to the work of the Glasgow University Media Group (1980). Their study highlighted how voices of union members have been historically marginalized and delegitimized through their representation as unruly, in contrast to articulate well-groomed managers. In this way we might also argue that media play a key role not only in facilitating communication from elites to the masses but also in framing ways in which it is possible for masses to communicate to elites. This attributes enormous power to media, in determining not only which public voices we hear but how they are represented.

Protest

Protest is a widespread form of political communication, with citizens dissatisfied with elite actors and unable to get their voices heard, or interests represented in other fora in the democratic system. While protests may often take the form of street demonstrations and marches, more recently, from Tahrir Square to Wall Street, protest camps have become a powerful mechanism for public expression of discontent, dissatisfaction with political (and other) elites. We have witnessed the emergence of 'new social movements' (Tarrow, 1998; Melucci, 1996) which have gone beyond the traditional realms of formal politics, as citizens express collective identities and call for broader social change (Diani, 1992) and there have been a variety of such movements with concerns as diverse as environmentalism, ecology, migration and economic inequality. In these spaces protest camps have emerged as a mechanism for citizens to imagine alternative worlds and 'articulate contentious politics' (Feigenbaum et al., 2013). Not only are these contentious politics discussed and articulated but historical learning from earlier protests camps, coupled with the emergence of new media technologies, have meant that protesters have found mechanisms by which to express their politics, without reliance on traditional media forms and the framing that sought to 'other' and present as deviant earlier protesters (such as the Greenham women as noted above). In their analysis of protests camps, Feigenbaum et al. (2013) explore how contemporary protestors seek to articulate their views both by 'adapting' to mainstream media demands and using 'alternative' media sources. They note the complexity and nuances of having mainstream media located within or near the camps, which 'inevitably changes a camp's dynamic' whereby activists 'tend to possess a reflexive awareness of the presence and logic of media and often attempt to adapt...accordingly' (Feigenbaum et al., 2013: 75). On the one hand, protestors recognize the need for mainstream media coverage and management; on the other, however, there was clearly tension in the camps about how journalists fulfilled their roles. And this is the paradox, that to articulate a political voice, protestors were reliant on a set of dominant practices and norms that could be antithetical to their agendas. But what was also interesting was how alternative media have come to play a more significant role in the communication and articulation of politics in protest camps (de Jong et al., 2005; van de Donk et al., 2004). One such example is that of Indymedia, which provided a platform for independent publication of digital images and texts, driven by an ethos that 'empowered activists not just to watch media but to *"be the media"'* (Feigenbaum et al., 2013: 91, original italics).

Citizens and social media

While political elites may seek to define the parameters of how citizens can communicate with them, media technologies have also played a significant role in shaping the context within which that communication takes place. More broadly it has been suggested that we have moved into a 'post-industrial' (Bell, 1973), 'information' or communications age, which is not only about developments in technology, but crucially is linked to the notion that these media technologies impact on the way our identities are formed, and how we organize socially, politically and economically. This technological space, it has been assumed, has opened up opportunities for two-way communication between elites and citizens, and to provide for possibilities for greater citizen self-actualization and intellectual pluralism (Neuman, 1991). More recently, new social media have been heralded as a mechanism whereby citizens can express their views and can communicate with each other in unprecedented ways. While there is long-running debate as to the emancipatory potential of new media, it could be argued that this opens up a space for global citizen dialogue in an unprecedented manner. The advent of the internet has facilitated opportunities for 'citizen journalism' (Allan and Thorsen, 2009) where 'ordinary' people caught up in 'extraordinary events or crises' can speak without censorship. As Allan and Thorsen's (2009) work shows, there is a variety of ways in which citizens are now using available technologies to not only bear witness to catastrophic events but to fight for justice, human rights and dignity in a variety of regions, including Palestine, Iran, India and China (to name but a few). We could suggest that the rise of this media technology facilitates unparalleled opportunities for 'ordinary people', for citizens, to communicate politically, both with elites, and with each other. New social media have also been lauded as playing a critical role in the Arab uprisings and as Howard et al. (2011) argue social media had the 'power to put a human face on political oppression. Bouazizi's self-immolation was one of several stories told and retold on Facebook, Twitter, and YouTube in ways that inspired dissidents to organize protests, criticize their governments, and spread ideas about democracy.' New social media was seen to play a critical role, especially in light of the absence of an open media and civil society (Khondker, 2011).

For proponents of new media technologies, the internet provided the opportunity to 'reinvigorate' democracy in the creation of 'virtual' public sphere(s) (Loader, 1997; Blumler and Gurevitch, 2001). This was because this space was assumed to provide a mechanism whereby open and free discussion could take place between elites and citizens (avoiding the mediation of mainstream media), and could provide the opportunity therefore to provide for a stronger participatory democracy (Hague and Loader, 1999). However, as usage of the internet progressed, it became clear that this was something of a utopian vision (Loader and Mercea, 2011) and that actually the (content on the) internet was shaped by existing entrenched social and economic interests (Hill and Hughes, 1998). Moreover, as feminist scholars have argued, this kind of 'public sphere' tends to privilege 'rational' communication; one which tends to favour white, wealthy males excluding other identities and interests (Pateman, 1989; Fraser, 1990; van Zoonen, 2005). So we see new technologies lauded as emancipatory for citizens, affording them new opportunities to communicate, to express their political identities. On one level, though, this might seem a bit technologically deterministic. It is not the technology itself that generates new debates, rather the people that use the technology. It would seem reasonably unsurprising that new technology, situated in existing social and political power structures, would reinforce rather than challenge those power structures, because the people who use this technology are also situated in those structures of power.

New social media (Twitter, Facebook and the blogosphere) have been met with similar optimism as the internet before them. This enthusiasm is located within assumptions that a different kind of democracy is available through these fora. This technology is assumed to connect to the 'private sphere' where the expression of identity or identities, social and/or political is possible. This technology provides a 'networked citizen centered perspective' (Papacharissi, 2010). This reverses some of the 'top-down' approaches made in respect of the internet, and our attention is drawn to how 'the citizen user [is] the driver of democratic innovation' (Loader and Mercea, 2011).

The expression and construction of political identity will be returned to below, but the ways social media have afforded the opportunity for activists and others seeking to communicate and articulate politics is an important aspect of this new technology. Not only is this about protest camps managing media strategies, but campaigns can be launched and effected without people needing to meet in public spaces. For example, in 2013 when the Bank of England announced that Winston Churchill would be on the new £5 note, Caroline Criado-Perez launched a campaign protesting that this would mean that there were no women featured on banknotes (apart from the Queen, who was there for the honour of not being born with any brothers [Elmhirst, 2015]). This was a campaign conducted largely via Twitter, and through social media, traction from citizens was gained, the political message was sent that this was not something the British public wished to see. And so in July of that year, the Bank of England announced Jane Austen would appear on the £10 note. This conforms to the optimism of Papacharissi's work (2013), in that indeed citizens networked to send a political message. Despite the emphasis on voting in democratic theory as a means of political expression, engagement and ultimately communication, there are those scholars who reject the masculinized construction of political activity, and reject the formal mechanisms of representational politics in favour of more participatory forms of engagement (Squires, 1999: 194); there are alternative ways in which politics can be communicated by citizens. For example, women have collectively mobilized to protest and speak out about and campaign for peace, against war, sexism and religious fundamentalism (to name but a few). Recognizing how formal politics may be gendered 'allows women to redefine politics and political participation' (Barriteau, 1995: 149), and new social media are just one example of an alternative platform for women to meet and mobilize politically.

However, there is another side, and one that is well documented on social media and the internet, where misogyny is a common theme (Filipovic, 2007). Criado-Perez was subjected to rape threats and other forms of violence. She was not alone in this experience; many female activists, journalists and public writers have been subject to similar levels of misogyny in this private/public sphere (Lewis, 2011; Friedersdorf, 2014). This kind of abuse to silence women from speaking out in public spaces is not new – as Laurie Penny reminds us, Mary Wollstonecraft was called a 'hyena in petticoats' (cited in Thorpe and Rogers, 2011). But what this does draw our attention to is how the opportunities for citizens to communicate are highly gendered. While the opportunities for citizens to create and innovate a networked form of democracy exists, how power relations remain ultimately gendered, where women's capacity to speak may become defined through existing assumptions about an Aristotelian conception of citizenship. The picture, of course, is more nuanced, and rather than be silenced, (some) women have chosen to speak out and speak back (e.g. Thorpe and Rogers, 2011). As Neuman observes, 'although new media make possible new forms of political and cultural communication, in the main they are not likely to be used in that way' (1991: 42).

Political identity

Identity is part of almost 'every contact between a government and its citizens' according to Harper (2006: 11), not only this but identity 'is so embedded in our daily interactions that people rarely give it much thought, but it is an essential social and economic process... [and] is part of nearly every meaningful encounter between people' (ibid). In this sense, identity is an essential part of what it means to be a citizen, as each time citizens communicate one of the features they are expressing is underlying political identity. Identities matter politically as they provide the backdrop through which we respond to our political elites and systems, as well as the extent to which we may play a role in shaping those political and social contexts. Moreover, identity is seen as important for an individual in providing a sense of well-being (Lewin, 1948). Collective identities have been referred to as explanatory factors for why people mobilize in political action (Polletta and Jasper, 2001). While collective identity may not be the property of individuals in groups but also states in the international arena (Wendt, 1994), the focus here is on how the identities of citizens within states is shaped and communicated. Identity politics revolves around group recognition rather than a universal understanding of humanity. Identity politics in its more narrow sense has been argued to highlight the benefits of diversity and the ethical value of pluralism (Jenkins, 2004: 14).

Our identities may be expressed in a variety of ways. Political identity, in its more formal sense, used to be closely associated with how we voted, and these loyalties were assumed to be fairly fixed. Initially, for example, in the United Kingdom, political identity was located in class: working class voted Labour and the middle classes voted Conservative. But increasingly partisan loyalties became eroded (Butler and Stokes, 1974) (for a variety of reasons, including the structural ways in which the Conservatives sought to attract the 'aspirational middle classes from the working class' [Dunleavy, 1991]). In this way, the political playing field changed, as Stuart Hall (1983) argued, the Conservatives and the New Right were not only able to shift the goalposts but the whole football pitch. As our political attachments loosened, so political identities became expressed in other ways. For example, consumption has become a significant means of articulating identity, giving voice and expression to beliefs through our purchasing habits. Increasing numbers of people engage in ethical consumerism: choosing to shop ethically where products are not sourced from sweatshops, or buying fair trade products or by boycotting Starbucks. For example, as an academic, I have the luxury of choice in the products I consume, which was not available to me in my earlier working life; and this is true for the thousands of people across the United Kingdom who have to use one of the 445 foodbanks in this country (with the numbers of users increasing at a rate of 19% a year [Butler, 2015]). In this sense, then, we could say our personal economic environment structures how we can express and communicate our political identities through consumption. Our choices of communicating politically may be determined by our structural circumstances. But this is not to deny the agency of individuals and their autonomy in creating and communicating their identities politically. But the key point here is that political identities are not something which we were born with, nor are they intrinsically fixed. Rather they are products of how we choose to engage with the social, political and economic environment around us, and how that environment structures the political choices that it is possible for us to make.

Identity matters as it becomes linked to the rights that we are afforded by the state. For example, there is a range of work that discusses the significance of ethnic identities, used as a conceptual category for a range of work around violence, democratic instability, individual well-being and economic growth, all argue that ethnicity matters (Chandra, 2006); crucially though, ethnic identity has also been used as a mechanism for groups to articulate and express rights. Kymlicka argues that democratic governments should afford ethnic minorities collective cultural autonomy; cultural recognition is an important right and ethnic minorities share distinctive cultures, therefore democratic governments should afford minority groups cultural rights (1995).

Our identities are also politically important as they have been historically used, biologically, as a way of positioning people in social and political systems. If we think about race and sex as categories through which our identities are constructed for us, we are born into systems which segregate the world based on the colour of our skin, or the gender that we express. For Stuart Hall, it is in 'the attempt to rearticulate the relationship between subjects and discursive practices that the question of identity recurs' and this subjectification entails a politics of exclusion (Hall, 1996/2000: 16). In this sense, politics is taking place in the ways we are able to articulate our identities – in response to existing structures of social practice. But for Hall, identities are not fixed, and do not have 'natural' properties, rather they are strategic and positional, located in historic and discursive sites. Laclau argues that the construction of identity entails an act of power in that 'an identity's construction is always based on excluding something and establishing a violent hierarchy between the two resultant poles – man/woman etc ... It is the same with the black/white relationship in which white, of course, is equivalent to "human being". Woman and black are thus "marks" (i.e. marked terms) in contrast to the unmarked terms "man" and "white"...' (1990: 33). In this way, we can see how identities are unified in oppositional terms, premised on the existence of an 'other' and a unity afforded to a group through differentiation from the 'other'. This also suggests a hierarchy of identities, whereby through the social demarcation of identities based on assumed biological attributes and expressed through language some identities become the 'norm' through which the 'other' is structurally positioned.

Foucault (1984) directs our attention to how identity is historically constituted and constructed through the body. Although as Hall observes 'the body has served *to function as the signifier of the condensation of subjectivities in the individual*' (Hall, 2000: 25, original italics). The body becomes a site through which identities are played out and, as Butler (1993) notes, the body is a site where politics is conducted. For Butler, our gender is constructed through the way it is 'performed' and that performativity takes place on and through the body. From the declaration at birth – 'it's a girl'; 'it's a boy' – gender is written onto our bodies. And the subsequent relations that take place serve to reinforce that performativity – such as dressing boys in blue, girls in pink, giving girls 'feminized' toys that relate to the private sphere (such as cookers and 'baby' dolls) and boys 'masculinized' toys (such as guns and cars) that relate to the public sphere, our genders are constructed and constituted through our experiences of them. Performativity is not a single act, rather it is a set of norms, and the reiteration of those norms (1993: 12–3). Moreover, this is not only about gender roles, but about the encoding of sexual norms which ensure the normalization of a hegemonic heterosexuality. It is at this site of performativity of gender and sexuality that politics takes place as power becomes imprinted upon the body. For Butler, then, asking political questions about the nature of our identities means that we '... think about how and to what end bodies are constructed as is it will be to think about how and to what end bodies are *not* constructed and, further, to ask after how bodies which fail to materialize provide the necessary "outside," if not the necessary support, for the bodies which, in materializing the norm, qualify as bodies that matter' (1993: 16). In the establishment that some bodies matter (and to that end, that some don't or are of lesser significance), we see the construction of identities which reinforce existing power relations.

So if we think about the expression of identity as a form of communicating politically, it might be useful to think about how these identities are constructed. Ontologically, the argument here is anti-essentialist: we are not born with political identities, rather they are the outcome of a densely structured and complex social, political and economic world (or set of structures) that we are born into. Language differs according to the country that we are born into, it is not something inherently natural at birth, and just as our language is socially constructed (cf. Wittgenstein, 2001/1953) so our political identities are the product of a series of experiences as we grow and learn. In the post-industrial era, there has been much discussion of the fragmentation of identities; this has meant that the stability that was linked to 'knowing one's place' in the production process has been replaced by disunity and instability, and the dismantling of previously stable identities (cf. Bauman, 1992). Following Bauman it might be that citizens themselves have been able to articulate identities, but the emphasis here is that these identities do not emerge from a vacuum and we witness tensions between challenging dominant identities which are imposed and attempts to forge identities which don't fit neatly into existing categorizations. And these identities don't always flow from the economic contexts that they are situated within. For example, the development of Queer theory points us towards how queer identities may develop in opposition to existing power structures, such as those of the family, heterosexuality and reproduction, and in this way 'queerness' opens up the possibilities of new narratives and opportunities for alternative kinds of relations (Halberstam, 2005: 1–2). To make sense of how identity is constructed and articulated enables us to reflect on how we express and communicate our politics. Collectively, and individually, the expressions of identity can provide a basis for resistance to dominant power structures.

Resistance as a form of political communication

Resistance to governments and states is a powerful way in which citizens can choose to communicate politically. Resistance, in short, means opposition or a refusal to accept something. Resistance in the political sense takes a variety of forms and spatially can take place globally, nationally or within local communities. It can also take the form of collective action, or can be individualized and personalized. Globally and nationally, in 1994 the uprising of the Zapatista National Liberation Army (EZLN) against the Mexican state was considered to be a 'game changer'; challenging long-held beliefs about the role of the state, identity and race relations and setting the ground work for a form of political activism that other movements would follow (Dellacioppa, 2012: 2). Using discourses of 'mutuality' they set the scene for the emergence of powerful anti-globalization movements (Dellacioppa, 2012: 2). One of those movements, 'the Battle of Seattle', has been cited as being at the root of new forms of global resistance (Della Porta and Diani, 2006), and this kind of resistance was marked not only by new tactics but a new form of resistance. Rather than overt resistance to states or governments, this was about the resistance to ideas and economic means of organizing (neoliberalism and globalization) and was directed at key economic actors (the World Trade Organization and IMF), rather than political elites. This kind of resistance 'from below' can take multiple forms and does not only rely on the capacity to organize globally, or indeed nationally. For Barriteau, women's resistance sends a highly political message for when 'women refuse to participate in politics which exclude their interests...women are...acting politically; they are rejecting politics that excludes their concerns' (Barriteau, 1995: 149). An example of women resisting and rejecting conventional forms of political organization, and articulating alternative politics can be found in the work of Isoke (2013). She provides a thoughtful and detailed account of the spatial components of political resistance, through analysis of Black women in Newark. She notes how transformative projects among these communities, such as sister-circles, rites of passage programmes and clothing exchanges, provide alternative liminal spaces where struggle is expressed, and leadership and political efficacy achieved. This offered opportunities for differing kinds of political engagement and participation; it is participation on their terms rather than those that have been structurally defined for these women. This site of enacting politics that is alternative to that enacted through the formal institutions of the state, also lays the basis for the possibilities of wider structural transformation.

For Rollock, the liminal space where racialized 'others' exist, provides a site of alterity: 'a position at the edges of society from which their identities and experiences are constructed' (Rollock, 2012: 65). But rather than this positioning being one where individuals and groups are disadvantaged, she argues this space is where identities are expressed and constructed, where a 'perspective advantage' is afforded these groups, enabling them to view the world more widely than a white majority may. This also affords the opportunity to advance a 'counter hegemonic discourse' (hooks, 1990: 149). We might then find a space where non-participation in formal existing structures of gendered and racialized politics becomes meaningful as politics is expressed in other sites. To do this politically means to 'name, reflect on and dismantle discourses of Whiteness' (Leonardo, 2002: 31). Deconstructing existing dominant discourses, naming them and challenging them afford the space for critical transformation as a form of resistance.

While the above centres on collective forms of resistance, we might also think about how individuals are able to resist. One of the difficulties in thinking that our political 'selves' are constructed through interaction with external discourses and socially constructed practices, played out through and on the body (cf. Butler, 1993), means that this raises the question: how is it ever possible to escape this, to enact resistance? In Foucault's and Butler's work (as above) the body forms a site where politics takes place; where discursive practices intersect around, for example, race, gender and sexuality. In their work on adolescent girls, Gilligan et al. (2013: 2) explore how young girls articulate forms of political resistance, which they see as a healthy response, as a mark of courage and, moreover, see the 'willingness to act on one's own knowledge when such action creates trouble' as indicative of the capacity to distinguish between authentic and inauthentic relationships. More broadly, resistance becomes an important psychological barrier in the development of identity and autonomy. There has been a barrage of literature that explores how media representations of young women create problems for the young women, and men, that they are aimed at. A capacity to critically evaluate the messages that are disseminated becomes a significant form of individual (and group) resistance to the wider politics that are at play in these messages. A recent All Party Parliamentary Group report, in the United Kingdom, highlighted some of the problems with media messages, from advertising to fashion, that focus on the way that women 'should' look to the extent that one in four seven-year-old girls have tried to lose weight. Resistance to these kinds of messages, it would seem, is necessary from an early age, reminding us political resistance is not something that is available to us once we reach the age of legal citizenship. According to Allen (2010), one of the ways collective action as resistance (or protests, as above) opens up a space where our identities can be deconstructed, negotiated and reconstructed is when this functions as a mechanism to make sense of the subordinating power relationships that may characterize our experience, and opens up a space where critical resistance and transformation is possible.

In thinking about the opening of alternative spaces through which citizens can communicate, it might also be worth reflecting on how citizens choose not to communicate. Baudrillard views passivity as a form of resistance, a form of political communication. While elites are creating meaning and social order, passivity by the masses becomes a form of resistance as through passivity the masses can neutralize or distort the meaning that permeates society. For Baudrillard, the masses do not have their own set of goals, rather they reconstruct phenomena which change the meaning, or strip meaning from that which elites intended. In this way, resistance and passivity become powerful forms of political communication; meaning is not absorbed as elites dictate, rather this is subverted by the masses. For Baudrillard, defeat of the system is possible through refusal to engage with it. If the masses refuse to desire anything, they do not seek knowledge or power, then they are able to defeat the system through a massive withdrawal of the will (Robinson, 2012). Rather than constructing non-participation in such terms, this suggests that refusal to take part in a system which does not recognize sufficiently the interests of diverse groups (and this could be extended across race and class) is in actuality a highly political statement.

Summary

Political communication has a tendency to focus on the actions of elite actors; primarily those involved with the mechanisms of the state, rather than the opportunities that citizens have to communicate politically, to each other and to those with whom they are in political relationships.

This chapter began with a reflection on the more formal mechanisms, as defined through democratic theory, to look at how citizens may communicate with elites, through formal process of participation and representation. But these processes are situated within structures which appear to be fixed. Citizens have looked for alternate mechanisms to express their politics, such as protest, when their voice or political viewpoints have not been heard, or sufficiently articulated. It is perhaps worth noting that in order to express their politics, citizens in protest camps, for example, still have to negotiate a mediated environment, which may impact the messages that they are able to disseminate, and the politics that they are able to articulate.

New media technologies have provided a 'virtual' space where the opportunity to behave politically and engage in like-minded communities is possible, irrespective of geographical distance. This does raise four key questions. Irrespective of the strength of political views that emerge through social media, how likely is it that those voices will be heard? It has been suggested elsewhere that the uprisings in the Middle East were facilitated by Facebook, and while revolution may well be the ultimate form of citizens communicating politically this does raise the question: does alternate politics ultimately require revolution? Moreover, the extent to which misogyny continues and indeed is flourishing in these virtual spaces, invites us to ask how can we really harness technology to challenge existing power structures? Do those power structures need to be weaker before collective voices can be effective?

But collective voices are an expression of identity, and the shaping and expression of identity is one which can be beneficial for both citizens and states. Harnessing collective identities can enable governments to control populations; yet the ways individuals may refuse to be defined by identities imposed upon them may also provide for a site in which individuals and groups may affect political communication. Deconstructing how our identities are constructed, and reconstructing them to articulate alternative means of communicating, can thus be a highly political act.

Reflection/seminar activities

Is political resistance possible? Desirable? Achievable?

How do you participate politically? How have you defined this? Could you do more/less?

Take a photo that symbolizes your political identity and write about what led you to take this picture. How does it define you politically? How does it link to the nation/state that you live in?

What contemporary examples of civil disobedience/political resistance or protest can you find? Are these effective forms of communication?

Conclusion: Politics and Power

One of the aims of this book has been to restate the centrality of politics within the field of political communication. In so doing, critical questions have been asked about the nature of politics and the way this is communicated. To ask questions about politics is to ask questions about the nature of power, the way it is distributed, operationalized, and how we as audiences, citizens, elite actors are implicated in and constructed by social and political relationships of subordination and domination. These questions have been raised, not as a mechanism to generate answers but as a means to problematize and critically interrogate the world around us. The list of topics covered in these pages is clearly not exhaustive but has provided a starting point for how we might think about what is taking place around us, and the nature of the politics that are being communicated to us. Asking questions about power is to ask fundamental questions about politics. But what is power? Is it something we can see? Is it a process or a thing? Who holds power? How does power work? In whose interests? The ways power has been referred to in these pages points us to a variety of ways in which power may be conceptualized. It is clear that power is not something that is fixed, rather it may be fluid, interactive and iterative. Power, in political science, media and cultural studies, sociology and other disciplines, is a contested concept and so the aim of this final chapter is to provide an overview of the different ways that we might think about how power operates and is distributed. We begin with an overview of Lukes' three faces of power, followed by a discussion of how poststructuralist theorists have drawn our attention to how power is socially and historically (and ultimately politically) constituted. Understanding power as a site of social and political relations also enables us to think about how we may articulate and communicate alternative forms of politics.

The three faces of power

Stephen Lukes' (1974) work on power provides the cornerstone of debates surrounding power. Lukes drew on two earlier pieces of academic research to make his argument that there were three faces of, or dimensions to, power. The first face relied on the work of Dahl (1961), who, in his study of decision making in New Haven, observed government officials making decisions as to who got what in public meetings.

It was in the capacity to achieve outcomes that Dahl argued that power lay, and in this way power became the property of agents who were making decisions: political actors in the policy-making process. So when we think about discussions in this book, from this perspective power can be seen to lie with politicians and, as in Chapter 4, those who exercise the capacity to control the political and media agenda. Dahl's work is often referred to as pluralist; power is assumed to be observable, dispersed evenly and differing groups benefit from its exercise at different points in the policy process.

In contrast to this, Bachrach and Baratz (1962) argued that actually power was the capacity to prevent decisions being made in the first place, power was the capacity to effect non-decision making. So, for the processes of political communication, in this sense we might think that power lies with media, in the decisions that are made what to communicate and what not to communicate. The silences and absences of media coverage about the nature of politics has been a key theme of this book, and so we might suggest that we can make sense of media activity through this 'second face' of power. The capacity to 'set the agenda' of what we do and don't publicly discuss is clearly an important facet of political communication. However, both the work of Dahl and Bachrach and Baratz assume the capacity for agency. That is, both assumed that agents were autonomous and free from any environmental constraints. Agents expressed their interests and were able to act on them, or able to prevent key issues from having decisions made about them. Ontologically, both sets of authors also made an assumption that power was observable.

Through critique, Lukes argued that rather than being located with decision makers, or non-decision makers, power is actually located structurally in the prevention of the emergence of 'real' interests. Ontologically, we cannot observe power; rather we can see only its effects. These effects were the obscuring of individuals' 'real interests'. This in turn meant that individuals (and groups) would act to advance the interests of the systems they were structured within, rather than have the capacity to act autonomously. This has been viewed as akin to Marx's notion of 'false consciousness' (notwithstanding the critique as to how it might be possible for Lukes and Marx to stand outside this false consciousness that afflicts the rest of us). Nonetheless, that structures militate, consciously or unconsciously, to ensure we act in their interests has been referred to throughout this book when references have been made to organizing narratives such as capitalism and patriarchy. We cannot see either of these structures but they have real effects, as has been documented by Wilkinson and Pickett's (2010) exposé of contemporary structures of social and economic inequalities and Banyard's (2010) work, for example, on gender inequalities.

The simplifying framework that Lukes provides us with is helpful in enabling us to ask questions about the location of power: does it lie with individuals or within social/political/economic structures? Wider discussions within sociology have drawn our attention to the interaction between individuals (or agents) and structures. Rather than seeing these as mutually exclusive or discrete analytic categories, rather we might see structures and agents as mutually reconstituting, mutually interdependent analytically and ontologically and this is a process rather than structures and agents existing as static entities.

Structures and agents

As noted in Chapter 1, Giddens (1984) advanced the argument that structures and agents were not separate from each other, rather they were interdependent. Rather than one or the other having the capacity to exercise power they were intimately bound in a process that was interactive and iterative. The actions of agents were constrained by the power structures they were situated in; but through action, agents had the capacity to reshape these power structures. Jessop (1990) argued that action occurs within a structure of context, but that context of structure is 'strategically selective', that is, positioning within a structure selects the strategies that may be available to an actor. For example, if you are a Black working-class woman you are less likely to be able to have power in a public space than a white middle-class man, as a consequence of how strategies and capacity for actions available to you, as a consequence of pre-existing (capitalist, patriarchal and racial) structures. This suggests a complexity to power and its operation; power is a process, and is also relational. That is, power is a product of social relations within a structure or context.

Mary Archer (1996) added another dimension to the debate around the relations between structure and agency. For her, culture (and discourses) plays a key role in mediating between structures and agents. This adds an extra layer to our analytical understandings of the constitution of reality. For Archer, culture is also fluid and contingent and vacillates between being 'the superordinate power in society' (performing a hegemonic role) and being 'reduced to a mere epiphenomenon (charged only with providing an ideational representation of structure)' (1996: 1). The way we perceive our structures, through a cultural lens of norms and values, also thus plays a key role in their constitution. So for example, the ways British Muslims' culture has been constructed constitutes a layer through which they are depicted in our news media as 'other' (see also Said, 1981). Our perceptions of these structures matter, as do the ideas we hold about these structures and cultures (cf. Hay,

2001). This of course raises the questions, ontologically, if culturally, we perceive structures to be fixed (as often implied in media coverage), does this deny the capacity for autonomous action, or the possibility of change?

Underlying Lukes' characterization of power as three-dimensional is also an assumption that power is located in the public sphere; its influence is in the realm of the public in contrast to the private. Lukes' work has been subject to critique and he addressed those concerns in a revised edition of his work published in 2005. His concern remained, though, to ask questions about how the powerful come to secure the compliance of those they dominate. And, more specifically, how they secure their *willing* compliance (Lukes, 2005: 12, 86). While Lukes engages with a variety of theorists, perhaps the two of greatest significance for this book are Foucault and Butler.

Power and the constitution of the subject

For Foucault, power 'is tolerable only on condition that it mask a substantial part of itself. Its success is proportional to its ability to hide its own mechanisms' (1980a: 86). That we cannot necessarily see power facilitates its effectiveness and in some ways this might be akin to Lukes' third face of power. However, Foucault suggests a greater complexity than power being located in structures. Rather we are all implicated in the production and construction of power relations. For him, power is manifest in society in everything we do in 'what he calls "micropractices", the social practices that constitute everyday life in modern societies' (Fraser, 1989: 18). That is, the practices we engage in as citizens serve to reproduce power structures. But power is not only repressive for Foucault; it also contains the capacity for positive effects, and he makes a distinction between how power may be repressive, constraining and setting limits to action and capacity for autonomy for agents. At the same time, power 'traverses and produces things, it induces pleasure, forms knowledge, produces discourses' (Foucault, 1980b: 119); in this sense, resistance is a possibility. But the dynamics of power as social relations ultimately mean, for Foucault, the production of 'subjects' and so power is played out on the body. Subjects are 'normalized' into subjects willing to adopt and adhere to norms of sanity and sexuality. These norms are policed through the micropractices of surveillance at the level of the self-regulating individual. In this sense, we cannot escape power. The subject is constructed through normalizing patterns of behaviour and this is a consequence of 'patterns that he [sic] finds in culture and which are proposed, suggested and imposed on him by his culture, his society and his social group' (Foucault, 1987: 11). These socialization practices are part of wider forms of 'governmentality' where governing takes place through 'micropractices' in school, by parents, at home, by employers. He argues that 'between the games of power and the states of domination, you have governmental technologies – giving the term a very wide meaning for it is also the way in which you govern your wife, your children, as well as the way you govern an institution' (Foucault, 1987: 19).

Despite extensive questioning of the nature of power, it seems somewhat strange that Foucault, while challenging and critiquing many social practices around sexuality, health, regulation of the body, failed to question his reproduction of power relations through gender in his work. As Braidotti observes, 'Foucault never locates woman's body as the site of one of the most operational internal divisions in our society, and consequently one of the most persistent forms of exclusion' (1991: 87). Foucault's failure to address this and his continued reference to the subject as 'he' means that 'sexual difference simply does not play a role in the Foucauldian universe, where the technology of subjectivity refers to a desexualized and general 'human subject' (ibid). In assuming that power is stamped onto the body, this 'leads to an oversimplified notion of gender as imposed rather than as a dynamic process' (McNay, 1992: 12), which limits discussion or opportunities to account for how individuals may act in an autonomous capacity despite wider overarching constraints. The possibility of emancipation from power structures has been a key theme of feminist scholarship and is written in Foucault's work, and it is through understanding of how the body forms a site of power relationships that these opportunities for emancipation are located. One of the ways that this is possible has been considered in this book, and in wider research, is in chapters where women's experiences are foregrounded, recognized as a legitimate site of study. For example, in reflecting on women's experiences in the production of news, in formal politics, in war situations, we are reminded that these are diverse and different from those of the universalized masculine 'norm'. In discussing these experiences we are able to offer a more complete analysis of how politics is communicated; challenging the notion that formal politics is, and can only be, the preserve of a white, middle-class man.

The subject and gender

For Judith Butler, power is also played out through the body, and again at this site we see issues of identity, experience, empowerment and disempowerment enacted through broader social structures of class, gender, race and sexual orientation. Butler argues that the subject is a subject 'of' power in two senses: power is both a condition of possibility for subjectivity and a force that the subject wields (Butler, 1997: 14). This means that the subject is '*neither* fully determined by power *nor* fully determining of power (but significantly and partially both)' (Butler, 1997: 17). Butler seeks to make sense of how the subordinated come to desire their subordination. For Butler, rational critique is insufficient as a mechanism of resistance, rather resistance is through the transformation of our desires, our wills and our basis of recognition. We might in the context of this book regard, for example, audiences and citizens as subjects of historically mediated, socially constructed power relations. As has been noted in the asking of questions, in the gaining of knowledge, in the act of becoming literate, all of these features may contribute to the contestation of positions as subordinate subjects.

Butler challenges the notion that identities first need to be in place for political action to be taken. She argues 'that there need not be a "doer behind the deed", but that the "doer" is variably constructed in and through the deed' (1999: 181). This means that how we perform our identities is the way they are constructed, our recognition of this facilitates alternative identities, and ultimately alternative politics. Butler reformulates questions of agency as questions about the way signification and resignification works. For her 'the substantive "I" only appears as such through a signifying practice that seeks to conceal its own workings and to naturalize its effects' (1999: 184). In this way, for example, I may be identified as a consumer, or a woman, but this identification is a product of an interrelationship of culture and discourses which mire the construction of this identity. She reminds us that there is nothing natural about such signification (e.g. as a woman, a citizen, a consumer) and in the roots of this recognition there is the possibility of alternative identities and conceptions of the political. It is the repetition of such identities which appears to foreclose alternatives, and in this way we might consider why, for example, women remain underrepresented in legislatures, in business, in other elite aspects of public life. If boys underachieve at school, what takes place that enables them to become overrepresented in the upper echelons of formal power structures? The repetition and normalization of MP to mean male MP and the use of term 'female' in front of MP to denote difference is an example of how the signification of identity conceals wider power structures about which there is nothing inherently natural. Throughout this book, the aim has been to encourage a reflection on how we are positioned, in respect of, and by, politicians, media and other elite actors who operate 'strategically selectively' (cf. Jessop, 2005). This takes place within historically culturally constituted structures, within which we are constructed as citizens and/or consumers through reference to our class, race, sexuality and gender. The point here is that we do not necessarily have to be determined by our positioning in these structures.

In the West, these structures are also informed by neoliberalism, and the body has become a site of regulation and its intersection with the neoliberal agenda is noted by a number of scholars. For Phipps, 'success is measured by individuals' capacity for self-care via the market, and those who do not achieve their potential are viewed as failures rather than victims of an oppressive social structure' (2014: 11). In this way, we are encouraged to view the social and political world around us as structured by individual and lifestyle choices, rather than based on inequalities structured around gender, race, class or sexuality. These structural inequalities for Brown serve a broader political function to achieve 'depoliticisation on an unprecedented level: the economy is tailored to it, citizenship is organized by it, the media are dominated by it, and the political rationality of neoliberalism frames and endorses it' (2006: 704). Not only, then, do we have a politically and socially, broadly unquestioned structure of inequality, but neoliberalism as a discourse also functions to ensure that it becomes difficult to questions this structure. Placing emphasis on the individual as culpable for their own situation effectively removes the politics of how individuals have been positioned in the first place. Consider, for example, headlines which focus on obesity. Here politics is played out on the body, as a site of individual responsibility, rather than a politics which recognizes this issue as a resource-based inequality (cf. Evans and Riley, 2013).

In seeking to destabilize, or 'trouble', norms of identity around gender and sexuality (Butler, 1999), Queer theory has developed to facilitate the asking of questions about that which constitutes 'normal' and who might be subordinated, oppressed or excluded by the construction of those norms. While Butler focuses her attention on gender and sexuality and how these 'norms' are performed and ritualized through repetition, Halberstam (2011) invites us to reflect on how 'success' and 'failure' are intimately linked to the social construction of gendered and heteronormative identities. Searle (2014) has argued that the terms success and failure have become normalized features of contemporary neoliberal discourse. As such, the ways subjects are culturally and historically constituted in a neoliberal context has consequences for how we may define what it means to be successful, and what failure means. For analysts of political communication, we might extend this logic to think about what success or failure within political communication may look like. In the preceding chapters, and within the field, there is often an underlying acceptance that success is often the achievement of elite goals. Success, conceived of in this way, thus continues to be something that perpetuates existing social structures. Halberstam argues that what this ultimately means is that 'feminine success is something that is always measured by male standards' (2011: 4). In so doing, we can perhaps reflect on the ways in earlier chapters we see critiques of how women are positioned in, by and through media as unsuccessful in an idealized version of femininity. Masculinized standards of what women should look like thus inform how women are constructed in mediated political discourses, from MPs to celebrities to soldiers. Yet for Halberstam, 'failure' can also offer unexpected pleasures, 'in being relieved of the pressure to measure up to patriarchal ideals' (2011: 4). Halberstam encourages us to think about avoiding the 'political grammar that insists on placing liberation struggles within the same logic as the normative regimes against which they struggle' (2011: 129). Rather a different logic is necessary, one which is articulated in terms of 'refusal, passivity, unbecoming, unbeing' (ibid). In this way, not only are we able to ask political questions about what is being articulated to us but also articulate and communicate alternate forms of politics.

Technologies of regulation in political communication

Within each chapter, the aim has been to ask critical questions about the nature of power in political communication. The starting point has been where much of the existing literature lies, and there has been a focus on elections, news production, audiences, celebrity politics, war and terror and how citizens communicate. In the academic field, much of the focus is on the role of material technologies in affecting what it is and, to a lesser degree, isn't possible to communicate. In contrast to the material technologies (such as TV, new social media) that form much of the focus within the literature around political communication, Foucault draws our attention to technologies as systems that regulate and govern our behaviours. The aim of this book has been to suggest that material technologies play a role in constituting ideational technologies and the term media has been used throughout this book to signify a set of social, cultural and political practices that form part of our daily lives. I use Couldry's definition to 'cover all institutionalized structures, forms, formats and interfaces for disseminating symbolic content' (Couldry, 2012: viii). This symbolic content plays a role in constituting us as subjects and positioning us not only as audiences but as consumers, often in place of citizenship. In reflecting on how we are positioned, there is capacity to reflect on how Foucauldian 'truth regimes' govern and regulate how our daily experiences are constituted. A key aim here has been to argue that critically unpacking these processes, and asking political questions of what is taking place, enables us to challenge power relations, so that we are able to choose (to a greater or lesser degree) the extent to which we wish to reproduce or seek to effect change in and on those structures of power. If we reflect on how we are socially and historically constructed through technologies of governmentality, regulation and domination:

> Maybe the problem of the self is not to discover what it is in its positivity, maybe the problem is not to discover a positive self or the positive foundation of the self. Maybe our problem is now to discover that the self is nothing else than the historical correlation of the technology built in our history. Maybe the problem is to change those technologies. And in this case, one of the main political problems would be nowadays, in the strict sense of the word, the politics of ourselves. (Foucault, 1993: 221–2)

In this way, understanding the technologies, the 'regimes of truth' that have come to shape our lives, is a way to make sense of how power relations are played out, they ways in which our very selves are effects or consequences of power; we are socially and politically constituted. In this way, as Foucault argues, 'It seems to me, that the real task in a society such as ours is to criticize the working of institutions which appear both neutral and independent; to criticize them in such a manner that the political violence which has always exercised itself obscurely through them will be unmasked, so that we can fight them' (cited in Rabinow, 1986: 6).

Politics plays a role in constructing our social reality. This is not simply the formal politics of the institutions and personnel of the state, but politics defined more broadly, as the circulation, negotiation and contestation of power. Politics is therefore a site where identities can be constructed, expressed and contested. These political identities are formed within discourses and can also shape discourses. I have sought to situate the asking of political questions in their wider discursive context; one in the West which is characterized by neoliberalism, capitalism and patriarchy. The aim has to be to think through how the discursive contexts within which we are socially situated are constructed, and how we might effect change within them. To do this is to ask fundamentally political questions about the nature of how power works within the politics that is communicated to us. Lazarsfeld and Merton (1969: 495) asked what are 'the effects of the existence of media in our society'? The aim of this book is to argue that they are incredibly significant, playing a crucial political role, in normalizing our behaviour, setting the limits of our imagination (cf. Lewis, 2013) and in shaping our ontologies, our lived experiences and capacities for political action. But that is not to say we as subjects are predetermined by this construction, and as political actors ourselves we have the capacity to effect political change.

Reflection/seminar activities

Draw or take a photo of 'reality'. What relations of power are depicted in your image?

How are we defined/constructed by dominant power structures, as individuals, groups, societies? Does this matter (how and why)? Can we step outside of/resist these power structures? Would we want to? Why/why not?

In Iron Maiden's 'Run to the Hills' the line 'White man came across the sea' uses six words from which we could derive a story about colonial masculine power relationships. Write your own six-word story that illustrates your own understanding of how political power works.

Bibliography

Adorno, M and Horkheimer, T W (1944/2002) 'The culture industry: Enlightenment as mass deception' in Gunzelin Schmid Noerr (ed.) *Dialectic of Enlightenment: Philosophical Fragments* pp. 94–136. Translated by Edmund Jephcott (Stanford, CA: Stanford University Press)

Allan, S (1998) '(En)gendering the truth politics of news discourse' in Carter, C Branston, G and Allan, S (eds) (1998) *News, Gender and Power* (London: Routledge) pp. 121–37

Allan, S (2010) *News Culture* 3rd edition (Maidenhead: Open University Press)

Allan, S and Thorsen, E (2009) *Citizen Journalism: Global Perspectives* (New York: Peter Lang)

Allen, A (2010) 'Rethinking resistance: Feminism and the politics of our selves' *Eurozine* http://www.eurozine.com/articles/2010-05-05-allen-en.html

Allen, H and Savigny, H (2012) 'Selling scandal or ideology? The politics of business crime coverage' *European Journal of Communication* 27(3) pp. 278–90

Almond, G and Verba, S (1963) *The Civic Culture: Political Attitudes and Democracy in Five Nations* (New York and London: Sage)

Althusser, L (1969) *Essays in Self Criticism* translated by Graham Locke (London: New Left Books)

Althusser, L (1971) *Lenin and Philosophy and Other Essays* (New York: Monthly Review Press)

Anderson QC, D (2014) *The Terrorism Acts In 2013. Report Of The Independent Reviewer On The Operation Of The Terrorism Act 2000 And Part 1 Of The Terrorism Act 2006* https://terrorismlegislationreviewer.independent.gov. uk/wp-content/uploads/2014/07/Independent-Review-of-Terrorism-Report -2014-print2.pdf

Ansolabehere, S and Iyengar, S (1995) *Going Negative: How Political Advertisements Shrink and Polarize the Electorate* (New York: Free Press)

Archer, M S (1996) *Realist Social Theory: the Morphogenetic Approach* (Cambridge: Cambridge University Press)

Arendt, H (1951/1968) *The Origins of Totalitarianism* (New York: Harcourt, Brace and Jovanovich)

Aristotle (2000) *The Politics (Penguin Classics)* (London: Penguin)

Armstrong, C (2004) 'The influence of reporter gender on source selection in newspaper stories' *Journalism and Mass Communication Quarterly* 8(1) pp. 139–54

Atton, C (2003) 'What is "alternative journalism"?' *Journalism: Theory, Practice and Criticism* 4(3) pp. 267–400

Bachrach, P and Baratz, M (1962) 'The two faces of power' *American Political Science Review* 56 pp. 947–52

Bandura, A and Walters, R (1963) *Social Learning and Personality Development* (New York: Rinehart and Winston)

Barker, M and Petley, J (eds) (1996) *Ill Effects. The Media/Violence Debate* (London: Routledge)

Barriteau, E (1995) 'Postfeminist feminist theorizing and development policy and practice in the Anglophone Caribbean: The Barbados case' in M. Marchand

and J. Parpart (eds) *Feminism: Postmodernism/Development* (London and New York: Routledge) pp. 142–158

Banakar, R (2010) 'Pre-empting terrorism? Two case studies of the UK's anti-terrorism legislation' in R. Banakar (ed.) *Rights in Context: Law and Justice in Late Modern Society* (London: Ashgate) pp. 193–214

Banyard, K (2010) *The Equality Illusion* (London: Faber and Faber)

Barnard-Wills, D (2012) *Surveillance and Identity: Discourse, Subjectivity and the State* (Farnham: Ashgate)

Barthes, R (1972) *Mythologies* (New York: Hill and Wang)

Bates, T R (1975) 'Gramsci and the theory of hegemony' *Journal of the History of Ideas* 36(2) pp. 351–366

Baudrillard, J (1994) *Simulacra and Simulation* (University of Michigan Press)

Baudrillard, J (1988) *The Consumer Society* (London: Sage)

Baum, M A (2005) 'Talking the vote: Why presidential candidates hit the talk show circuit' *American Journal of Political Science* 49(2) pp. 213–34

Bauman, Z (1976) *Towards a Critical Sociology: An Essay on Commonsense and Emancipation* (London: Routledge)

Bauman, Z (1992) *Intimations of Postmodernity* (London: Routledge)

Bauman, Z (2007) *Consuming Life* (Cambridge: Polity)

Bechdel, A (1985) 'The Rule' *Dykes to Watch Out For* http://alisonbechdel.blogspot.co.uk/2005/08/rule.html

Bechdeltest.com (2015) statistics http://bechdeltest.com/statistics/

Beck, U (1992) *Risk Society: Towards a New Modernity* translated by M. Ritter (London: Sage)

Beetham, D (1992) 'Liberal democracy and the limits of democratization' *Political Studies* 40(5) pp. 40–53

Bell, D (1973) *The Coming of Post-Industrial Society: A Venture in Social Forecasting* (New York: Basic Books)

Bennett, W L and Iyengar, S (2008) 'A new era of minimal effects? The changing foundations of political communication' *Journal of Communication* 58 pp. 707–31

Beresford, Q (1998) 'Selling democracy short: Elections in the age of the market' *Current Affairs Bulletin* Feb–March 74(5) pp. 24–32

Bernays, E (1928/2005) *Propaganda* (Brooklyn: Ig Publishing)

Bimber, B (2014) 'Digital media in the Obama campaigns of 2008 and 2012: Adaptation to the personalized political communication environment' *Journal of Information Technology and Politics* 11(2) pp. 130–50

Bloom, M (2005) *Dying To Kill: The Allure of Suicide Terror* (New York: Columbia University Press)

Blumenthal, S (1980) *The Permanent Campaign* (Boston, MA: Beacon)

Blumenthal, M (2005) 'Toward an open-source methodology. What we can learn from the blogosphere' *Public Opinion Quarterly* 69(5) pp. 655–69

Blumler, J and Gurevitch, M (1995) *The Crisis of Public Communication* (Abingdon: Routledge)

Blumler, J and Gurevitch, M (2001) 'The new media and our political communication discontents: democratizing cyberspace' *Information, Communication and Society* 4(1) pp. 1–13

Blumler, J and Katz, E (eds) (1974) *The Uses of Communications* (Beverly Hills, CA: Sage)

Blumler, J and Kavangh, D (1999) 'The third age of political communication: Influences and features' *Political Communication* 16 pp. 209–30

Bode, L and Dalrymple, K E (2014) 'Politics in 140 characters or less: Campaign communication, network interaction, and political participation on Twitter' *Journal of Political Marketing* http://www.tandfonline.com/doi/abs/10.108 0/15377857.2014.959686?src=recsys#.VP67lHysUTZ

Bode, L and Epstein, B (2015) 'Campaign klout: Measuring online influence during the 2012 election' *Journal of Information Technology and Politics* http://www.tandfonline.com/doi/abs/10.1080/19331681.2014.994157#.VP672XysUTa

Boucher, D and Kelly, P (2009) *Political Thinkers* (Oxford: Oxford University Press)

Bourdieu, P (1979) 'Public opinion does not exist' in A. Mattleart and S. Siegelaub (eds) *Communication and Class Struggle 1: Capitalism, Imperialism* (New York: International General)

Boyd-Barrett, O; Herrera, D and J Baumann, (2012) 'Hollywood, the CIA and the "War on Terror" in D. Freedman and D K Thussu (eds) *Media and Terrorism: Global Perspectives* (London: Sage) pp. 116–33

Boyle, K (2015) 'Representing gender based violence. Challenges and possibilities' *LSE Commission on Gender, Inequality and Power* 17 April

Braidotti, R (1991) *Patterns of Dissonance: A Study of Women in Contemporary Philosophy* (Cambridge: Polity Press)

Brants, K (1998) 'Who's afraid of infotainment?' *European Journal of Communication* 13(3) pp. 315–35

Brants, K and Voltmer (2011) 'Introduction: Mediatisation and de-centralization of political communication' in K Brants and K Voltmer *Political Communication in Postmodern Democracy* (Basingstoke: Palgrave) pp. 1–18

Breyer, S (2010) *Making our Democracy Work: A Judge's View* (New York: Kopf)

Brooks, A (1997) *Postfeminisms. Feminism, Cultural Theory and Cultural Forms* (London: Routledge)

Brooks, D J (2006) 'The resilient voter: Moving toward closure in the debate over negative campaigning and turnout' *Journal of Politics* 68(3) pp. 684–696

Brooks, M (2012) 'If you can play a video game, you can fly a drone' *New Statesman* 13 June http://www.newstatesman.com/sci-tech/sci-tech/2012/06/play-video-game-fly-drone

Brown, W (2006) *Regulating Aversion: Tolerance in the Age of Identity and Empire* (Princeton, NJ: Princeton University Press)

Brownmiller, S (ND) *Making Female Bodies the Battlefield* http://www.learningshark.com/WebDocs/Web%20PDF/MakingFemaleBodiesTheBattlefield.pdf

Brunson, C (1997) *Screen Tastes: Soap Opera to Satellite Dishes* (London: Routledge)

Burchell, G; Gordon, C and P Miller (1991) *The Foucault Effect: Studies in Governmentality* (Chicago, Ill: University of Chicago Press)

Butler, D and Stokes, D (1974) *Political Change in Britain* (London: Macmillan)

Butler, J (1993) *Bodies that Matter* (London: Routledge)

Butler, J (1997) *The Psychic Life of Power: Theories in Subjection* (Stanford, CA: Stanford University Press)

Butler, J (1999) *Gender Trouble* (New York: Routledge)

Butler, P and Collins, N (1994) 'Political marketing: Structure and process' *European Journal of Marketing* 28(1) pp. 19–34

Butler, P and Collins, N (2001) 'Payment on delivery: Recognising constituency service as political marketing' *European Journal of Marketing* 35(9/10) pp. 1026–37

Butler, P (2015) 'Food bank use tops million mark over the past year' *The Guardian* http://www.theguardian.com/society/2015/apr/22/food-bank-users-uk-low-paid-workers-poverty

Butsch, R (2009) 'Introduction: How are media public spheres?' in ed R. Butsch *Media and Public Spheres* (Basingstoke: Palgrave) pp. 1–14

Byerly, C (2004) 'Feminist interventions in newsrooms' in K Ross and C. Byerly (eds) *Women and Media International Perspectives* (Oxford: Blackwell) pp. 109–31

Capella, J N and Jamieson, K H (1997) *Spiral of Cynicism: The Press and the Public Good* (New York and Oxford: Oxford University Press)

Cardo, V M (2011a) "Voting is easy, just press the eed button": Communicating politics in the age of Big Brother' in K Brants, K Voltmer (eds) *Political Communication in Postmodern Democracy: Challenging the Primacy of Politics* (Basingstoke: Palgrave Macmillan) pp. 231–48

Cardo, V M (2011b) 'The amazing Mrs Politician: Television entertainment and women in politics' *Parliamentary Affairs* 64(2) pp. 311–25

Cardo, V M (2014) 'Celebrity politics and political representation: The case of George Galloway MP on Celebrity Big Brother' *British Politics* 9 pp. 146–60

Carlin, D B and Winfrey, K L (2009) 'Have you come a long way, baby? Hillary Clinton, Sarah Palin, and sexism in 2008 campaign coverage' *Communication Studies* 60(4) pp. 326–43

Carr, C (2000) *The Book of War: Sun Tzu The Art of Warfare and Karl Von Clausewitz On War* (New York: The Modern Library)

Carruthers, S (2011) *The Media At War* (Basingstoke: Palgrave)

Carter, C Branston, G and Allan, S (eds) (1998) *News, Gender and Power* (London: Routledge)

Cassidy, J (2002) *Dot.Con: The Greatest Story Ever Told* (London: Penguin/Allen Lane)

Cassidy, S (2006) 'Teenagers beguiled by false dreams of instant fame on reality TV' *The Independent* http://www.independent.co.uk/news/education/education-news/teenagers-beguiled-by-false-dreams-of-instant-fame-on-reality-tv-522770.html

Castells, M (1996/2010) *The Rise of the Networked Society* (West Sussex: John Wiley and Sons)

Chandra, K (2006) 'What is ethnic identity and does it matter?' *Annual Review of Political Science* 9 pp. 397–424

Childs, S and Krook M L (2006) 'Gender and politics: The state of the art' *Politics* 26(1) pp. 18–28

Childs, S and Krook, M L (2009) 'Analysing women's substantive representation: From critical mass to critical actors' *Government and Opposition* 44 (2) pp. 125–45

Chomsky, N and Achar, G (2008) *Perilous Power* (London: Penguin)

Civil Rights Movement (2015) 'What is hate speech?' http://www.civilrights movement.co.uk/faq-what-classed-hate-speech.html

Cohen, S (2011) *Folk Devils and Moral Panics: The Creation of Mods and Rockers* (London: Routledge)

Coleman, S (2003) 'A tale of two houses: the House of Commons, the Big Brother house and the people at home' *Parliamentary Affairs* 56(4) pp. 733–58

Condit, C M (1989) 'The rhetorical limits of polysemy' *Critical Studies in Mass Communication* 6(2) pp. 103–22

Connell, R (1987) *Gender and Power* (Sydney, Australia: Allen and Unwin)

Connell, R W (1993) *Masculinities* (Berkeley: University of California Press)

Connell, R W (1993) 'The big picture: Masculinities in recent world history' *Theory and Society* 22 (5) pp. 597–623

Coughlan, S (2015) 'Schools face new legal duties to tackle extremism' *BBC News* http://www.bbc.co.uk/news/education-33328377

Couldry, N (2010) *Why Voice Matters: Culture and Politics after Neoliberalism* (London: Sage)

Couldry, N (2012) *Media, Society, World Social Theory and Digital Media Practice* (Cambridge: Polity)

Couldry, N and Markham, T (2007) 'Celebrity culture and public connection: Bridge or chasm?' *International Journal of Cultural Studies* 10(4) pp. 403–21

Couture, T (1995) 'Feminist criticisms of Habermas's Ethics and Politics' *Dialogue* XXXIV pp. 259–79

Cranny-Francis, A; Waring, W; Stavropoulos, P and Kirby, J (2003) *Gender Studies: Terms and Debates* (Basingstoke: Palgrave)

Crenshaw, M (ed.) (1995) *Terrorism in Context* (Philadelphia: Pennsylvania University Press)

Critcher, C (ed.) (2006) *Moral Panics and the Media* (Maidenhead: Open University Press)

Crouch, C (2004) *Post Democracy* (Cambridge: Polity)

Curran, J (2002) *Media and Power* (London: Routledge)

Curran, J (2010) 'Entertaining democracy' in J Curran (ed.) *Media and Society* 5th edition (London: Bloomsbury) pp. 38–62

Cushion, S and Lewis, J (eds) (2010) *The Rise of 24-hour News Television: Global Perspectives* (New York: Peter Lang)

Dahl, R (1961) *Who Governs? Democracy and Power in an American City* (New Haven: Yale University Press)

Dahl, R A (2000) *On Democracy* (New Haven and London: Yale University Press)

Dahlgren, P (2009) *Media and Political Engagement* (Cambridge: Cambridge University Press)

Dalton, R (2004) *Democratic Challenges, Democratic Choices: The Erosion of Political Support in Advanced Industrial Democracies* (Oxford: Oxford University Press)

Dalton, R (2006) 'Citizenship norms and political participation in America: The good news is ... the bad news is wrong' *Occasional Paper Center for Democracy and Civil Society* (Washington DC; Georgetown University)

Davis, A (2002) *Public Relations Democracy* (Manchester: Manchester University Press)

Davis, A (2005) 'Media effects and the active elite audience: A study of media in financial markets' *European Journal of Communication* 20(3) pp. 303–26

Davis, A (2007) *The Mediation of Power: A Critical Introduction* (London: Routledge)

Davies, N (2008) *Flat Earth News* (London: Chatto and Windus)

Debord, G (1967) *Society of the Spectacle* http://www.marxists.org/reference/archive/debord/society.htm

Dietz, T (1998) 'An examination of violence and gender role portrayals in video games: Implications for gender socialization and aggressive behavior' *Sex Roles* 38(5–6) pp. 425–42

de Jong, W, Shaw, M and Stammers, N (eds) (2005) *Global Activism, Global Media* (London: Pluto Press)

Dellacioppa, K Z (2012) 'Local communities and global resistance. Social change and autonomy struggles in the Americas' in Dellacioppa, K Z and Weber, C (eds) *Cultural Politics and Resistance in the 21 Century* (New York: Palgrave Macmillan) pp. 1–120

della Porta, D and Diani, M (2006) *Social Movements An Introduction* (Oxford: Blackwell)

Delli Carpini, M X and Keeter, S (1996) *What Americans Know about Politics and Why it Matters* (New Haven: Yale University Press)

de Sousa, R (1987) 'When is it wrong to laugh?' In J Moreall (ed.) *The Philosophy of Laughter and Humor* (Albany, NY: State University of New York) pp. 226–49

Deuze, M (2007) *Media Work* (Cambridge: Polity)

Devereux, E (2009) *Understanding the Media* (London: Sage)

Diani, M (1992) 'The concept of social movement' *The Sociological Review* 40(1) pp. 1–25

Donaldson, M (1993) 'What is hegemonic masculinity?' *Theory and Society* 22(5) pp. 643–57

Dorling, D (2010) *Injustice: Why Social Inequality Persists* (Bristol: Policy Press)

Douglas, S (2010) *The Rise of Enlightened Sexism: How Pop Culture Took us from Girl Power to Girls Gone Wild* (New York: St Martin's Griffin)

Downs, A (1957) *An Economic Theory of Democracy* (New York: Harper and Row)

Dow, B J (1996) *Prime-time Feminism* (Philadelphia: University of Pennsylvania Press)

Drake, P and Higgins, M (2012) 'Lights, camera, election: Celebrity, performance and the 2010 leadership debates' *British Journal of Politics and International Relations* 14(3) pp. 375–91

Du Bois, W (1989/1903) *The Souls of Black Folk* (New York: Bantam)

Dunleavy, P (1991) *Democracy, Bureaucracy and Public Choice* (New York: Prentice Hall)

Edelman, M (1988) *Constructing the Political Spectacle* (Chicago, Ill: University of Chicago Press)

Engels, F (1884/2010) *The Origin of the Family, Private Property and the State* (London: Penguin)

Enloe, C (2013) *Seriously! Investigating Crashes and Crises as if Women Mattered* (Berkeley: University of California Press)

Entman, R (1993) 'Framing: Towards clarification of a fractured paradigm' *Journal of Communication* 43(4) 51–8

Evans, A and Riley, S (2013) 'Immaculate consumption: Negotiating the sex symbol in postfeminist celebrity culture' *Journal of Gender Studies* 22(3) pp. 268–281

Fairclough, N and Wodak, R (1997) 'Critical discourse analysis' in T A van Dijk (ed.) *Discourse as Social Interaction* (London: Sage) pp. 258–84

Faludi, S (1991) *Backlash: The Undeclared War against American Women* (New York: Crown)

Farrell, N (2014) "Conscience capitalism" and the neoliberalisation of the non-profit sector' *New Political Economy* 20(2) pp. 254–72

Farrell, N (2013) 'Navigating the stars: The challenges and opportunities of celebrity journalism' in Fowler-Watt, K and Allan, S (eds) *Journalism: New Challenges*. Poole: CJCR: Centre for Journalism and Communication Research, pp. 367–383

Featherstone, M (1991) *Consumer Culture and Postmodernism* (London: Sage)

Feigenbaum, A; Fremzel, F and McCurdy, P (2013) *Protest Camps* (London: Zed Books)

Filipovic, J (2007) 'Blogging while female: How internet misogyny parallels "real world" harassment' *Yale Journal of Law and Feminism* 19 pp. 295–303

Fish, S (1994) *There's No Such Thing as Free Speech ... And It's a Good Thing Too* (New York: Oxford University Press)

Fiske, R (1987) *Television Culture* (New York: Methuen)

Forde, S (2011) *Challenging the News: The Journalism of Alternative and Community Media* (Basingstoke: Palgrave Macmillan)

Foucault, M (1961/1967) *Madness and Civilisation: A History of Insanity in the Age of Reason* (London: Tavistock)

Foucault, M (1975/1977) *Discipline and Punish: The Birth of the Prison* (Harmondsworth: Pelican)

Foucault, M (1976/1990) *The History of Sexuality: Volume One: An Introduction* (Harmondsworth: Penguin)

Foucault, M (1980a) *The History of Sexuality vol. 1* translated by R. Hurley (New York: Random House)

Foucault, M (1980b) *Michel Foucault: Power/Knowledge. Selected Interviews and Other Writings 1972–77* (New York: Harvester Wheatsheaf)

Foucault, M (1984) 'Nietzsche, genealogy, history' in P Rabinow (ed.) *The Foucault Reader* (Harmondsworth: Penguin)

Foucault, M (1987) 'The ethic of care for the self as a practice of freedom: An interview with Michel Foucault on 20 January 1984' in J Bernauer and D Rasmussen (eds) *The Final Foucault* (Cambridge, MA and London: MIT Press) pp. 1–20

Foucault, M (1991) *The Foucault Effect: Studies in Governmentality* Edited by G Burchell, C Gordon and P Miller (Chicago: University of Chicago Press)

Foucault, M (1993) 'About the beginnings of the hermeneutics of the self: Two lectures at Dartmouth' *Political Theory* 21(2) pp. 198–227

Fox, J C (2007) *Film Propaganda in Britain and Nazi Germany: World War II Cinema* (Oxford: Berg)

Francois-Cerrah, M (2015) 'The absurd hunt for "Muslim toddler terrorists" exposes the extent of anti-Muslim prejudice' *New Statesman* http://www.newstatesman.com/politics/2015/06/absurd-hunt-muslim-toddler-terrorists-exposes-worrying-trend-our-attitude-extremism

Franklin, B (1994) *Packaging Politics* (London: Edward Arnold)

Franklin, B (2001) 'The hand of history: New Labour, news management and governance' in Ludlam, S and Smith, M (eds) *New Labour in Government* (Basingstoke: Palgrave) pp. 130–44

Fraser, N (1985) 'What is critical about critical theory? The case of Habermas and gender' *New German Critique* 35 pp. 97–131

Fraser, N (1992) 'Rethinking the public sphere: A contribution to the critique of actually existing democracy' in C Calhoun (ed.) *Habermas and the Public Sphere* (Cambridge, MA: MIT Press) pp. 109–42

Fraser, N (1989) *Unruly Practices: Power, Gender and Discourse in Contemporary Political Theory* (Cambridge: Polity Press)

Freedman, D and Thussu, D K (2012) *Media and Terrorism: Global Perspectives* (London: Sage)

Friedersdorf, C (2014) 'When misogynist trolls make journalism miserable for women' *The Atlantic* http://www.theatlantic.com/politics/archive/2014/01/when-misogynist-trolls-make-journalism-miserable-for-women/282862/

Fuchs, D and Klingeman, H-D (1990) 'The left-right schema' in M Kent Jennings and J W van Beth (eds) *Continuities in Political Action* (Berlin: deGruyter)

Gaber, I (1998) 'A world of dogs and lamp-posts' *New Statesman* 19 June p14

Garcia-Blanco, I and Wahl-Jorgensen K (2011) 'The discursive construction of women politicians in the European press' *Feminist Media Studies* 12(3) pp. 422–41

Gauntlett, D (1998) 'Ten things wrong with the effects model' in Dickinson, R; Havindranath, R and Linne, O (eds) *Approaches to Audiences* (London: Arnold)

Gauntlett, D (2008) *Media, Gender and Identity: An Introduction* (London: Routledge)

Gay, R (2014) *Bad Feminist* (New York: Harper Collins)

Gershkoff, A and Kushner, S (2003) 'Shaping public opinion: The 9/11-Iraq connection in the Bush administration's rhetoric' *Perspectives on Politics* 3(3) pp. 525–37

Gerodimos, R and Justinussen, J (2014) 'Obama's 2012 Facebook campaign: Political communication in the age of the like button' *Journal of Information Technology and Politics* http://www.tandfonline.com/doi/abs/10.1080/19331681.2014.982266?src=recsys#.VP68RnysUTY

Giddens, A (1984) *The Constitution of Society: Outline of the Theory of Structuration* (Cambridge: Polity)

Gill, R (2007) *Gender and the Media* (Cambridge: Polity Press)

Gill, R (2008) 'Empowerment/sexism: Figuring female agency in contemporary advertising' *Feminism and Psychology* 18(1) pp. 35–60

Gill, R (2011) 'Sexism reloaded, or it's time to get angry again' *Feminist Media Studies* 11(1) pp. 61–71

Gilligan, C; Rogers, A G and Tolman, D L (2013) *Women, Girls and Psychotherapy: Reframing Resistance* (New York: Routledge)

Gitlin, T (1980) *The Whole World is Watching* (Berkeley: University of California Press)

Glasgow University Media Group (1980) *More Bad News* (London: Routledge and Kegan Paul)

Goldman, E (1910/2013) *Anarchism and Other Essays* (USA: Rough Draft Printing)

Goldstein, J (2001) *War and Gender* (Cambridge: Cambridge University Press)

Goldstein, J (2004) 'War and gender' *Encyclopedia of Sex and Gender* pp. 107–116

Gramsci, A (2011) *Prison Notebooks* translated by Joseph A Buttigieg (Columbia: Columbia University Press)

Gray, J (2011) 'Perpetual warfare' *New Statesman* 8 September http://www.newstatesman.com/global-issues/2011/09/afghanistan-iraq-west-world

Gould, P (1998) *The Unfinished Revolution* (London: Little, Brown and Company)

Gronbeck, B E (1990) 'Popular culture, media, and political communication' in D L Swanson and D Nimmo (eds) *New Directions in Political Communication* (California: Sage) pp. 185–222

Grossman, D (1995) *On Killing: The Psychological Cost of Learning to Kill in War and Society* (Boston: Little Brown)

Habermas, J (1989) *The Structural Transformation of the Public Sphere* (Cambridge, MA: MIT Press)

Hague, B and Loader, B D (1999) *Digital Democracy: Discourse and Decision Making in the Information Age* (London: Routledge)

Halberstam, J (2005) *In a Queer Time and Place. Transgender Bodies, Subcultural Lives* (New York and London: New York University Press)

Halberstam, J (2011) *The Queer Art of Failure* (Durham and London: Duke University Press)

Hall, S (1996/2000) 'Who needs "identity"?' in du Gay, P; Evans, J and Redman, P (eds) *Identity: A Reader* (IDE: Sage Publications Inc.) pp. 15–30

Hall, S (1983) 'The great moving right show' in S Hall and M Jacques (eds) *The Politics of Thatcherism* (London: Lawrence Wishart) pp. 19–39

Hall, S (1981) 'Notes on deconstructing "the popular"' in J Storey (ed) (2009) *Cultural Theory and Popular Culture: A Reader* (Harlow: Pearson) pp. 508–18

Hall, S; Durham, M G and D M Kellner (eds) (2001) *Encoding/Decoding, in Media and Cultural Studies: Keyworks* (London: Wiley)

Hall, S (1988) 'Brave New World' *Marxism Today* October pp. 24–9

Hallin, D C and Mancini, P (2004) *Comparing Media Systems: Three Models of Media and Politics* (New York: Cambridge University Press)

Halman, L and Heinen, T (1996) 'Left and right in modern society' in L Halman and N Nevitte (eds) *Political Value Change in Western Democracies: Integration, Values, Identification and Participation* (Tilburg: Tilburg University Press)

Hamilton, M (2012) 'Does Tomb Raider's Lara Croft really have to be a survivor of a rape attempt?' *The Guardian* http://www.theguardian.com/commentisfree/2012/jun/13/tomb-raider-lara-croft-rape-attempt

Haraway, D (1991) *Simians Cyborgs and Women* (London: Free Association Books)

Harcup, T and O'Neill, D (2001) 'What is news? Galtung and Ruge revisited' *Journalism Studies* 2(2) pp. 261–80

Harmer, E and Wring, D (2013) 'Julie and the cybermums: Marketing and women voters in the 2010 election' *Journal of Political Marketing* 12(2–3) pp. 262–73

Harris, M (2014) 'The legal definition of terrorism threatens to criminalise us all' *The Independent* 24 July http://www.independent.co.uk/voices/comment/the-legal-definition-of-terrorism-threatens-to-criminalise-us-all-9626325.html

Harper, J (2006) *Identity Crisis: How Identification Is Overused and Misunderstood* (Washington: Cato Institute)

Harris, R (1988) *Language: Saussure and Wittgenstein* (London: Routledge)

Harris, P and Wring, D (2001) 'Editorial: The marketing campaign. The 2001 British general election' *Journal of Marketing Management* 17 pp. 909–12

Harrop, M (1990) 'Political marketing' *Parliamentary Affairs* 43(3) pp. 277–91

Hartley, K (2007) 'The arms industry, procurement and industrial policies' *Handbook of Defence Economics* (eds) T Sandler and K Hartley (Amsterdam: North-Holland) pp. 1139–1176

Harvey, D (2007) *A Brief History of Neoliberalism* (Oxford: Oxford University Press)

Haworth, A (1998) *Free Speech* (London: Routledge)

Hay, C (2002) *Political Analysis* (Basingstoke: Palgrave)

Hay, C (2007) *Why We Hate Politics* (Cambridge: Polity)

Held, D (2006) *Models of Democracy* (Cambridge: Polity) 3rd edition

Hellinger, D and Judd, D (1991) *The Democratic Facade* (Pacific Grove, CA: Brooks/Cole)

Herman, E and Chomsky, N (1988) *Manufacturing Consent: The Political Economy of the Mass Media* (Cambridge: Cambridge University Press)

Higgins, M (2008) *Media and their Publics* (Maidenhead: Open University Press)

Higgins, M and Smith, A (2013) '"My husband; my hero": selling the spouses in the 2010 general election' *Journal of Political Marketing* 12(2/3) pp. 197–210

Hobbes, T (1651/2014) *Leviathan* (Oxford: Oxford University Press)

Hoffman, J and Graham, P (2006) *Introducing Political Concepts* (Harlow: Longman Pearson)

hooks, b (1981) *Ain't I a Woman?* (London: Pluto Press)

hooks, b. (1990) *Yearning: Race, Gender and Cultural Politics* (Toronto, Ontario: Between the Lines)

Hopgood, S (2013) *Keepers of the Flame: Understanding Amnesty International* (New York: Cornell University Press)

Howard, P; Duffy, A; Freelon, D; Hussain, M; Mari, W and Mazaid, M (2011) 'opening closed regimes: What was the role of social media during the Arab Spring?' *Project on Information Technology and Political Islam* Available at SSRN: http://ssrn.com/abstract=2595096

Hutchinson, J R (2002) 'En-gendering democracy' *Administrative Theory and Praxis* 24(4) pp. 721–38

Isoke, Z (2013) *Urban Black Women and the Politics of Resistance* (Basingstoke: Palgrave)

Isserlis, S (2013) 'Music in the shadow of war' *The Guardian* http://www.theguardian.com/music/2013/sep/16/chamber-music-in-the-shadow-of-war-steven-isserlis-wigmore-hall 16 September

Iyengar, S. (2005) 'Speaking of values: The framing of American politics' *The Forum* (Stanford University) 3(3)

Jackson, R (2005) *Writing the War on Terrorism: Language, Politics and Counter-Terrorism* (Manchester: Manchester University Press)

Jamieson, K H (1992) *Packaging the Presidency: A History and Criticism of Presidential Campaign Advertising* (Oxford: Oxford University Press)

Jenkins, R (2004) *Social Identity* (London and New York: Routledge)

Jenssen, A D Aalberg, T and Aarts, K (2012) 'Informed citizens, media use, and public knowledge of parties' policy positions' in T Aalberg and J Curran (eds) (New York and London: Routledge) pp. 138–58

Jessop, B (2005) 'Critical realism and the strategic-relational approach' *New Formations: A Journal of Culture, Theory and Politics* (56) pp. 40–53

Kaid, L L (2004) 'Political advertising' in L L Kaid (ed.) *Handbook of Political Communication Research* (Mahwah, NJ: LEA) pp. 155–202

Karp, Jeffrey A and Banducci, Susan A (2008) 'When politics is not just a man's game: Representation and political engagement' *Electoral Studies* 27 pp. 105–15

Kavanagh, D (1995) *Election Campaigning: The New Marketing of Politics* (Oxford: Blackwell)

Kallis, A A (2005) *Nazi Propaganda and the Second World War* (Basingstoke: Palgrave)

Katz, D and Mair, P (1995) 'Changing models of party organization and party democracy: The emergence of the cartel party' *Party Politics* 1(1) pp. 5–28

Kellner, D (1990) *Television and the Crisis of Democracy* (Boulder: Westview)

Kertzer, D (1988) *Ritual, Power and Politics* (New Haven, CT: Yale University Press)

Khiabany, G and Williamson, M (2012) 'Terror, culture and anti-Muslim racism' in D Freedman and Thussu, D K (eds) *Media and Terrorism* (London: Sage) pp. 134–50

Khondker, H H (2011) 'Role of the new media in the Arab Spring' *Globalizations* 8(5) pp. 675–79

Kiesler, S; Sproull, L and J S Eccles (1985) 'Pool halls, chips, and war games: Women in the culture of computing' *Psychology of Women Quarterly* 9(4) pp. 451–62

Kim, S T and Weaver, D H (2003) 'Reporting on globalization: A comparative analysis of sourcing patterns in five countries' newspapers' *Gazette: The International Journal for Communication Studies* 65(2) p121–44

Kitschelt, H (1996) *The Transformation of European Social Democracy* (Cambridge: Cambridge University Press)

Klapper, J (1960) *The Effects of Mass Communication* (Glencoe, IL: Free Press)

Kline, D and Burnstein, D (2005) *Blog! How the Newest Media Revolution is Changing Politics, Business, and Culture* (New York: CDS Books)

Knight, B Harding, L and Willsher, K (2015) 'Germanwings co-pilot Andreas Lubitz "wanted to make everyone remember him"' *The Guardian* 28 March http://www.theguardian.com/world/2015/mar/27/germanwings-co-pilot-andreas-lubitzs-background-under-scrutiny

Knutsen, O (1995) 'Left-right materialist orientations' in J W van Deth and E Scarborough (eds) *The Impact of Values* (Oxford: Oxford University Press) pp. 160–96

Koc-Michalska, K, Gibson, R and Vedel, T (2014) 'Online campaigning in France, 2007–2012: Political actors and citizens in the aftermath of the Web.2.0 evolution' *Journal of Information Technology and Politics* 11 (2) pp. 220–44

Kotler, P and Andreasen, A (1996) *Strategic Marketing for Non-Profit Organisations* 5th edition (New Jersey: Prentice Hall)

Kotler, P and Levy, S (1969) 'Broadening the concept of marketing' *Journal of Marketing* 33 pp. 10–15

Kundnani, K (2009) *Spooked! How Not to Prevent Violent Extremism* (London: Institute of Race Relations)

Kymlicka, W (1995) *Multicultural Citizenship* (Oxford: Oxford University Press)

Laclau, E (1990) *New Reflections on the Revolution of Our Time* (London: Verso)

Lakoff, G (1996) *Moral Politics: What Conservatives Know that Liberals Don't* (Chicago, Ill: University of Chicago Press)

Lance Bennett, W and Iyengar, S (2008) 'A new era of minimal effects? The changing foundations of political communication' *Journal of Communication* 58 pp. 707–31

Lasswell, H (1927) *Propaganda Technique in the World War* (New York: Kopf)

Lasswell, H (1936) *Politics: Who Gets What, When, How* (New York: McGraw-Hill)

Lasswell, H (1995) 'Propaganda' in R. Jackall (ed) *Propaganda* (London: Macmillan) pp. 13–25

Lau R R and Pomper, G M (2001) 'Effects of negative campaigning on turnout in U.S. Senate elections, 1988–1998' *Journal of Politics* 63(3) pp. 804–19

Lazarsfeld, P, Berelson, B and Gaudet, H (1944/1969) *The People's Choice: How the Voter Makes Up His Mind in a Presidential Campaign* (3rd edition) (New York and London: Columbia University Press)

Lazarsfeld, P and Merton, R (1969) 'Mass communication, popular taste and organised social action' in W. Schramm (ed.) *Mass Communications* (2nd ed.) (Urbana: University of Illinois Press) pp. 494–512

Le Bon, G (1896) *The Crowd: A Study of the Popular Mind* (London: Ernest Benn)

Lees-Marshment, J (2001) *Political Marketing and British Political Parties: The Party's Just Begun* (Manchester: Manchester University Press)

Leavis, F R and Thompson, D (1933/1977) *Culture and the Environment: The Training of Critical Awareness* (Westport, CT: Greenwood Press)

Leftwich, A (2004) *What is Politics?* (Cambridge: Polity)

Leiss, W; Kline, S and Jhally, S (1990) *Social Communication in Advertising: Persons, Products and Images of Well Being* (New York: Routledge)

Leonardo, Z (2002) 'The souls of white folk: Critical pedagogy, whiteness studies, and globalization discourse' *Race Ethnicity and Education* 5(1) pp. 29–50

Levy, A (2005) *Female Chauvinist Pigs: Women and the Rise of Raunch Culture* (New York: Free Press)

Lewin, K (1948) *Resolving Social Conflicts* (New York: Harper)

Lewis, H (2011) '"You should have your tongue ripped out": the reality of sexist abuse online' *New Statesman* http://www.newstatesman.com/blogs/helen-lewis-hasteley/2011/11/comments-rape-abuse-women

Lewis, J (2008) 'The role of the media in boosting military spending' *Media, War and Conflict* 1(1) pp. 108–17

Lewis, J (2001) *Constructing Public Opinion* (New York: Columbia University Press)

Lewis, J (2013) *Beyond Consumer Capitalism: Media and the Limits to Imagination* (Cambridge: Polity)

Lewis, J; Inthorn, S and K Wahl-Jorgensen (2005) *Citizens or Consumers? What the Media Tell us about Political Participation* (Maidenhead: Open University Press)

Lewis, J; Mason, P and Moore, K (2009) '"Islamic terrorism" and the repression of the political' in L Marsden and H Savigny (eds) *Media, Religion and Conflict* (Farnham: Ashgate) pp. 17–38

Lijphart, A (1984) *Democracies: Patterns of Majoritarian and Consensus Governments in Twenty-One Countries* (New Haven: Yale University Press)

Lilleker, D and Lees-Marshment, J (2005) *Political Marketing: A Comparative Perspective* (Manchester: Manchester University Press)

Lindblom, C E (1977) *Politics and Markets: The World's Political Economic Systems* (New York: Basic Books)

Lippmann, W (1922/1977) *Public Opinion* (New York: Free Press)

Lloyd, J (2004) *What Are the Media Doing to our Politics?* (London: Constable and Robinson Ltd)

Loader, B D and Mercea, D (2011) 'Networking democracy? Social media innovations and participatory politics' *Information, Communication and Society* 14(6) pp. 757–69

Loader, B (ed.) (1997) *The Governance of CyberSpace: Politics, Technology and Global Restructuring* (London: Routledge)

Lock, A and Harris, P (1996) 'Political marketing – vive la difference' *European Journal of Marketing* 30(10/11) pp. 28–9

Lukes, S (1974) *Power: A Radical View* (London: Macmillan)

Lukes, S (2005) *Power: A Radical View. Second edition* (Basingstoke: Palgrave)

Maarek, P J (1995) *Political Marketing and Communication* (London: John Libbey and Company)

Mac An Ghial, M and Haywood, C (2007) *Contemporary Femininities and Masculinities* (Basingstoke: Palgrave)

Macedo, S et al. (2005) *Democracy at Risk: How Political Choices Undermine Citizen Participation, and What We Can Do About It* (Washington DC: Brookings Institution Press)

Macharia, S (2010) 'Editorial' *Media and Gender Monitor* (April) http://cdn. agilitycms.com/who-makes-the-news/Imported/reports_2010/highlights/ highlights_en.pdf WACC, Global Media Monitoring Project

Machiavelli, N (1532/2003) *The Prince* (London: Penguin Classics)

Maloney, W; Jordan, G and A McLaughlin (1994) 'Interest groups and public policy: The insider/outsider model revisited' *Journal of Public Policy* 14(1) pp. 17–38

Mancini, D and Swanson, P (1996) 'Introduction' in D Swanson and P Mancini (eds) *Politics, Media and Modern Democracy* (Westport, CT: Praeger) pp. 1–28

Mannheim, K (2013) *Ideology and Utopia: 1 (Routledge Classics in Sociology)* (London: Routledge)

Marçal K (2015) *Who Cooked Adam Smith's Dinner?* (London: Portobello Books)

Marquand, D (2004) *Decline of the Public* (Cambridge: Polity)

Marsh, D and Furlong, P (2010) 'A skin not a sweater: Ontology and epistemology in political science' in D Marsh and G Stoker (eds) *Theory and Methods in Political Science* 3rd edition (Basingstoke: Palgrave) pp. 184–211

Marx, K (1888/2002) *The Communist Manifesto* (London: Penguin)

Marshall, P D (1997) *Celebrity and Power: Fame in Contemporary Culture* (Minneapolis: University of Minnesota Press)

McAnulla, S (2002) 'Structure and Agency' in D Marsh and G Stoker (eds) *Theory and Methods in Political Science* (Basingstoke: Palgrave) pp. 271–91

McChesney, R (1997) *Corporate Media and the Threat to Democracy* (New York: Seven Stories Press)

McChesney, R (2008) *The Political Economy of Media: Enduring Issues, Emerging Dilemmas* (New York: Monthly Review Press)

McCombs, M E and Shaw, D L (1972) 'The agenda setting function of mass media' *Public Opinion Quarterly* 36(2) pp. 176–87

McGinnis, J (1969) *The Selling of the President, 1968* (New York: Trident Press, Inc.)

McKay, F (2007) '"Thick" conceptions of substantive representation: Women, gender and political institutions' Paper presented at *European Consortium of Political Research Joint Sessions of Workshops* 2007 Helsinki May 7–12

McLuhan, M (1964) *Understanding Media: Extensions of Man* (New York: McGraw Hill)

McNair, B (1996) *Mediated Sex: Pornography and Postmodern Culture* (London, New York: Arnold)

McNair, B (2002) *Striptease Culture: Sex, Media and the Democratization of Desire* (London, New York: Routledge)

McNay (1992) *Foucault and Feminism* (Cambridge: Polity)

McQuail, D (2005/1983) *McQuail's Mass Communication Theory* (London: Sage) 5th edition

McRobbie, A (2008) *The Aftermath of Feminism* (London: Sage)

McRobbie, A (2007) 'Post-feminism and popular culture' *Feminist Media Studies* 4(3) pp. 255–64

Mead, M (1967) 'Epilogue' in Fried, M; Harris, M and Murphy, R (eds) *War: The Anthology of Armed Conflict and Aggression* (Garden City, NY: Natural History Press) pp. 235–7

Mearsheimer, J and Walt, S (2006) 'The Israel lobby' *London Review of Books* 28(6) 23 March

Melucci, A (1996) *Challenging Codes: Collective Action in the Information Age* (New York: Cambridge University Press)

Merrin, W (2005) *Baudrillard and the Media* (Cambridge: Polity)

Meyer, T (2002) *Media Democracy: How the Media Colonize Politics* (Cambridge: Polity)

Mill, J S (1978) *On Liberty* (Indianapolis: Hackett Publishing)

Miller, D (2004) 'Information dominance: The philosophy of total propaganda control' in Y R Kamalipour and N Snow (eds) *War, Media and Propaganda: A Global Perspective* (Lanham, MD: Rowman and Littlefield) pp. 7–16

Miller, T (2012) 'Terrorism and popular culture' in D Freedman and D K Thussu (eds) *Media and Terrorism: Global Perspectives* (London: Sage) pp. 97–115

Millett, K (1985) *Sexual Politics* (London Virago)

Milne, K (2005) *Manufacturing Dissent: Single Issue Protest, the Public and the Press* (London: Demos)

Moeller, S (2009) *Media Literacy: Understanding the News* (Washington: Center for International Media Assistance)

Monbiot, G (2011) 'The corporate press are fighting a class war, defending the elite they belong to' *The Guardian* 13 December p29

Moon, N (1999) *Opinion Polls: History, Theory and Practice* (Manchester: Manchester University Press)

Morley, D (1980) *The Nationwide Audience* (London: British Film Institute)

Morris, D (1999) *Behind the Oval Office: Getting Re-elected Against All Odds* (Los Angeles: Renaissance Books)

Mortimer, J and Terry, C (2015) 'Women in Westminster: Predicting the number of female MPs' *Electoral Reform Society* http://www.electoral-reform.org.uk/publications/

Mulvey, L (1975) 'Visual pleasure and narrative cinema' *Screen* 16(3) pp. 6–18

Murphy, R (2014) *The Tax Gap: Tax Evasion in 2014 – And What Can Be Done About It* (Public and Commercial Services Union | pcs.org.uk)

Muntz, D (2001) 'The future of political communication research. Reflections on the Occasion of Steve Chaffee's retirement from Stanford University' *Political Communication* 18 pp. 231–6

Negrine, R and Stanyer, J (2006) *The Political Communication Reader* (London: Routledge)

Neilson, B and Rossiter, N (2008) 'Precarity as a political concept, or, Fordism as exception' *Theory, Culture and Society* 25(7–8)pp. 51–72

Nettleton, S (2006) *Sociology of Health and Illness* (Cambridge: Polity)

Neuman, W R (1991) *The Future of the Mass Audience* (Cambridge: Cambridge University Press)

Newman B (2001) 'Commentary: Image-manufacturing in the USA: Recent US presidential elections and beyond' *European Journal of Marketing* 35(9/10) pp. 966–70

Newton, K and Brynin, M (2001) 'The national press and party voting in the UK' *Political Studies* 49 pp. 265–86

Nicholson, L (ed.) (1990) *Feminism/Postmodernisim* (New York/London: Routledge)

Niemi, R G and Junn, J (1998) *Civic Education: What Makes Students Learn* (New Haven: Yale University Press)

Noelle-Neuman, E (1974) 'The spiral of silence. A theory of public opinion' *Journal of Communication* 24(2) pp. 43–51

Noelle-Neumann, Elisabeth (1977) 'Turbulences in the climate of opinion: Methodological applications of the spiral of silence theory' *Public Opinion Quarterly* 41 pp. 143–58

Norris, P (1997) *Women, Media and Politics* (Oxford and New York: Oxford University Press)

Norris, P (1999) 'Institutions and political support' in P Norris ed. *Critical Citizens: Global Support for Democratic Governance* (Oxford: Oxford University Press)

Norris, P (1999) 'New politicians? Change in party competition at Westminster' in Evans, G and Norris, P (eds) *Critical Elections: British Parties and Voters in Long-Term Perspective* (London: Sage)

Norris, P; Curtice, J; Sanders, D; Scammell, M and Semetko, H (1999) *On Message: Communicating the Campaign* (London: Sage)

Norton, A (2010) 'Politics against history: Temporal distortions in the study of politics' *Political Studies* 58(2) pp. 340–53

Nunn, H and A. Biressi (2010) '"A trust betrayed": Celebrity and the work of emotion' *Celebrity Studies* 1(1) pp. 49–64

Nye, J; Zelikow, P and King, D (eds) (1997) *Why Americans Mistrust Government* (Cambridge, MA: Harvard University Press)

Oborne, P (2015) 'Why I have resigned from the Telegraph' *Open Democracy* https://www.opendemocracy.net/ourkingdom/peter-oborne/why-i-have-resigned-from-telegraph

O'Neill, D and Savigny, H (2014) 'Female politicians in the British press: The exception to the "masculine" norm?' *Journalism Education* 3(1) pp. 6–16

Ormrod, R (2006) 'A critique of the Lees-Marshment market-oriented party model' *Politics* 26(2) pp. 110–8

Orwell, G (2013) *Nineteen Eighty-Four* (London: Penguin)

O'Shaughnessy, N (1990) *The Phenomenon of Political Marketing* (London: Macmillan)

O'Shaughnessy, N J and Henneberg, S C (2007) 'The selling of the president 2004: A marketing perspective' *Journal of Public Affairs* 7 pp. 249–68

Page, B and Shapiro, R (1983) 'Effects of public opinion on policy' *American Political Science Review* 77 pp. 175–90

Page, B and Shapiro, R (1992) *The Rational Public* (Chicago: University of Chicago Press)

Panebianco, A (1988) *Political Parties: Organisation and Power* (Cambridge: Cambridge University Press)

Papacharissi, Z (2010) *A Private Sphere: Democracy in a Digital Age* (Cambridge: Polity)

Pateman, C (1988) 'The patriarchal welfare state' in A Gutmann (ed.) *Democracy and the Welfare State* (Princeton: Princeton University Press) pp. 231–60

Pateman, C (1989) *The Disorder of Women: Democracy, Feminism and Political Theory* (Cambridge: Polity)

Peck, M (2010) 'Why the army doesn't train on Xboxes' *Wired* 9th February http://www.wired.com/2010/02/why-the-army-doesnt-train-on-xboxes/

Penny, L (2013) 'Laurie Penny on Steubenville: This is rape culture's Abu Ghraib moment' *New Statesman* http://www.newstatesman.com/laurie-penny/2013/03/steubenville-rape-cultures-abu-ghraib-moment

Perloff, R M (2014) *The Dynamics of Political Communication* (New York: Routledge)

Pietrykowski, B (1994) 'Consuming culture: Postmodernism, postFordism and economics' *Rethinking Marxism: A Journal of Economics, Culture and Society* 7(1) pp. 62–80

Phipps, A (2014) *The Politics of the Body* (Cambridge: Polity)

Phillips, A (1991) *Engendering Democracy* (Cambridge: Polity Press)

Plato (2007) *The Republic* (London: Penguin)

Polanyi, K (1944/2001)*The Great Transformation* (Boston: Beacon Press)

Polletta, F and Jasper, J (2001) 'Collective identity and social movements' *Annual Review of Sociology* 27 pp. 283–305

Power, M (2007) 'Digitized virtuosity: Video war games and post 9/11 cyber-deterrence' *Security Dialogue* 38(2) pp. 271–88

Power Inquiry (2006) *Power to the People: The Report of Power: An Independent Inquiry into Britain's Democracy* (York: York Publishing)

Prior, M (2005) 'News vs entertainment: How increasing media choice widens gaps in political knowledge and turnout' *American Journal of Political Science* 49 pp. 577–92

Projansky S (2001) *Watching Rape* (New York: New York University Press)

Putnam, R (2000) *Bowling Alone: The Collapse and Revival of American Community* (New York: Simon and Schuster)

Quinn, T (2004) *Modernising the Labour Party: Organisational Change since 1983* (Basingstoke: Palgrave)

Rabinow, R (1986) *The Foucault Reader* (Harmondsworth: Penguin)

Ranciere, J (2009) *The Emancipated Spectator* (London: Verso)

Rayner, L and Easthope, G (2001) 'Postmodern consumption and alternative medications' *Journal of Sociology* 37(2) pp. 157–76

Richardson, J (1993) 'Pressure groups and government' in J Richardson (ed.) *Pressure Groups* (Oxford: Oxford University Press)

Ritzer, G (1988) 'Introduction' in Baudrillard, J (1988) *The Consumer Society* (London: Sage)

Robinson, A (2012) 'Jean Baudrillard: The masses' *Ceasefire* https://ceasefiremagazine.co.uk/in-theory-baudrillard-12/

Robinson, P (1999) 'The CNN effect: Can the news media drive foreign policy?' *Review of International Studies* 25 (i) pp. 301–9

Robinson, W I (2004) *A Theory of Global Capitalism* (Baltimore and London: The Johns Hopkins University Press)

Rojek, C (2001) *Celebrity* (London: Reaktion Books)

Ross, K. (2005) 'Women in the boyzone, gender, news and *herstory*' *Journalism: Critical Issues* (Maidenhead: Open University Press) pp. 287–98

Ross, K (2007) 'The journalist, the housewife, the citizen and the press' *Journalism* 8(4) pp. 440–73

Ross, K (2010) 'Danse macabre: Politicians, journalists and the complicated rumba of relationships' *International Journal of Press/Politics* 15 (3) pp. 272–94

Ross, K (2011) 'Silent witness: News sources, the local press and the disappeared woman' in Krijnen, T; Alvares, C and S Van Bauwel (eds) *Gendered Transformations* (Bristol: Intellect) pp. 9–24

Ross, K and Carter, C (2011) 'Women and news: A long and winding road' *Media, Culture and Society* 33(8)pp. 1148–65

Ross, K; Evans, E; Harrison, L; Shears, M and Wadia, K (2013) 'The gender of news and news of gender: A study of sex, politics, and press coverage of the 2010 British general election' *The International Journal of Press/Politics* 18(1) pp. 3–20

Rowe, K (2011) *Unruly Girls, Unrepentant Mothers: Redefining Feminism on Screen* (Texas: University of Texas Press)

Ryfe, D M (2001) 'History and political communication: An introduction' *Political Communication* 18 pp. 407–20

Said, E (1978) *Orientalism: Western Representations of the Orient* (London: Routledge, Kegan and Paul)

Said, E (1981) *Covering Islam. How the Media and the Experts Determine How We See the Rest of the World* (London: Routledge and Kegan Paul)

Sanders, K (2009) *Communicating Politics in the 21st Century* (Basingstoke: Palgrave)

Saussure, F de (1966) *A Course in General Linguistics* translated by W Baskin (New York: McGraw-Hill)

Savigny, H (2004) 'Political marketing: A rational choice?' *Journal of Political Marketing* 3(1) pp. 21–38

Savigny, H (2008) *The Problem of Political Marketing* (New York: Continuum)

Savigny, H and Marsden, L (2011) *Doing Political Science and International Relations* (Basingstoke: Palgrave)

Savigny, H and Temple M (2010) 'Political marketing models: The curious incident of the dog that doesn't bark' *Political Studies* 58(5) pp. 1049–64

Savigny, H and Warner, H (eds) (2015) *Popular Culture and Feminism: The Politics of Being a Woman in the 21st Century* (Basingstoke: Palgrave)

Sartori, G (1973) 'What is "politics"' *Political Theory* 1 (1) pp. 5–26

Scammell, M (1995) *Designer Politics. How Elections Are Won* (London: Macmillan)

Scammell, M (1998) 'The wisdom of the war room: US campaigning and Americanization' *Media, Culture and Society* 20(2) 251–75

Scammell, M (1999) 'Political marketing: Lessons for political science' *Political Studies* 47(4) pp. 718–39

Schudson, M (2011) *The Sociology of News* (New York: W.W. Norton and Company)

Searle, K (2014) *Attitudes to Identity in Men's Gay Lifestyle Magazines* Unpublished PhD thesis (Birmingham: University of Birmingham)

Seib, P (2008) *The Al Jazeera Effect: How the New Global Media Are Reshaping World Politics* (Virginia: Potomac Books, Inc)

Sender, K (1999) 'Selling sexual subjectivities: Audiences respond to gay window advertising' *Critical Studies in Mass Communication* 16 (2) pp. 172–96

Schiller, H (1989) *Culture Inc – The Corporate Takeover of Public Expression* (Oxford: Oxford University Press)

Senft, T (2008) *CamGirls. Celebrity and Community in the Age of Social Networks* (New York: Peter Lang)

Shenkman, R (2008) *Just How Stupid Are We? Facing the Truth about the American Voter* (New York: Basic Books)

Shepherd, L (2008) *Gender, Violence and Security: Discourse As Practice* (London and New York: Zed Books)

Simons, J (2000) 'Ideology, imagology and critical thought: the impoverishment of politics' *Journal of Political Ideologies* 5(1) pp. 81–103

Sjoberg, L and Gentry, C (eds) (2011) *Women, Gender, and Terrorism* (Athens and London: The University of Georgia Press)

Smith, A (1776/2008) *Wealth of Nations* (Oxford: Oxford University Press)

Smith, A and Higgins, M (2013) *The Language of Journalism* (London: Bloomsbury)

Soueif, Ahdaf (2011) 'Image of unknown woman beaten by Egypt's military echoes around world' December 18 *The Guardian* http://www.guardian.co.uk/commentisfree/2011/dec/18/egypt-military-beating-female-protester-tahrir-square

Sparrow, N and Turner, J (2001) 'The permanent campaign: The integration of market research techniques in developing strategies in a more uncertain political climate' *European Journal of Marketing* 35(9/10) pp. 984–1024

Spivak, G (1985) 'Three women's texts and a critique of imperialism' *Critical Inquiry* 12 pp. 243–61

Spivak, G (1988) 'Can the subaltern speak?' In C Nelson and L Grossberg's *Marxism and the Interpretation of Culture* (Basingstoke: Macmillan) pp. 271–313

Squires, C (2002) 'Rethinking the black public sphere: An alternative vocabulary for multiple public spheres' *Communication Theory* 12(4) pp. 375–486

Squires, J (1999) *Gender in Political Theory* (Cambridge: Cambridge University Press)

Stafford Smith, C (2008) 'Welcome to "the disco"' *The Guardian* http://www.theguardian.com/world/2008/jun/19/usa.guantanamo 19th June

Standing, G (2011) *The Precariat: The New Dangerous Class* (London: Bloomsbury)

Steans, J (1998) *Gender and International Relations: An Introduction* (New Brunswick, NJ: Rutgers University Press)

Stewart, C (2011) 'Saudi women gain vote for the first time' *The Independent* http://www.independent.co.uk/news/world/middle-east/saudi-women-gain-vote-for-the-first-time-2360883.html

Stohl, M (2008) 'Old myth, new fantasies and the enduring realities of terrorism' *Critical Studies on Terrorism* 1(1) pp. 5–16

Stohl, R and Grillot, S (2009) *The International Arms Trade* (Cambridge: Polity)

Street, J (1997) *Politics and Popular Culture* (Cambridge: Polity)

Street, J (2004) 'Celebrity politicians: Popular culture and political representation' *British Journal of Politics and International Relations* 6(4) pp. 435–452

Street, J (2010) *Mass Media, Politics and Democracy* (Basingstoke: Palgrave) 2nd edition

Street, J (2012) 'Do celebrity politics and celebrity politicians matter?' *The British Journal of Politics and International Relations* 14(3) pp. 346–56

Street, J (2012) *Music and Politics* (Cambridge: Polity)

Sussman, B (1988) *What Americans Really Think and Why Our Politicians Pay No Attention* (New York: Pantheon)

Tarrow, S (1998) *Power and Movement: Social Movements and Contentious Politics* (Cambridge: Cambridge University Press)

Thorpe, V and Rogers R (2011) 'Women bloggers call for a stop to "hateful" trolling by misogynist men. Anonymous trolls regularly threaten female writers with rape' *The Observer* 6 November http://www.guardian.co.uk/world/2011/nov/05/women-bloggers-hateful-trolling?newsfeed=true

Trotter, W R (2005) 'The music of war' *Military History* June pp. 58–64

Tsesis, A (2009) 'Dignity and speech: The regulation of hate speech in a democracy' *Wake Forest Law Review* 42 pp. 497–534

Tuchman, G; Daniels, A K and J W Benet (eds) (1978) *Hearth and Home: Images of Women in the Mass Media* (New York: Oxford University Press)

Turner, G (2003) *British Cultural Studies* (London: Routledge)

Turner, G (2010) 'Approaching celebrity studies' *Celebrity Studies* 1(1) pp. 11–20

van de Donk, W; Loader, B; Nixon, P and D Rucht (eds) (2004) *Cyberprotest: New Media, Citizens and Social Movements* (London and New York: Routledge)

van Zoonen, L (1994) *Feminist Media Studies* (London: Sage)

van Zoonen, L (1998) 'One of the girls? The changing gender of journalism' in C Carter; G Branston and S Allan (eds) *News, Gender and Power* (London: Routledge) pp. 33–46

van Zoonen, L (2005) *Entertaining the Citizen, When Politics and Popular Culture Converge* (Oxford: Rowman and Littlefield)

van Zoonen, L (2006) 'The personal, the political and the popular: A woman's guide to celebrity politics' *European Journal of Cultural Studies* 9(3) pp. 287–301

van Zoonen, L And E Harmer (2011) 'The visual challenge of celebrity politics: Female politicians in Grazia' *Celebrity Studies* 2(1) pp. 94–96

Von Clausewitz, C (1832/1989) *On War* (Princeton, NJ: Princeton University Press)

WACC (World Association for Christian Communication) (2010) *Who Makes the News?* (London: World Association for Christian Communication)

Wajcman, J (1991) *Feminism Confronts Technology* (Pennsylvania: Pennsylvania State University Press)

Wajcman, J (2002) 'Addressing technological change: The challenge to social theory' *Current Sociology* 50(3) pp. 347–63

Walker, A (1985) *The Color Purple* (New York: Pocket books, Simon and Schuster)

Walter, N (2010) *Living Dolls* (London: Virago)

Walton, D (2012) *Doing Cultural Theory* (London: Sage)

Wängnerud, L (2009) 'Women in parliaments: Descriptive and substantive representation' *Annual Review of Political Science* 12 pp. 51–69

Waters, M (1995) *Globalisation* (London: Routledge)

Weaver, C. K (1998) '*Crimewatch UK*: Keeping women off the streets' in Carter, C; Branston, G and Allan, S (eds) *News, Gender and Power* (London: Routledge) pp. 248–63

Weaver, D (1996) 'Media agenda setting and elections' in D Paletz (ed.) *Political Communication: Approaches, Studies, Assessments* Vol II (Norwood, NJ: Ablex Publishing) pp. 211–24

Wendt, A (1994) 'Collective identity formation and the international state' *The American Political Science Review* 88(2) pp. 384–96

Wheeler, M (1997) *Politics and the Mass Media* (Oxford: Blackwell)

Whitaker, B (2002) 'Islam and the British press After September 11' *Islam and the Media* (London: Central London Mosque)

Williams, R (1958/1987) *Culture and Society: Coleridge to Orwell* (London: Hogarth)

Williams, R (1983) *Keywords: A Vocabulary of Culture and Society* (London: Flamingo)

Williamson, J (1998) *Decoding Advertisements* (New York: Marion Boyars Publishers Inc)

Wilkinson, R and Pickett, K (2010) *The Spirit Level: Why Equality is Better for Everyone* (London: Penguin)

Wilson, A (1992) *The Culture of Nature: North American Landscape from Disney to the Exxon Valdez* (Cambridge, MA, and Oxford: Blackwell)

Wittgenstein, L (2001/1953) *Philosophical Investigations* (London: Blackwell)

WMEAT, (2014) *World Military Expenditures and Arms Transfers, 2014 edition* http://www.state.gov/documents/organization/237437.pdf

Wolf, N (1991) *The Beauty Myth* (London: Vintage)

Wolinetz, Steven B (2002) 'Beyond the catch-all party: Approaches to the study of parties and party systems in contemporary democracies' in R Gunther; J R Montero and J Linz (eds) *Political Parties: Old Concepts and New Challenges* (Oxford: Oxford University Press)

Wollstonecraft, M (1792/ 2008) *A Vindication of the Rights of Woman* (Oxford: Oxford World Classics)

Wring, D (1996) 'Political marketing and party development in Britain: A "secret" history' *European Journal of Marketing* 30(10/11) pp. 100–11

Wring, D (2001) 'Labouring the point: Operation victory and the battle for a second term' *Journal of Marketing Management* 17 pp. 913–27

Wring, D (2004) *The Politics of Marketing the Labour Party* (Basingstoke: Palgrave)

Yates, C (2015) *The Play of Political Culture, Emotion and Identity* (Basingstoke: Palgrave)

Young, A (1990) *Femininity in Dissent* (London: Routledge)

Young, R J C (2004) *White Mythologies* (London and New York: Routledge)

Zakaria, F (2003) *The Future of Freedom: Illiberal Democracy at Home and Abroad* (New York: W. W. Norton)

Zaller, J R (1992) *The Nature and Origins of Mass Opinion* (Cambridge: Cambridge University Press)

Index

183